I Know What to Do, I Just Don't Do It

How to Break Free from the Lies that Keep You Frustrated, Overweight, and Out of Shape

SUE MARKOVITCH

BALBOA
PRESS

A DIVISION OF HAY HOUSE

Balboa Press books may be ordered through booksellers or by contacting:

Balboa Press
A Division of Hay House
1663 Liberty Drive
Bloomington, IN 47403
www.balboapress.com
1-(877) 407-4847

Because of the dynamic nature of the Internet, any web addresses or
links contained in this book may have changed since publication and
may no longer be valid. The views expressed in this work are solely those
of the author and do not necessarily reflect the views of the publisher,
and the publisher hereby disclaims any responsibility for them.

The author of this book does not dispense medical advice or prescribe the use
of any technique as a form of treatment for physical, emotional, or medical
problems without the advice of a physician, either directly or indirectly. The
intent of the author is only to offer information of a general nature to help
you in your quest for emotional and spiritual well-being. In the event you use
any of the information in this book for yourself, which is your constitutional
right, the author and the publisher assume no responsibility for your actions.

Any people depicted in stock imagery provided by Thinkstock are
models, and such images are being used for illustrative purposes only.
Certain stock imagery © Thinkstock.

Printed in the United States of America.

ISBN: 978-1-4525-8106-4 (sc)
ISBN: 978-1-4525-8108-8 (hc)
ISBN: 978-1-4525-8107-1 (e)

Library of Congress Control Number: 2013915726

Balboa Press rev. date: 10/16/2013

Dedication

For every woman who feels she must cross a Grand Canyon to be good enough.

Table of Contents

Standing at the Edge

Afraid, I stood at the edge and looked across. I knew I had to go but I knew from step one that it would be difficult. I knew there would be times I would want to quit, I knew I would break down and cry, and I knew I would doubt myself and my ability to keep going.

But I also knew I had to do it. I was standing on the south rim of the Grand Canyon about to hike across it. But for me, it wasn't just a hike.

When we lose a loved one, we know we have to go through the grief, yet we can put it off and hold it down for years like I did. When we are addicted and chained to compulsive behaviors, we know we have to do the work to get clean, yet we put it off and make excuses and wait for the magical "as soon as" to happen so it will be easier. When we are stuck, we look around and find all the reasons outside of ourselves that explain why we can't move forward.

But putting off grief doesn't make it any less painful. Putting off recovery doesn't make getting clean any easier. And staying in our comfort zone doesn't make us at all comfortable.

The way to move forward is to step out.

When I did take that first step, just that very first one, I knew I had done something important in my life. I just didn't know what. I wouldn't know that until 12 hours into the hike as I was climbing the steep north rim, when it became evident that I made two big mistakes. One, I failed to climb at my pace. Two, I didn't eat enough. At that point in the hike, as it was getting dark, my body said "no more". My mind said "no more". And I stopped.

Well, stopping isn't an option. But I couldn't move forward on my own.

I was with three fellow hikers. Two went on to the top while one came back for me and began talking me through each step. He said, "I know how you feel, I've been there." He walked very slowly with me as I took my ten small steps. Then he waited as I bent over, hands on my knees, trying to catch my breath. He tried to carry my backpack for me, I wouldn't let him. He tried to get me to eat something. And he said, "You are going to finish."

My head was screaming, "Let him go finish his hike at his pace, you are ruining his experience! Tell him, 'don't worry about me'." But I couldn't finish alone, and I wanted to finish this hike. My life depended on it.

I already knew what quitting felt like. I already knew what failing felt like. I wanted success. I wanted to stand on the other side with my arms held high, knowing that I didn't give up.

So I kept walking.

Learning to Walk

I am a personal trainer and fitness coach and I own a studio that offers specialized fitness training for women over 40. I realize that means people think I have my act together all the time, but I don't. I am in the process of growing, healing and changing just like everyone else.

Part of my weekly routine was to send out a schedule of classes offered at the studio, in an email. It was the summer of 2009, and I had been training women for enough years to start hearing the same things repeated over and over. Things like, "Weight Watchers works great for me, I've done it seven times!" and "I know what to do, I just don't do it." I was starting to form some strong beliefs about what it really takes to change, and many of these beliefs were contrary to what was being marketed and talked about in the media and among women.

That same summer, a major magazine published a cover article that frustrated me so much I wrote up a response to it and sent it out with my weekly schedule. The responses I got from my clients were incredibly interesting. I wanted to share them with everyone. So, I was officially inspired to write again the next week and I included all of their responses. Thus began our conversation.

And that is what this book is; it is a peek inside the conversation I have had with hundreds of women who are seeking the same things that I am.

You will share in four years that go by, and as we work through another Thanksgiving and New Year, winter and summer, the message gets stronger. I actually get more rooted in the truth from working with all these inspiring women and hearing their stories.

You will see a running streak that actually has nothing to do with running, and eventually switches to a love of walking. You will see my good days and bad days. You will see as I dig deeper into my own junk and share it with everyone, how it touches others and heals me, too.

★★★

One of the things I hear the most when you allow me to share in your journey is that you want it to go faster. I understand wanting it NOW. But consider the journey for a moment. Could it be that health is not a destination, but a direction? Are we ever really "there"?

Some of you have seen me use the visual of taking small, consistent steps until I have crossed the room. Then, I go back to where I started and try to get to the other side in one big jump. It doesn't work. I can't jump that far.

But I can step. One small step forward. Another small step forward. Right foot, left foot, right foot, left foot. Monday, Tuesday, Wednesday. September, October, November. And if I am heading in the right direction and taking consistent steps, I will see small changes. If I keep heading in the right direction over a long period of time, I will be able to step back and see major changes.

I don't believe that creating a healthy, fit lifestyle requires one major change. It requires many little changes. Imagine you are writing a book for your very best friend who wants to live a healthier life. Your book is 100 pages long. On each page, write one small change you've made that she can make and stick with. Keep writing small changes until you have filled up your book. Now you have the guidance for making a lifestyle change that's all yours.

We tend to look outside of ourselves for the answer. Wouldn't it be great if we could find that one *thing* that would help us change for good? Instead, we have to create our own personal formula that incorporates our foods, our family, and our lifestyle.

Believe that the answers lie within you. Create your own healthy lifestyle and get moving in the right direction. Take your time and enjoy the gifts along the path of your transformation.

★★★

I am an athlete. Can you say it? Do you believe it? Or do you have certain criteria that must be met to consider yourself a real athlete?

I used to think to be a real runner you had to be a good runner, or a fast runner, or run all the time. Then I started running. I ran trails and hills. I ran on my treadmill. Some of those miles, I walked because my lungs were on fire or my knee was killing me. I slogged along slowly. I fought. I cried.

I've never won a race. When I joined the running club, I was one of the slowest. I walked the last 9 miles of my last marathon. So what! I have the exact same finisher's medal as the person who was first.

Running has changed my life. My soul loves to run. My heart is healed during my trail runs. Running makes me happy.

If that's not a real runner, I don't know what is. No matter how slow or clumsy or frightened you feel, get up and move your body. In my mind, as soon as you take that first step—whether it's walking or running, you, my dear, are a real athlete.

★★★

Changing your life is a bit like climbing a mountain. You look at it ahead of you and it's tempting to think, "no way!" It's too big. But if you take one step and then another, next thing you know, you are doing it.

I believe that we are all on the same journey and that on this journey we will come upon many mountains to climb.

Some we choose. I get on an airplane once a year to fly out West to purposefully climb mountains. It is something my soul needs to grow and be happy. Some people sign up for a distance race that is very far outside their current ability, yet something in them feels ready to step out there.

Some we don't choose. I had to climb the mountain of grief from the death of my parents, but I'm doing it and am finding healing and grace. I have friends who have climbed the mountain of illness, and some are still in the battle.

What we can't do is expect our journey to be without mountains.

If we are moving along and find ourselves standing at the foot of one, we cannot let ourselves or each other stand there stuck, wondering why we've come upon this challenge. It is meant to be there. It is part of the journey. Don't be afraid to start climbing, whatever your mountain may be.

★★★

When I was in California last week, I got up early and went for a run.

I didn't take anything with me except my iPod with inspirational music and my cell phone just in case I got hurt or lost. I found a road that headed up into the hills behind the inn where we stayed and turned onto it. I settled into an easy pace to warm up and took time to enjoy the view. The sun had just come up so the shadows were long across the hills. The higher I climbed, the more I could see of the valley full of vineyards and country homes.

My body warmed up so I could kick it up a notch to match the intensity of the songs. Climbing and climbing these hills, my body found the groove. It felt easy. I don't know why. Some days it feels so difficult. In this moment, I would endure a hundred difficult runs for just a taste of this sweet freedom of movement. Complete inspiration and peace.

In this state of mind I was hoping the road would go on forever, but it turned into a path which came to an end at a private property, so I stopped to rest. If you have climbed much in your lifetime, you know that there is a moment when you turn around to take a look. Oh, the joy of discovering how high you have climbed and how gorgeous the view!

If you have been climbing and climbing, turn around. Take a look. There is such beauty in seeing how far you have come. Don't let any voice tell you, "But you still have so far to go." Who cares? You're moving. You're climbing. You are a beautiful creature that is part of this amazing world. Find what inspires you to keep climbing.

★★★

I heard an interesting concept this weekend that I sort of knew but have never heard phrased like this before. "What you focus on grows."

What, I wondered, have I been focusing on? I wasn't feeling my best. In fact, I was having a bit of an "I suck" time of it, and I didn't know why. I know I always have a little let-down after a big event, and the half marathon had been awesome this year. I also had taken a great vacation but got off track with workouts and sleep, my food wasn't organized, and I had gone several days without doing cardio.

For me, cardio is not optional. Way back in my 20s, I sought the help of a therapist to deal with the pain I was in regarding the death of my parents and some other things that were going on in my life. We talked about medication, but, not feeling ready for that, I asked her if there was another option for me. "Yes," she said, "walk or run outside or on a treadmill for 45 minutes every day."

Because I was a heavy smoker, that was not something I thought I could do. But I was committed and also scared of the alternative, so I joined the Y and started my daily 45 minutes. I kept a journal during this time, and it's remarkable to look back and see the difference it made to get my body moving every day and to focus on something positive.

Knowing that, I decided to light a fire of motivation in my gut for this winter. It would be too easy to focus on the cold, the dark, my fears, my mistakes, what I can't do, what I didn't do.

What can I do? I can walk or run. So, I am going to walk or run every day between now (I started 11/1) and my birthday, which is Feb. 28th. Today is day 8, and I feel like a new person. The funk is completely gone, I feel excited about the winter, and I am pumped up that I made a challenge for myself and I'm sticking with it.

I want the same for you. The past is gone. We all have limitations, fears, and failures. There is a time to claim them, but too much focus and they become so BIG. Let's move forward. See if you can lift your gaze off the obstacles right at your feet and focus on the horizon. I believe we can do it together. It's really beautiful up ahead.

★★★

I'm ready to challenge myself to lose every excuse and stay moving over the winter months.

Thanks to the newsletter and Facebook, I am excited to report that a lot of you are joining me! I love receiving your daily updates and hearing about all the stuff that comes up. It feels like we're shaking something loose, doesn't it?

One of the first things that has come up for me is duration. How many miles do I have to do to make it a run and to fulfill the streak? It's come up for others as well. One of my clients wrote me this:

"I may not be getting in the 45 minutes each time, but the challenge is keeping me to at least doing something! (Two days I only got 30 minutes in.) If I can at least commit to that, eventually I might begin to take time for myself again and not cut my time short because I'm worrying about what else needs to be done. I might realize again that 45 minutes is not being selfish—it is what I need; the rest can wait."

I think this is so fascinating. How often do we skip a workout because we don't have the full hour? I know I do it, but I'm not skipping workouts right now because of the streak. I'm realizing how missing workouts deprives myself of one of life's greatest pleasures, which is being able to spend the entire day saying to myself and out loud, "I did it!!"

By Friday of last week, my legs needed a break, so I planned a one- miler on the treadmill. Once I got going, I ended up walking 1.5, and I was surprised that the rest of the day I felt fabulous. I worked up a good sweat, did what I said I was going to do, and carried on. And it took less than 20 minutes.

There is something about wanting to do it but not doing it, that is very painful to me. My self-esteem plunges. I struggled for years with it, and I see it often in women who want to lose weight but aren't ready to make a change. It wouldn't be a problem except we start hating ourselves or berating ourselves for not doing what we say we'll do, whether it's doing cardio or staying within your calories. If you find you've been beating yourself up, do something for your self-esteem. Do *something*. Trust me when I tell you it doesn't matter how much you do or for how long you do it.

You can change your life *right now*. You don't ever have to wait for some monumental thing to happen. Just show up, every day, and make a choice to support your own goals. Starting on the very first day, you get to say "I did it!" And there is one less thing to beat yourself up about.

Keep doing that day after day, one day at a time, and you have just changed your life!

★★★

What an incredible experience this is turning into! I love knowing I am going to get my workout in. It's not a wish. It's not a hope. I am just doing it no matter what.

I am overcoming.

I am overcoming the momentum to skip workouts on cold, dark evenings. I am overcoming the negative voice that always lurks in my shadow ready to tell me that I will never be good enough. Every step I take is a step closer to becoming the woman I want to be.

How can this be? All from walking or running? If you don't believe me, try it. I challenge you: walk or run at least one mile every day. By day 22, you will be amazed at how your confidence will have skyrocketed. You will see that it is actually all a choice, your choice. That you are creating your life by each and every decision you make. And that every step counts.

There is only one way to move forward and that is to take a step forward. If you feel like that first step is not worthwhile because it doesn't get you very far, take another. And another. Find a way to keep going. You will see that the first step was huge!

If you feel stuck and are thinking you are never going to get "there", take another step. Keep moving forward. Once you really get moving, you will see that there is no "there." There is only the ability to move in one direction or another. And the beautiful thing is that you get to pick the direction at any moment.

★★★

I am so proud of those of you who have joined me. It feels much easier knowing I am not the only one on this quest. It's true that it happens one day at a time.

I really had to face and conquer my excuses this week. Here's what some of my thinking sounded like. It was fascinating to observe:

"I'll run in the morning so it's done for the day oops I hit snooze and overslept that's OK I'll run at lunch oh but I got invited out to lunch I hate to miss that I'll run as soon as I finish lunch ugh I am way too full I'll run right after work man I am so tired and hungry I just want to make myself something to eat and relax."

or "It's Sunday I really want to sleep in so I'll run after church but I'm already showered and my hair is done I'd rather go to breakfast and run later whew I have so much to do to get ready for my week I have to do my laundry and shop for groceries and prepare my food and walk to dogs I will run as soon as I finish all these things but it was so nice outside earlier and now it's raining how can I run in the rain?"

Sound familiar? Been there, too? I find it interesting that with a shift in my thinking, all these excuses have become irrelevant. This week, instead of caving into all these excuses, I ran anyway! I ran when I was full, I ran when I was tired, I even ran in the rain today. And it was awesome.

What was the shift in my thinking? It was commitment. I made a promise to myself that I would walk or run every day *no matter what* because I want the result that this type of consistency brings. I want the feeling I get when I can say, "I did it!"

Feeling frustrated? Feel like you spend all your time thinking about getting fit but not enough of your time doing something about it? Change your thinking. Starting today, make a choice that exercise is no longer optional. Find the time, fit it in, and I guarantee you will feel so much better about yourself you'll be shocked. And very happy.

★★★

I am so thankful and happy January 1 will not be Day One.

I used to hate New Year's Day. It usually meant a new diet and another quit smoking attempt; the beginning of yet another program that was finally going to be the one to give me the body and the life that I wanted.

I have a plan to never, ever be at Day One again. Not with smoking and not with weight loss.

If you start today and don't stop, you will never have to deal with Day One again, either. No more staring anxiously at the long road ahead, wondering how you are ever going to get anywhere.

I have been thinking about what keeps us from starting. It's so hard to find the right time. I understand this. I was always going to start as soon as things became less stressful. As soon as the weekend was over. As soon as I got through the holidays. As soon as I had a different job.

To change my mind-set, I had to think differently. In my quit smoking days, I learned to call excuses and the lies we tell ourselves "stinkin' thinkin.'" Now, I identify these things as false beliefs. A perfect example of a false belief for me was, "I will exercise every day as soon as I have more time."

The lie—as soon as I find the time, I will begin.

The truth—as soon as I begin, I'll find the time.

How can this be? Adding exercise to my already crazy busy day will only subtract another hour, right? You would think so, but no. I don't know why, it's one of the little miracles of this journey, but I promise you as soon as you begin, you will find the time.

Experience it for yourself. Start today. Don't make a big deal out of it, don't demand perfection, and don't think about it too much. Just throw on your shoes and move your body. You just put your very last Day One behind you. Now make a commitment to keep going *no matter what* and keep believing. Pretty soon, those little miracles will start showing up.

★★★

I used to be slightly obsessive about getting ready for a walk or run. It was a big deal. Get the right clothes on, download music, find the good shoes, the perfect socks, the Garmin GPS, the heart rate monitor, water, water bottle holder, phone, bee sting kit, gum, tissues. It was like I was packing to climb Everest.

In the last few weeks I have run without music. I've walked in old shoes and new shoes. I've run at work. I've run in my neighborhood. I've run in pajama pants on my treadmill. I've gone to work sweaty. I've skipped the sports bra. I've walked at night. All my rules have been broken.

Somehow it simplified everything. Now I can decide to run and be out the door in five minutes. I can run up the road to my sister's driveway, turn around, and come home with my two-miler done.

I didn't realize how I was weighed down. I am a huge fan of heart rate monitors. I also love my Garmin to track pace and distance. It's great to have inspiring music for a workout. But for me, these things had become reasons not to go. It had all become too complicated. Too much work.

I had forgotten that the beauty of a walk or a run is that you don't need any of these things. All you need is the desire to do something good for yourself. Today, throw on your shoes and go for a walk or a run. Leave everything else behind for a short period of time and see what happens.

★★★

Why does this challenge bring up so much junk, I wonder? Do you know what I mean? I mean it triggers stuff in my mind and my heart that I have to deal with. Stuff I didn't know was there.

If you are doing this challenge with me, have you also experienced this? Perhaps it has highlighted for you how difficult it is to get time to yourself. Or maybe it has shown you that your excuses can often override your best intentions.

When we attempt to change, why is there a part of us that seems to be resistant? I want to run every day but there is a part of me that fights. Have you experienced this with food? I want to eat healthy, but I just wolfed down something that I feel awful about.

Yesterday I battled and battled in my mind, probably wearing myself out just by thinking about running, until I finally just put on my shoes, gloves, and coat, and with a crappy attitude, I went out the door to get it over with.

It was about 19 degrees yesterday. My face was cold and my first mile was into the wind. I was not comfortable. Then the light bulb came on. Changing means being uncomfortable. I had to step out into something new, away from my comfort zone.

I realized if I want to continue to progress, I have to get OK with being uncomfortable.

How many of us eat some "comfort food" the moment we feel an upsetting emotion? How many of us avoid workouts if we might get too hot, too cold, or too tired? How many of us can't take the feeling of hunger very long at all? Is this really serving us?

It was 19 degrees yesterday. But by the end of my run, my heart was dancing and my feet were flying. My body adjusted to the cold, and I was actually sweating. If I would have stopped and turned around like I wanted to, I would have missed a life-changing experience. I would have missed out on the joy I felt from being outside and pushing myself past my same old, same old.

If you are ready to make a change in your life, prepare to trigger some junk. Allow it to come to the surface. Stop reacting in the same way to the same old feelings, and try something new. It will feel uncomfortable. It's supposed to.

★★★

I am not a fan of the whole New Year—New You thing. I understand it is a time that motivates many people finally to take action that previously they had only just thought about, which is good.

But how do we turn this eruption of motivation into long-term consistent behavior?

I want to share with you an email from a woman who lost 57 pounds last year.

"I was always successful for a short while, and then I would fall back into old habits. I would choose to eat foods that I knew were hurting my body. I tried no carb/low carb diets, I tried cutting sugar out of my diet...every once in a while, I would even try exercising. All this would work for a few months, and then I would slip up and fall back into old ways. This "yo-yo-ing" was torture both physically and emotionally. I finally reached a point of giving up on myself. I would try again but inside I was telling myself I would never be able to lose the weight and, sure enough, I would fail again. As I re-read that last sentence, I am currently starting to cry. How horrible was I to myself that I would set myself up for disaster. Always putting myself down inside. Never believing that I could do this. What is worse, I had no self-worth. I didn't believe I was worth it."

How true. Don't we quickly give up on ourselves? What would change is we decided never, ever to give up on ourselves?

First, I believe we would learn to slow down. All the weight does not have to be lost by your deadline for your journey to be a success. Every pound is a victory, and it is a slow process. Change is gradual. This is not the Biggest Loser.

Then, I believe we would learn to receive forgiveness. To me that means when we had a crappy day and didn't do a thing we had told ourselves we would do, we would wake up the next day with the outlook that it is a new day. And never again would we let the tapes inside our head beat us up. It's a new day!

I believe we would take the time to organize and plan for our success. If you don't believe you can succeed, why bother? But if you believe in yourself and never give up, you are going to need some things in order for this to work. Time scheduled to exercise? Check! Healthy food in the fridge prepared and ready to go? Check! Water bottle? Check!

I believe we would learn to eat and not deprive ourselves. If you know you are in this for the long haul, you are going to learn to eat and develop a healthy relationship with food. I believe in adding lots of healthy, whole, fresh, satisfying foods. Add, add, add. Then the few treats are not a big deal.

I believe we would heal. We've been putting ourselves down for a long time. We've been putting ourselves through the roller coaster of dieting for a long time. These harsh words and harsh lifestyles leave scars, but they can heal. If you are going to think about a new you this New Year, decide to become the person who never, ever gives up on herself.

★★★

I am amazed at how the accountability of this streak gets me out the door.

On days when I am busy or tired, I still run. On days when it is snowing, I hit the treadmill. Bad mood? Walk or run anyway. Feel like being a coach potato? Walk.

Why? Because it is important to me to be able to report to all of you positive results. I could not stand sitting down to write my newsletter and have to write "broke streak on day 76 because I didn't feel like it."

What is your accountability? I believe that we all need it. Maybe not in the same aspects of our lives, but having someone to be accountable to helps people stay the course.

Personal training is a lot about accountability. After one or two sessions, you know how to do a bicep curl, right? I did, but I worked out with my personal trainer for four years. Having that appointment meant that I would get a workout, even if the rest of the week went to hell.

It also meant having someone to report to. I always loved being able to show up for my workout and report that I ran a whole mile, or worked out twice on my own. I also had weeks where I didn't do anything on my own and got the encouragement I needed to do better next week.

There is power in stating your intentions to someone. Think about what you want to accomplish. Then decide on a few small steps you are willing to commit to this week. Write them down. Share them. Do them.

That's how to feel fabulous about yourself.

★★★

SUE MARKOVITCH

I feel like I've written this sentence a lot lately, but again this was the hardest week so far. Back from hiking, I was a bit jet-lagged and not as well organized as when I have all day Sunday to prepare for the week.

When I got home from Utah, the battle began. I don't know why, but my psyche stared to rebel. All of a sudden, this week I didn't want to walk or run at all. There are times when I don't want to run a lot or don't want to run a particular day. But this was more like "I don't want to run at all."

Even though I had jet lag, on Monday I got up a few minutes early to run a mile on my treadmill in the basement. I think it was one of those miles where I was in pajamas and running shoes, eyes half-shut. Tuesday, similar story. Wednesday I stayed after class to run one mile on the treadmill at the studio when all I really wanted to do was go home and crawl under about 12 blankets with a giant bowl of macaroni and cheese. Thursday, another forced one-miler. Friday, one mile. Saturday, one mile.

If Monday through Saturday were my battles, Sunday was the all-out war. Several thoughts went through my mind. I could skip the day and write about how important it is to be able to keep going even when you blow it one day. Or I could use my tight hamstring muscle as a good excuse to take a "planned" day off. Or I could just lie—the bad thoughts in my head said. Who would know?

I remember living this way, pinned down under all the excuses and I-don't-feel-like-it thinking and lies I told myself. I would do it tomorrow. It was too cold. I was too tired. Too busy. Too stressed. I remember giving in day after day only to end up years later wishing I were a different person. A fit, healthy, happy, joy-full person.

I walked to my closet and I just stared at my running shoes. I wanted to cry for some reason. I normally love my running shoes. But I didn't feel like putting them on. I knew this was the moment of choice. The one small moment that, when added up with all my other choices, would determine how I felt about myself tomorrow, next week, maybe next year.

That was enough. Remembering the pain of wishing and hoping I could change, but feeling stuck, was enough to get my shoes on.

I could do this. Then, I put on my hat and gloves, and I ran to my sister's house and back. It was an emotional run. I was happy I had chosen the right thing and shaken that it had been so difficult. It reminded me that if I choose according to how I feel, versus what I know to be best for me, I will not stay on the right path.

This week is the coldest, roughest week of the year. It's so cold! I felt it and I struggled. But looking back, those one- milers seem like successes. Who cares how far I went? I went. Who cares if those miles weren't pretty? They were miles. Who cares if I had epic mental battles while trying to make the right choice? I made the right choice for me.

If you are struggling, I want to remind you that I know how hard this is, and I encourage you to battle through it. *Choose what's good for you* no matter how you feel. Let's do this together.

★★★

Ah, it's such a relief to want to run again instead of that long week of making myself do it. I got in a few two- and three-milers and was feeling excited about ramping things up this weekend and getting in a long workout.

Unfortunately, I woke up Friday with a bug. Sore throat and cough.

Now I had the opposite problem. I wanted to walk or run, but I had this physical obstacle preventing me from doing so. Throw in a foot of snow and suddenly my ramp up just became a serious slow down.

Must this process be so hard? Some days it feels like one step forward, two steps back. I remember early on in my weight loss getting sick could really derail me. It wasn't just the time off of working out, but the lack of energy and then the difficulty in getting back on track mentally.

I don't want this streak to be unhealthy for me either, so I wanted to be careful to take time off if that was what I really needed. I was finding this balance a challenge. What do I really need? Rest? Or to keep the streak alive?

I decided on both. I did my mile each day over the weekend, but I did it very slowly and in agreement with myself that if I felt that I was pushing too hard, I would stop. Then I added lots of rest and relaxation this weekend. As I was running nice and easy up my street the day after the big snowstorm, one phrase kept going through my head. "This too shall pass."

The snow will soon melt making room for sunny spring days and long enjoyable walks and runs. This cold will be gone tomorrow (I hope!) and I will once again be able to take big deep breaths without coughing. Another mental battle may come and go. More obstacles will pop up, guaranteed. They, too, shall pass.

I believe what's important is that I don't quit no matter what obstacle I encounter. It's so easy to get discouraged. It is no fun to take one step forward, two steps back. But these setbacks are temporary. When I refocus and allow myself to see the bigger picture, I can see that I am moving in a direction that I chose. It is not always a straight line, but that doesn't matter.

One hundred days. 330 miles. I like those numbers, but when I really think about what all this means to me, it's about keeping a promise I made to myself. I'm honoring my commitment. There is no better feeling to me than being able to say I did what I set out to do, despite all the setbacks. Remember, this too shall pass.

★★★

No more streak. I made it to Day 100 and then stopped due to the nasty respiratory virus that's going around. The doctor prescribed rest, and I listened.

A few interpretations of this:

1) I quit and failed. The goal was to run at least one mile every day from November 1–February 28, and I didn't make it.

2) I had a perfectly good excuse, so I don't have to call it a failure. No one should be expected to exercise when they are ill.

3) My self-discipline sucks. With only 20 days to go, couldn't I toughen up and run one slow mile each day? I could have done that.

4) I always fail. I don't know why I even try. Never again.

5) My friend Mandy has made it longer than me. So has Michele. And Greg is about to pass me.

6) I ran 100 consecutive days through Thanksgiving, Christmas, New Years, vacation, and snow. YAY!

7) I am proud of myself for giving a workout streak a good shot. I learned a lot.

All of these thoughts have spent time in my head this week, some for a split second, others for days. In the past, I could have easily latched on to some of the darker interpretations. Number 4 used to be one of my favorites—attempting to quit smoking would usually send me into that kind of pit. I would spend months gearing up to quit again. I would get sick of smoking to the point that I was ready. Then I would have a ceremonial last cigarette and go to bed determined to quit the next morning. Usually by 2:00 p.m. the next day, I was at a gas station buying smokes, hating myself for failing, and for even trying because now look what I caused— a major self-esteem meltdown and nothing was worth feeling like this.

But I haven't allowed myself to go there. To do that, I had to really think about why I started this to begin with. I began the running streak to find a way to stay focused on exercise through the holidays and the winter. I wanted to come out of the other end of winter feeling better about myself than I had going in. I wanted to feel empowered by winter, not depressed by it.

Here's the paragraph from my earlier newsletter:

"I decided to light a fire of motivation in my gut for this winter. It would be too easy to focus on the cold, the dark, my fears, my mistakes, what I can't do, what I didn't do.

What can I do? I can walk or run. So, I am going to walk or run every day between now (I started 11/1) and Feb. 28th. Today was day 8 and I feel like a new person...I feel excited about the winter, I am pumped up that I made a challenge for myself, and I'm sticking with it."

As I meditate on these words and allow myself to dig into their meaning, what I remember is my purpose. This work is my purpose and it is something I need to be at the center of my life. And it is my passion to bring it to other women as well.

So, then my question becomes: how did creating a 100-day workout streak support my passion and purpose? And the exciting answer is that it changed me. I was transformed. Every week, week after week, I learned another lesson, fought another battle, and took another step.

And as I communicated this journey with others, they, in turn, learned lessons, fought battles, and took steps and then shared it. We were all changed, if only in some small way. Your circumstances may say one thing, but dig deeper and find your purpose. Find your reason. What seems like a momentary shortcoming may indeed be part of some transformation, and all you need is to be able to see it.

★★★

Here was my Saturday: I got to sleep in, which was wonderful and relaxing. It was the first morning that I've awoken feeling almost recovered from this bug. I lounged around drinking coffee and reading. I got some things done around the house. I connected a bit on Facebook while eating breakfast.

After I showered, I pulled a few pieces of warmer-weather clothing out of the back of my closet to try on. Not sure if it was the flu or the running streak or a combination, but my clothes were fitting great, and I felt like a lean mean machine.

I ventured out to meet a friend for a great conversation, and then I headed to the mall to spend some of the gift cards I received over the holidays. While there, I stopped at Starbucks and got my skinny latte. All was well with the world.

Shopping went great. Things I tried on fit, and it felt really good to feel good about myself in the dressing rooms. Those places used to be dreaded, dreaded places. Many a Saturday afternoon would I leave frustrated and near tears from shopping. Not so on this day.

But I shopped too long. By the time I reached the car, I was starving. I had been having too much fun shopping to think about stopping for lunch at the mall. So I went through the McDonald's drive-through. I was so hungry I didn't really care what I was ordering or how many calories were in it, so I ordered the Fish Value Meal.

As I pulled out of the drive-through, I reached in the bag and ate a few fries. Ick. They were cold, salty, and greasy. Disgusting. So, I waited through the light, turned around, went back through the drive-through and politely got my money back.

You would think that would end it. However, I knew I had nothing in the fridge at home. All my prepared food for the week was gone. I hadn't been to the grocery store yet, so I had to find something. (For all the times I have offered you all suggestions to stop and get a protein bar, a piece of fruit, anything that's considered a good choice: I understand when your mind goes blank and all you can think of is fast food.)

So I drove past my house, and instead of turning left and going to Raisin Rack for a smoothie, some sushi, something from their salad bar, etc.), I went to KFC! I hate KFC. I am not kidding. It was like there were two parts of me. The one who knows what to do and the one doing the doing. Who *was* this person?

So I order this disgusting wrap with fried chicken and cheese, fried potato wedges, and a diet coke. I got home and opened up the bag. I took a bite of the chicken wrap. I ate two wedges. And I threw the entire thing in the trash. $5.99 to the landfill.

The end, right? I got a grip and had a bowl of cereal and skim milk, right? No. I went to a birthday party hungry and had pizza and two pieces of cake. My stomach still hurts thinking about it. I felt the self-loathing creep in that I remember too well. Not a good feeling. Driving home I kept thinking, "Do not melt down. Do not melt down." I just could not wait to get to bed and start a new day.

When I got up today, I thought about the episode. Was I feeling too good about myself and I had to bring it down a notch? Did I get so hungry that I lost all control of making good choices? Was I losing control since I wasn't running? Or is this battle something that can rise up any time that I am unorganized, unprepared, or let my guard down? I would guess it is a combination.

Happily, since I have been through this before, I know that one day does not change anything if you don't let it. So I got my act together today. I went grocery shopping for fresh food, I made turkey and black bean chili for the week, and I got organized. It was an interesting reminder that although I feel like I have conquered a lot of my issues with food, they still lurk and I have to stay vigilant.

Note to self: Stay committed. Receive forgiveness immediately when you blow it. You're not crazy, just human. Recommit as soon as possible.

★★★

Back on track after almost three weeks off of working out due to one nasty little bugger of a virus. It felt great to lift three days last week and run a few miles. Ah...nothing like sore triceps to feel like I've done something.

I am happy the streak is over, and I believe it was successful in that it kept me active all winter. I am still amazed that by focusing on walking or running at least one mile every day how the miles added up.

Why do the miles seem to add up but the pounds lost don't? I know many of you have the experience of working out every week, watching what you eat, and still the weight loss feels excruciatingly slow. That was certainly my experience. What's going on here?

I lost about 45 pounds in 7 years. I wanted to lose 45 pounds in 45 days, but that didn't happen. I worked out three times a week with my trainer. I walked and ran marathons, I walked at Highbanks, and still it came off slowly. That's about a pound every 8 weeks.

If it comes off that slowly, is it worth the work? How do you stick with it, even though you aren't getting instant results or much encouragement from the scale? Is there anything you can do to speed up the process?

I believe we lose weight when we are ready to lose weight, and at the pace that is right for us. But I also believe there are many things we can do to prepare ourselves for transformation, instead of just waiting for some kind of magic to appear.

★★★

Last week, I asked if you felt like you are doing the work but the results are slow or not there at all. Here is a sample of the many, many responses I received:

"Like I said at our last meeting, it is like you are spelling out my own thoughts! I have been trying to shift my thinking to "fueling my body" versus just feeding my cravings. Hopefully this will work. I am also not going to weigh myself for a month and see where that gets me. Hopefully obsessing less!"

"Okay, I guess I need to get back in the swing of things...you have motivated me. Especially when you said you lost 45 pounds in 7 years, but you wanted to lose 45 pounds in 45 days. Gee, I thought that was an option!! I certainly have fallen off the wagon since my wedding. But now I need your positive attitude to help me get my 'groove' back."

"In response to your newsletter....I am doing the work and disciplined with it but I am not as so with my eating habits. I eat mostly good things but can't get a grip on whether I should eat 3 square meals a day or 6 small meals and stop the snacking. I feel that I work out so I can eat the sweet stuff! That is my struggle. Any insight would be helpful."

"Yes, please continue to address the time/weight issues. I've just started doing the work, but I know that this is going to be a process, so I'm trying not to focus on the time it's going to take or what the scales have to say. But, the question is: how do you keep that from creeping in and derailing the progress?"

Thank you for all the responses I received. I hope you can see that if you are working hard but the results are slow, you are not alone. I work with a lot of women, and I think it's safe to say that the number one question I receive when I first start working with someone is, "How long did it take you to lose the weight?"

I lost 45 pounds, but it was over several years and it was very slow. From the beginning of this transformation, I was willing to exercise. I liked the way it made me feel. Like I have mentioned before, cardiovascular exercise was something that I started doing when I was seeing a therapist and she recommended it for mental health. It worked well for me and still does.

Just because I was exercising, however, doesn't mean I was losing weight. I lost a few initial pounds but I was doing so many things wrong that progress stopped shortly after it started. Of the many things I was doing wrong, I believe the main things that were holding me back were not getting enough sleep, not drinking enough water, doing my cardio inconsistently and in the wrong heart rate range, and not taking responsibility for what I was eating.

Among all of those, taking responsibility for my food was the hardest of all and like you saw in my confession newsletter, my food issues can still flare up. Thankfully, those flare-ups are infrequent, and I have learned how to move past them (and move forward).

I believe there are many reasons why it is so difficult to get the food aspect under control.

— Food was a major source of comfort for me, especially when I was lonely.
— I did not take time to be organized so I was often grabbing something quick.
— I was totally confused about what I should eat to lose weight.
— I was unaware of how many calories were in the foods I ate.
— I did not want to be deprived and miss out on treats.
— I ate out at restaurants whenever possible because I didn't like to eat at home.
— I was either on a diet or in a food free-for-all.

For these reasons, I had what I call an unhealthy relationship with food. I felt anxious about my eating, when I was dieting it leaned towards the obsessive, and what I ate could make me feel horrible about myself. If I ate too much and got too full, I could have a full-blown self-hatred meltdown.

So to go from that unhealthy way of relating to food to a healthy, mindful approach to eating took a long time. For me, I believe it had to take that long because there was so much stuff to deal with. If you haven't noticed yet, when you choose to change your life, all sorts of stuff starts coming up. And the longer you stick with it, the more stuff comes up. It's hard.

The good news is: the only way out is through. So every time something new comes up, whether it is a fear, an obstacle, or an excuse, if you choose to deal with it, you come one step closer to being through it. And freedom awaits you at the end of that road.

So what does that mean for today? What should I do now to get started or make something happen? I believe a great way to prepare for the changes ahead are these:

Start or continue exercising consistently because becoming stronger physically will help you become stronger emotionally, and you will need that to stick with this for the long haul.

Count calories. But not for the reason you think. Not so you know the exact amount of calories you take in so you can keep under 1452 calories, or whatever. Count calories to become aware of how many calories are in the foods that you eat. Once you are aware, you can make much better decisions about what is healthy for you.

Find someone you feel comfortable sharing all your emotional junk with to talk to and start sharing. Say to someone, "I am a mess and would like to tell you about it!" Go for a walk and tell someone that you are afraid to try to make a change because you have failed so many times and don't know if you can handle it again. Then ask them to be there to support you.

Make a commitment to yourself right now to never, ever give up and to keep believing that you are strong enough.

★★★

Last week I said I would dive into the specifics of healthy eating; what to eat, when to eat, and why. This is a complicated topic because we are all unique, so what I am presenting here are my personal beliefs and my own experience in finding a formula that works for me. Here goes.

When you ask me what, how, when, and why to eat, I believe my answer must be a question which is, "Where are you now?" Learning to have a healthy relationship with food is a progression through various stages. Here is how I look at them.

Stage One—Stop the Bleeding

When I was just getting started, I felt very out of control. I had been gaining weight for some time, wishing I could change, and feeling very bad about myself. So I relate to women that come to me feeling like this. I believe at this stage, you need to get a little control back in small doable steps. Weight Watchers points or calorie tracking works well for this stage. Small successes are the key to turning things around.

A 250-pound woman is probably eating between 2500–3000 calories a day to be gaining weight, so even cutting 500 calories a day can add up to big successes. Often, just the act of writing down what you eat and adding up the points or calories (I prefer calories) creates a new mindfulness that can lead you to the next stage.

If you feel like you are stuck in this stage and cannot get any control at all, I suggest you talk to someone about why your relationship with food has become so unhealthy.

Stage Two—Heal and Grow

I progressed very slowly through this stage because I had so much emotional stuff that needed to heal. I would come upon these long periods of plateau in my weight loss. I realize now that I never stopped working or progressing, I just couldn't see what was happening. Layers were being stripped away and I was deep into the reasons why my relationship with food had become so unhealthy.

There were times when I got so frustrated because it seemed like I was working out so hard and the weight wouldn't budge. But I was still learning how to not depend on food for emotional comfort, trying to get organized, trying to stop punishing myself, becoming more aware of what to eat and when, and getting out of the all-or-nothing diet mentality. As I progressed through these things, I became more honest with myself about what I was really eating, and as that happened, more weight came off.

If you feel like you are stuck in this stage, I suggest you ask yourself what needs to heal or grow within you to move forward.

Stage Three—Optimize

This is the place where you've gotten through a lot of emotional work and now are tweaking your lifestyle continuously. There may be times you are thinking about optimizing your performance, your health, or your confidence.

Once I progressed to this point, I began to think more about food in terms of how to fuel my body. I don't count calories anymore, I know for the most part what to eat, I know how to comfort myself without using food, I know how to receive forgiveness and move on when I have a bad day. In other words, I have finally developed a healthy relationship with food.

The personal formula that works best for me is what I call *Never Too Hungry, Never Too Full*. It is very simple. Eat correct portions of whole, fresh foods often enough to send the signal to your brain and body that nutrition is abundant—no need to store fat.

You may find you can "eat clean" about 75% of the time, which is great. If you want to, you may have to increase your clean eating to 85% of the time. I've found that my struggles here have to do with priorities. For example:

Which is more important to you: eating and drinking what you want in social situations or your weight loss?

Which is more important to you: rewarding yourself with sweet treats or fitting into your jeans?

I know from my experience I may be spending a lot of mental energy thinking about improving my body composition, but I haven't gotten brutally honest about eating clean when I am out with the girls on a Friday night.

If you are struggling at this stage, I suggest you ask yourself if losing those last stubborn pounds or firming up that body part is worth making the changes that need to be made to get there. And if it is worth it to you, stop thinking about it and get serious about it.

You know it when you eat the right thing because you feel great! No sugar highs and lows. Just good energy. Think about that apple slice with all-natural peanut butter. Or a grilled chicken breast with steamed broccoli. A salad with avocado, almonds, and veggies. Yum.

We must send the signal to our bodies and brains that food, water, and nutrition are abundant. No need to store fat. Deprivation is not necessary. Once you fall in love with eating healthy, the junk doesn't have the same pull that it used to. Be aware of how many calories are in the foods you choose. Be aware of the reasons you eat. Be aware of portion sizes. Remember; shoot for progress—not perfection. There is no such thing.

★★★

Last week I dove into the specifics of healthy eating; what to eat, when to eat, and why. Did you find you could identify with one of the stages? Do you see why the process can take so long? Even though at the most basic level losing weight requires a calorie deficit, usually there is a transformation that must occur on the inside to make this happen.

To further complicate the process, there is an avalanche of information being thrown at us constantly about what to eat, what is healthy, and what will help us lose weight. I find it can be so overwhelming and confusing to read article after article of food advice. There are a few things I try to keep in mind.

First, I try to remember that food companies are trying to make money and they do not care about my health and fitness as long as I am buying their product. Just because an ad claims something doesn't mean I believe it. There is no losing 30 pounds in 30 days. There is no shortcut. There is no secret.

There is only eating fresh, whole foods and working hard. If you keep looking for the magic pill or diet that will allow you to eat junk (food that contains more calories than nutrition), you are wasting time that could be spent on things that matter.

Second, I try to remember to think in terms of health and fitness, not scales and weight loss. Can I live on Lean Cuisines and Weight Watchers desserts and lose weight? Sure, for awhile. Will my overall health suffer? Yes, it will. There is not enough nutrition in these products to optimize my overall health and fitness.

What I find happens when I focus on nutrition is that I am rewarded with a metabolism boost. I also do not feel at the mercy of cravings. There were many times that I would eat my Lean Cuisine only to wander to the snack machine an hour later and eat a package of M&Ms, which have more calories than the lunch did. But when I eat a whole foods lunch of lean protein and complex carbs plus water, I send the signal to my brain that what I needed has been received. No more food needed. Free to move on to other things.

Third, I try to remember that all foods are not created equal. Fruit is a great example. How many of us are confused about fruit! Can I eat it? Should I eat it? What about the sugar? Here's how I think about fruit. Fruit is awesome in its whole, natural form in proper portions. The combination of fiber, fructose, vitamins, and water is just what our body needs. But what happens when we strip the fiber out and just get the sugar? The body reacts differently.

According to the science, you will get a higher insulin response when you have fruit juice as opposed to whole fruit. Then there is dried fruit with added sugars, canned fruit with added syrup, fruit-flavored Kool Aid, and Fruit Roll Ups. We can't make the mistake of thinking these are all equal. Whole, natural fruit is best. Add some natural peanut butter to your apple slices with the skin on and now you have the optimal combination (fiber + natural sugar + protein).

Chicken is another good example. Is chicken good for you? I believe natural chicken breast without hormones or antibiotics is good for you. I dislike that they inject chicken with 15% salt solution to plump it up for sale. Then once you start to bread it, fry it, add cheese and bacon to it, it gets away from being good for you.

So how can we simplify all the information and choices available to us? Repeat it again and again. Fresh, whole foods. Fresh, whole foods. Remember the advice—stick to the perimeter of the grocery store. Don't fall for the commercials. If it comes in a box or a bottle, it was probably messed with enough to diminish its nutritional value for the sake of profit and marketability. Read the labels.

Or just fill up your cart with apples, bananas, cantaloupe, beans, nuts, peppers, squash, cucumber, fish, chicken, lettuce, eggs, avocados, onions, sweet potatoes, and all those wonderful things the Earth has managed to provide all this time without Stouffers, Weight Watchers, Nabisco, or Kraft.

★★★

We spent the last few weeks talking about food. Remember; eat as many whole, natural foods as possible. Lean meat, low-fat dairy, vegetables, fruit, whole grains, nuts, healthy fats, and coffee, tea, water. Everything else is probably processed in some way (which in my mind means stuff has been added that adds calories), and we need to watch how much of that we allow into our daily nutrition because those calories tend to add up much faster.

Eat healthy foods, be aware of your portion sizes, get your exercise in, drink lots of water, get good sleep, and find healthy ways to deal with your stress. We can dig into each of these, but my belief is that we know what to do.

The problem occurs when we know what to do, but don't do it. Why is it so hard to decide to exercise and then stick with it? Or to decide to eat clean and stay committed to it? Wouldn't all this be so much easier if we just did what we asked ourselves to do?

I spent many years thinking a lot about dieting and exercise. I was convinced that I would be happy as soon as I got to my goal weight. At the same time, I was quite good at thinking about exercise while I sat on the couch, or at thinking about eating healthy while pounding down some junk food.

There is a very good reason it took me over 7 years to lose 45 pounds. It's because I was changing. I had to allow this process of change to happen in my life if I was ever going to stop overeating and start exercising consistently. The reason I could not lose the weight without changing on the inside is that I was using food to feel better.

There were times in my life that I felt very lost and in a lot of pain. When I look back, the lonely times were the worst. Like the year I lived in Detroit with very few friends, away from family, with a new job, in my own apartment. Pizza, nacho chips with queso dip, White Castles, and ice cream are what got me through a lot of lonely evenings. Or, the year leading up to my divorce, when I felt isolated and disconnected at home. Several evenings a week I would go alone to Panera and sit there filling up on bread and cookies.

I didn't realize there were healthier ways of filling myself. Now if I feel lonely, I call a friend and we go for a walk at Highbanks or go to the coffee shop. When I feel unmotivated to exercise, I take a class or work out with a friend. It's a much better experience.

We are not meant to take this journey alone. Nearly every woman I work with has some struggle she is working through. We all are. It's really one of the amazing things that connect us all. One of the reasons I share some of the emails I receive from clients is to remind all of us that we are not alone. If you feel stuck, remember there are people around you. Grab the hand of someone, squeeze it, and ask them to do this with you.

★★★

Have you seen this in the news this week: "Women need an hour of exercise daily to maintain weight in midlife"?

If you struggle with your weight, the fight just got a little tougher. The latest advice from researchers regarding women and their weight is that we need to exercise an hour a day, 7 days a week, to maintain our weight without dieting and to avoid the weight gain that comes with aging. An hour; as in 60 minutes. Have you seen a woman lately with an extra hour in her day?

Me either. Nonetheless, that's the recommendation released online Tuesday in the Journal of the American Medical Association.

"We wanted to see in regular folks—people not on any particular diet—what level of physical activity is needed to prevent weight gain over time," said the lead author of the study, Dr. I-Min Lee, an epidemiologist at Brigham and Women's Hospital in Boston and an associate professor of medicine at Harvard University. "It's a large amount of activity. If you're not willing to do a high amount of activity, you need to curtail your calories a lot,' Lee told the Los Angeles Times."

How do you feel about that? I worry about studies like this. Actually, I worry about our response to them. How many of you have the initial reaction that this is impossible, you are already overwhelmed, so you might as well give up now?

The other problem is the reporting of the study. The news has the study but gives you only a small part of it, not the whole. For example, if you read the report, they count an hour of walking equal to a half hour of running. Did that then just cut the recommendation in half? What if you can power walk and get to the same heart rate as when you run? Or walk on hills? Is 30 minutes enough then? The report also talks about breaking up the 60 minutes into small, intense workouts being equivalent but the news did not report that.

In a way, the study is common sense. I am sure that before McDonald's was on every corner, we drove everywhere, and sat at desks all day, it was the norm for a woman to have at least an hour of intense physical activity every day. I would think in many cultures women spend their days actively growing and preparing food, walking to the market and back, and venturing out for clean water. But we don't.

So, what can you do if this is too much right now? The study is basically saying to make sure you get a lot of exercise or you will need to cut your caloric intake year after year. Um, I'm 45 and I already know this from experience. Didn't need the study to tell me that it gets more challenging. Right, ladies?

Don't let these studies get you down. This one reminds me a little bit of the magazine cover story that got me going last summer. Whoever is doing the writing, they are not writing with our hearts in mind. They forget that we don't operate logically when it comes to these matters.

I suggest you ignore all this, even though it was in the news day after day last week. Let it go in one ear and out the other. Stay on YOUR path. Keep taking your small, doable steps. Keep working in the right direction. This is a very personal journey and a difficult one if you have failed many times before. Don't let information like this discourage you.

If it doesn't help you, move on. Find the stuff that helps you. Do you get inspired by watching The Biggest Loser? Then watch it! Are you just getting started exercising? Keep going! Are you struggling with your weight? Don't give up! Information is fine if it's helpful, but what really matters is that you keep believing.

★★★

We talk a lot about food. I get a lot of questions about food. I ask a lot of questions about food. Too bad it's not about food.

Have you ever gone to the grocery store with renewed determination to buy fresh, healthy foods only to get home and order a pizza? Have you worked hard to prepare a very healthy dinner, ate it, and a half hour later wandered into the kitchen and ate something else just because you weren't satisfied?

The most common phrase I hear from every woman I know is this, "I know what to do, I just don't do it." What's going on here?

Here is the fact: If you eat more than your body uses, it stores that energy as fat. So logically, knowing exactly how many calories your body needs and then following that precisely would completely solve the problem. No one would be overweight. No one would feel crappy about themselves. So why doesn't it work?

For me, I knew I wanted to eat healthier. I knew I wanted to eat less. I knew I wanted to stop eating compulsively. I knew I wanted to be thinner. But it never would have worked to just rip that extra food from me. It would not have changed anything because the underlying problem still existed. My broken heart was still there.

If you are struggling, I want to challenge you to find what it is in you that has you eat when you aren't hungry. Where is your emptiness? What is your hunger? We all struggle to find ways to cope with our pain, our loneliness, our guilt, our shame, our stress, our anger, our disappointment, and our fear. One way to cope is to eat.

I used eating to cope. I have used many things to cope. The problem with using is that our drugs of choice have consequences. Using cigarettes to cope leads to disease. Using shopping to cope leads to out- of-control debt. Using people-pleasing to cope leads to losing ourselves. Using food to cope leads to being overweight.

It was not easy to look at myself like this. I had to admit that because I ran away from my feelings, I ran to other things. And the outcome of that was a very unhealthy, unhappy, worthless-feeling woman. I had to get really honest and say that I had lost my way.

I had given up on myself. I thought the best was behind me, and I had missed my chance at happiness. What a lie! Don't believe it for a second.

Here's what happened. My dad died when I was 13, my mom died when I was 23. And because I was young and didn't know any better, I let these losses define me. I was damaged. I was not good enough. I would never be whole. So what difference did it make if I smoked? What difference would it make what I ate and ate and ate? It made no difference to me. I was never going to truly like or accept myself anyway.

Then I found the truth. I was hurting. I was in pain. My heart was broken. I said these things out loud to other people over and over, and my heart began to heal. "I am afraid, I am angry, I am lonely", I said. And the more I shared my story, the less power these feelings had over me. I figured out that although I am the daughter of two parents who died young, that it didn't have to define me. I could be a survivor. A fighter. An overcomer! I like that much better.

And as I healed, my extra weight came off. I know now that no matter how badly I wanted to, I could not have willed myself off food. I had to heal from the inside out. The way to that for me was to remember who I was, to realize that I was strong enough to feel what I was feeling instead of running away from it, and to always believe that the best was yet to come.

★★★

I have two stories. One story sounds something like this. My parents died when I was young. I dropped out of high school. I was broke and in terrible debt in my twenties. My marriage failed in my thirties. I made bad decisions. I smoked for seventeen years. I went from job to job. I was diagnosed with a kidney disease. I was overweight and struggling. Why me?

My other story goes like this. I have always had amazing people around me. No matter what I went through, I had friends and family to support and encourage me. I was forgiven for things I didn't deserve to be forgiven for. When I got in trouble financially, someone was there to help me. I not only went to college, I earned a master's degree. I quit smoking and got healthy. The long and winding road of various jobs led me to my dream career. I am loved beyond measure. I am very, very blessed.

I am aware that both these stories exist. At any given moment, I can be living in one or the other. For most of my life, I saw my life from within the first story. A few years ago, I experienced a major shift and began seeing my life from the second story. And with a wave of gratitude my life changed forever.

I had a meeting with a client this week. I began the session with congratulations because she had just hit the 40-pound weight loss mark. She made a face back at me and turned the corners of her mouth down with a groan. Too slow, she said. Not enough. Still so far to go.

I understand this. To me, this is seeing life from the first story. How could this be going so badly for her, right? Only 40 pounds in one year. Nothing to celebrate. It's taking too long. Not good enough. Never good enough.

Here's the interpretation of the same facts from the second story. This wonderful woman found encouraging people to help her get on track. She worked incredibly hard and lost 40 pounds! Her life is changing dramatically for the better. She feels stronger, healthier, younger, and more energetic. She is heading in the right direction and inspiring others while doing it. She will stick with it and reach her goals.

Maybe you interpret your life or your body or your fitness journey from the first story. I want to challenge you this week to be grateful. Find the gifts. Even if you feel like you have nothing to be grateful for, start looking. Be grateful for the taste of your breakfast. Be grateful for your pretty eyes. Be grateful for legs that work. Be grateful for the sunshine. Be grateful you went for a walk.

Once you do that, try to reinterpret whatever is going on from the second story. Can you see the gifts? Can you see how far you have come? Can you see that all the stops and starts were leading you towards your dreams? Can you see all the mistakes and failures were just part of the journey?

At any given moment, we can be in one story or the other. When you get stuck in the first one, it gets very difficult to move forward. The energy is negative, and it is hard to receive the gifts of love, encouragement, and support from the people around you. I believe you can create a new story any time, no matter what your circumstances.

★★★

When I am walking up mountains, a wonderful thing happens. I become fully present. I believe it has something to do with the hard work of climbing, as well as the fear of falling off a very high cliff. But suddenly I find myself without the baggage of my past. And without the worries of the future. I am focusing on each step.

Walking is a slow way to get somewhere, especially when climbing. We did a hike called Observation Point at Zion National Park, and at the very beginning I was focused on the destination: Observation Point. It was hard not to think about how long it would take to get there (about three hours). But rather quickly into the hike, we rounded a corner and came upon an incredible hidden canyon. There was a sheer cliff reaching upward on one side, and spectacular rock formations on the other. We stood in the silence of the canyon and I thanked God that I got to experience this beauty. My heart was filled with wonder.

When I was unhappy with my weight and my life, I was always looking for instant solutions. If I tried something and it didn't fix things immediately, I gave up on it. It's one of the reasons I stayed stuck for quite a long time. Then I discovered walking. It became such a symbol for me and my journey. Slow, steady, just pressing on.

I learned that one step isn't walking. You have to stick with it step after step after step to get somewhere. There are no instant solutions. But I learned if you keep walking, amazing changes take place. If I keep walking, sometimes I turn the corner and am presented with an amazing gift of beauty that stays with me forever. If I keep walking, I am blessed with the gift of endurance. If I keep walking, my belief in my own abilities to persevere changes and grows. I receive the gift of self-confidence.

After about three hours, we did reach the summit of Observation Point, and the view was indescribable. My friend said to me, "Our feet got us here." It was an amazing feeling of accomplishment. I could never feel that way sitting somewhere thinking about doing it. Sometimes we want so badly to change the direction of our path that we get stuck in our heads. I believe the way to make changes in our life is to move forward.

If you feel stuck, remember one choice can put you on a new path. If you are that person sitting in one place trying to figure out how to pole vault to the next place, spinning your wheels because you can't figure out how to do it, look to where you are trying to go. Is it possible that if you start taking one step after another after another, you will get there? I believe you will, and you will be changed along the way.

★★★

I read a definition of "power" recently that really hit me: "the ability to bring about a desired result." Are we each living in that kind of power? Knowing that we have the ability to bring about what we want for our lives?

When you think about fitness, what do you want? Do you want to be strong? Fit? Athletic? Healthy? Confident? A role model? Are your reasons big enough to get you to lace up your shoes every day and put in your miles or time in the gym?

For me, when I felt my worst, I not only hated how I looked but I was stuck in a pretty bad spiral of beating myself up. I just didn't feel good about myself. When I started walking at Highbanks, I started feeling a little more empowered on every walk. What I thought had gotten away from me completely—my ability to be fit and confident—started to feel possible again.

Now, when I have that moment of choosing whether to work out or not, I remember those times when I felt lost to myself, and it makes it a joy (most days) to lace up my shoes and start moving because nothing was worse than the thought of living the rest of my life under that cloud of self-loathing.

If you feel at all stuck, just put your shoes on. Then step outside. Then start to walk. This is not something you can reason your way out of. In fact, our minds are only in the way. Walk, walk, walk. One step and then another. Pretty soon, you will feel the power that was inside you all along. It's never too late.

★★★

You work out hard. You walk miles and miles. You make good food choices. But if you don't do it consistently, you probably will not see results.

We all tend to have a similar approach to fitness. We get jazzed up for Monday. We "are good" for a few days, then by Thursday or Friday we are back to our bad habits. We have fun with those bad habits for the weekend, and then berate ourselves into starting all over again on Monday.

What I see with this repeating cycle is that over time, it is very destructive. It is most definitely not marked by harmony or peace. There is a battle going on. One part of me wants to work out consistently, eat clean, and enjoy optimal fitness and health. The other part of me wants to eat a giant bowl of vanilla ice cream with Hershey's syrup and whipped cream every night and not care about the consequences.

The problem is that, for me, the consequences became very real. I was being fitted for a dress for my sister's wedding. Did you know they charge extra for excess material over a certain size? I learned that. I also learned that it was no fun to shop when I was overweight. And I didn't have much self-confidence. I turned down invitations to things because I didn't feel good enough about myself.

Turning that around was not easy. I had developed lots of bad habits and false beliefs about food and fitness. I had excuse after excuse about why I wasn't at a healthy weight. I have the image in my mind of a giant ship going full-steam ahead and then trying to do a U-turn. That's how it felt to get consistent with exercise and eating healthier.

But it is possible. I believe we are all capable of making those changes if the reason is important enough. This is really hard work. It takes time. It requires sweat and sometimes tears. Losing weight was never enough of a reason for me to consistently make better choices. I had to come to the point where I was so sick of feeling bad about myself. I couldn't stand the battle anymore, I wanted harmony.

I know there are a million reasons not to walk or lift today. There are as many reasons to eat a giant ice cream sundae or to order a pizza. There may be only one reason to take the time to go to the grocery store, stock up on healthy foods, cook a fabulous dinner, lace up your shoes and go for a walk. But that one reason, if it means enough to you, is the only thing that will get you to choose what's best for you. Remember, you are worth it.

★★★

I am afraid.
I am afraid of being humiliated.
I am afraid of failing.
I am afraid of looking stupid.
I am afraid of being uncomfortable.
I am afraid I can't finish.
I am afraid I'll never start.
I am afraid I'll never be good enough.

And so, to some extent, is every other woman who has set foot in a gym or laced up their shoes to try something new. It's all so intimidating. But it can be overcome.

The first thing that helps me is to realize the fears that pop up are normal. And they are universal. If I can face them, they lose their power.

The second thing that works is to go my own pace. It is *so* important to start where you are and do what you can do. When I am training clients, I say two conflicting things. The first thing I say is "Push! Try! Knock out a few more...you can do it!" The second thing I try to get across is, "Don't compete with others." Pick a level based on what you can do, so it pushes you outside of your comfort zone but doesn't injure you or make you quit. It's a hard balance.

I believe that a lot of the time, our excuses are just mechanisms to hide our fear. It's easier to say, "I don't have time," than it is to say, "I am afraid I will fail." This week, I encourage you to picture whatever barriers are standing in your way and like a ninja warrior, roundhouse kick them to the ground and step into a new life.

★★★

Do you have a difficult decision to make? One tough choice puts you on a new path. Ten tough choices create the life of your dreams.— Debbie Ford

When I read this quote from a favorite author of mine, it reminded me of how important my choices are. I am actually creating my life out of my choices. I may not have control over things that happen in life, but I can choose how to respond.

Ugh. That may not always feel like good news if you want to get in shape. You mean to tell me it's all up to me? It's one of those things that no one can do for you, and you have to find your personal reason for wanting it.

I used to want to be thin so I would look better. But it was never reason enough to make better choices. Once I started walking regularly, I started to feel better about myself. Now that was something I found motivating! Sit on the couch all evening eating: feel crappy for days. Get up, put my shoes on and walk: feel proud of myself for days. Get a strength training workout in with my trainer: feel strong. Eat too much over the weekend: beat myself up for days.

There is always something else to do instead of exercise. There is always bad food around, too much food around. There is always stress. There is never enough time. So what is important enough to you to overcome all that? To kick down the obstacles and make the tough choices anyway?

Grab a pencil and paper. Make two columns. Left side column: How I Feel Now. Right side column: How I Want to Feel. For a long time, my left column looked like this, and I only dreamed about feeling strong and confident and motivated.

How I feel	How I want to feel
Fat	Confident
Scared	Important
Lazy	Brave
Unmotivated	Strong
Out of control	Disciplined
Undisciplined	Motivated
Unhealthy	Determined
Unhappy	Joyful

Then I made one tough choice. ONE. And that one choice led me to make another. And another. Then, I would slip up, and I learned to receive forgiveness and move on. I always wanted to find the magic, quick way to pole vault to fitness. One giant jump and I would be there. But it only works taking many, many little steps.

Get consistent. If you are not consistent over a long period of time, you won't see the changes you are dreaming about. If you are struggling to get consistent, your job is to figure out what you need in your life to help you find motivation, encouragement, strength, confidence, and discipline. These things are available to us all.

Now that I feel better about myself, I would not give that up for anything. Nothing! When I am tired or tempted to slip back to my old ways, I close my eyes and remember what it felt like to feel awful about myself. I remember all it takes is one tough choice to keep going. Right now is all that matters. Believe that it's worth the work. Trust in the process. I believe you can do it.

★★★

June is almost over. I can't believe it. This weekend is the Fourth of July! What does that mean to you if you were planning on your summer clothes fitting better by now, and they don't? Or if you were hoping that this was the year you would feel great in a bathing suit and you don't?

Sometimes it feels like time is getting away from me. The summer goes so quickly and along with it all my hopes for walking every evening, eating super clean, and feeling better about myself. Right about this time of year, I am reminded that this fitness thing doesn't come easily to me and if I lose focus, I go the other way.

In the middle of February it is so easy to blame the lack of activity on winter. I always vow that as soon as it is nice enough and light enough to be outside in the evenings, that's where I'll be. Then the summer comes, and suddenly it's too hot. The humidity is too high. Bugs are out. There are ball games, graduation parties, and showers to plan and attend. And there is food everywhere.

There is no better feeling than moving in the right direction, however. No matter what speed I movie, if I am heading the right way, I feel good. It's when things start heading the wrong way that I feel out of control, undisciplined, and extremely disappointed with myself.

So what is a good approach to refocus when headed in the wrong direction? Here are some strategies that work for me:

Recommit to eating clean for three days. This is usually what it takes for me to get the sugar out of my life and to get back to clean eating. I usually feel so much better after three days that I remember why I make healthy choices, and it becomes part of my life again.

Drink a ton of water. Being dehydrated can make my workouts feel like torture and give me the false signal that I'm hungry when really I am craving water. When I get out of the habit of carrying my water bottle, I struggle. So I dig the water bottle back out of the cupboard and recommit to staying hydrated all day long.

Stay off the scale. When I am heading in the wrong direction, the scale is not my friend. Trying to control the measurement won't help me make the changes I need to make. Focusing on my behavior is what works. Whether it is going back to my food journal, logging miles in a spreadsheet or pedometer, or counting servings of fruits and veggies, what helps me is to refocus on my behavior. I can measure the results of my behavior change later, once I have some consistency (I say wait at least 4 weeks). If you are hooked on the scale, you're missing the point. Get off it.

Start measuring your heart rate every single workout. The best way to do this is with a heart rate monitor, but you can also measure your heart rate manually. Take your pulse for 6 seconds and add a zero. So, 13 beats plus a zero is 130 beats per minute, which is right in the aerobic zone for most of us. Don't waste your time working out anaerobically (too high of a heart rate). When I do that, I feel like crap, get a headache and sore muscles, crave sugar, and am much less likely to work out next time. Stay aerobic.

Know your aerobic range. Here's the math:
220 − your age = (MAX)
0.65 x (MAX) = low limit
0.85 x (MAX) = high limit

So my aerobic range (I am 45 years old) is
Low Limit: 0.65 x (220 − 45) = 114
High Limit: 0.85 x (220 − 45) = 149

Get consistent. Stops and starts are the nemesis of weight loss and fitness. Last week I set my alarm for 5:00 a.m., so I could get a run in on Thursday. If you know me, you know that is not my happy time to run or even be awake. But I know that if it's going to be 90 degrees and humid, the morning is my best shot at getting it done. I really didn't want to, but if I can do that, you can overcome your excuses and busy life and do it too.

★★★

We all deserve the right to indulge from time to time; just consciously ask yourself first, "Will taking this action rob me of the future I desire?"
—Debbie Ford

How true. But what happens when we feel like we deserve the right to indulge more than our body can metabolize? We all know that answer—our bodies store the extra as fat. A few pounds of fat can hardly rob me of the future I desire. But here's what can happen.

I overindulge and promise myself I will work extra hard tomorrow to burn it off. Tomorrow comes, life happens, and I don't work out. I store the extra 500 calories as fat. I beat myself up for not making time to work out. I regret saying yes to something I really wanted to say no to. I feel like I have no control over my time. I feel stressed out and tired. So I overindulge and promise myself I will work extra hard tomorrow to burn it off. Tomorrow comes and life happens....

If I get stuck in this cycle, a week goes by and I have gained a pound. Two weeks, two pounds. My clothes feel tight and my energy dips. Three weeks, three pounds. I start to feel bad about myself. Four week, four pounds. I start to pick on little things about myself in the mirror. Five pounds. I put away my cute clothes and pull out the oversized hide-me clothes. Six pounds. What's the point of working out?

The same thing can happen when trying to lose weight. I might work really hard at my training session. I worked so hard I feel the right to indulge, so I do and promise myself I will work extra hard tomorrow. Tomorrow comes, life happens, and I don't work out. If I am stuck in this cycle, I can be working out really hard but never losing weight.

That is why every moment counts. Every calorie counts. Being conscious of these things and being honest with yourself about what and how much you are eating is crucial to weight loss and overall fitness.

One of my clients recently told me that she heard me say that I had eaten crappy over a weekend, so I couldn't wait to work out and burn it off. That is something I would say because I know that if I overindulge, I have a very small window of opportunity to burn it off before it's stored. For me, having lived a significant portion of my life stuck in these cycles of broken promises and being dishonest with myself, I know I have to. I don't have a choice.

But when I do, I am living consciously and choosing the future I desire. One in which I am healthy and fit, enjoying clothes and shopping, hiking and running, and feeling good about myself. No overindulgence is worth giving that up for ever again.

★★★

Losing weight and getting in shape is hard work. It requires mental focus that takes a long time to work up to and maintain. Once you have that sharp focus, it can be difficult to keep a healthy perspective.

It's like a street map online. If I click on the [+] too many times and zoom in too far, I can't tell where I am. Instead I am obsessed with the tiniest details, even if they don't matter in the long run. Unhealthy restrictive diets, daily weigh-ins, and obsession with calories or points are examples of that.

If I click on the [−] too many times, I zoom out so far that I am lost. This might look like being unaware of how many calories are in the foods I eat, why I overeat, and why I skip exercising.

To make lifestyle changes and have them stick with you long term, I believe you must find the right amount of zoom. Stay focused on the things that matter. These things are your consistent daily behavior. Eating clean. Eating mostly plants and lean protein. Strength training. Walking. Drinking water. Getting good rest and relaxation. Being aware of what is in the food you eat. Being aware of your heart rate and how many calories you burn during exercise.

If you find yourself getting weighed each morning or obsessing over every calorie you eat, zoom out a bit and see if you can see the bigger picture in a healthy perspective.

If you are not focused and are just spending time thinking about making changes but not backing it up with the behavior change, zoom in and see what you can make a little bigger priority.

★★★

You miss 100% of the shots you don't take. —Wayne Gretzky

You may have noticed I have an appreciation for words like *Dream, Rock*, and *Believe.* You will notice that they are prominent in the studio. They are there for a reason.

For me, fitness used to be something I should be doing but

wasn't. It was among a *long list* of things I felt I should be doing but wasn't. It was one of my reasons for thinking I wasn't as good as others. It was one of my reasons for thinking I didn't have enough discipline or determination for my dreams to come true.

Then I walked. Not far at first, not fast. But I did it. And I felt a little tiny something in me light up. I heard a very small "I did it."

Then I lifted some weights. Just enough to challenge me. No Olympic records, but I did it. And the very small "I did it" grew just a little bit.

Then I took a yoga class.

I jogged for two minutes.

I rode my bike. I swam laps.

I tried spinning. I tried Zumba.

I went hiking. I climbed a rock.

Then I started to believe.

It wasn't that I couldn't do things; I didn't try. I lived in my head and found all the reasons in the world why I couldn't.

Fitness can be transformational. If you want it to, fitness can change your life. It's a wonderful thing because the changes take place by doing. There is no figuring out required. You just have to take the shot.

If you feel like you are not where you want to be in your life, fitness is a tool available to each one of us no matter what our current fitness level. It can move you from "I should" to "I am." It can transform you from "I can't" to "I did it!" And that belief in yourself can be applied to every area of your life.

The Struggle to Keep Going

The fight is won or lost far away from the witnesses, behind the lines, in the gym, and out there on the road; long before I dance under those lights.
—Muhammad Ali

Why isn't getting fit easier? I don't know. There are days I wish it all came easy, but it doesn't for me. This morning was quite a mental battle to get out of bed early enough to run before the heat got too bad. I did it, but only after hitting the snooze for thirty minutes and finding all kinds of excuses to stay in bed. Finally I got sick enough of listening to the internal fight that I got up and ran. It felt great. I knew it would, but it's still a battle.

Same with food. Ten years into my journey and I still have an angel on one shoulder and a little devil on the other when it comes to food choices. Take my favorite rationalization: How bad can it be? Oh, trust me, it can be bad. Here are a few examples that I can recall ordering over the years and then checking online when I got home. It's a sinking feeling to realize you just blew a whole day's worth of calories in one meal. Especially if you thought you were making a good choice.

— MiMi's Cafe lunch portion Chicken Sundried Tomato Penne: 1800 calories, 99 grams of fat
— Bob Evans Cranberry Chicken Pecan Salad: 1100 calories/63 grams of fat
— Chipotle loaded Chicken Burrito: 1200 calories/53 grams of fat
— Scrambler Marie's Veggie Omelet w/Hash Browns: 1200 calories/68 grams of fat

I believe one of the most important weapons in this battle is awareness. Keep taking the time to look up how many calories are in the foods you eat. Try to do your research ahead of time. Keep a mental list of "go-to" places where you know what to order and how many calories are in the meal. Prepare for it like you are in a fight for your life.

Another important part of this is your reason. Why do you want to change? Why is this important enough to you to put your time, your sweat, your financial resources towards it? For me, it has always been about feeling better about myself. Exercise does that for me. Making informed, healthy food choices does that for me. I hate beating myself up, but I do it if I start skipping my workouts or eating a lot of junk. So I refocus over and over and over, knowing that I have a say in whether I am moving in a positive or negative direction.

Two years ago this month, I injured my back. It has taken a long time to heal, but the worst part was thinking my fitness was somehow being taken from me. I couldn't run. I couldn't lift. Suddenly, I would give anything to do the same workouts I had been dreading a month ago. I realized how important moving my body is to me. I am willing to fight for it, so I have. That meant working out on the Step-Mill for 45 minutes, which was not fun, but worth it to keep going.

Being healthy and feeling good about myself is worth fighting for. I defend it, I cherish it, and I am committed to it. I am not perfect at it, but I'll never give up. My fight is life long, but it gets easier. I learn from my mistakes. I believe in myself a little more every day and trust in my ability to make choices that support my health, my fitness, my soul, and my life.

You may feel like you are struggling. Take a moment and be thankful. Don't take your ability to go out for a walk or to lift some weights for granted. It's a gift worth fighting for.

★★★

Move the tank tops to the back of the closet and dig out long sleeved shirts—check. Pack the shorts away in the bottom drawer and get the jeans out—check.

Hooded sweatshirt—check. Salad ingredients replaced in the shopping cart with ingredients for chili and soup—check. Exercise plan for fall—check. Renewed commitment to eating clean—check.

Can you feel it in the air? The change of season and all that it brings. I personally am happy to say goodbye to summer this year and hello to my favorite time of year in Ohio. It's much easier to walk and run outside without the heat and humidity, and the parks are gorgeous.

How did your summer go? Did you hope to eat a lot of salads and fresh fruit and then end up eating burgers and potato salad? Were you hoping to "get on track" this summer? Did you? If you did, great! Renew your commitment to keep it going. If you didn't, it's in the past. Let it go and let's move on. Repeat after me: "I'm moving forward."

It's a good time to renew. If you are bored with your exercise, try something new. Add something new to your arsenal and switch things up a bit. If you are sick of your normal foods, don't buy the same things out of habit. Get some new ideas from Cooking Light or The Eat Clean cookbooks and try something different.

Don't make a September resolution about all the things you are going to change, eliminate, or lose. Start adding. Add some veggies to your day. Add water. Add a new exercise. Add 10 minutes to your walks. Add fish once a week. Add some healthy fats. Add more rest. Add 2 minutes of stretching. Add, add, add.

It has never worked for me to focus on restriction. As soon as I try to not eat sugar, all I want is donuts. As soon as I try to cut calories, all I want to do is eat a Chipotle burrito and chips. I am rebellious and resistant. What I have found that works is to fill myself up with all the healthy stuff I want so that I am full, nourished and satisfied. Once I have that good feeling about myself and my healthier choices, I tend to not obsess about the other stuff and it falls away more easily.

Then I screw up, refocus, let it go, and move forward. Again and again and again. Repeat after me: "Progress, not perfection."

★★★

Last year on this day I started a workout streak. My goal was to walk or run at least one mile every day from November 1 to February 28. It was my strategy for staying motivated through the winter. I wrote about it each week, and I learned a lot from the experience.

I learned that it only took about 12 minutes of cardio a day to feel like I had done something. I learned that once I got going, sometimes I kept going. And I learned that if it wasn't optional, I found a way to fit exercise in every day. It was great to get through the holidays and the New Year exercising consistently.

This season can be a free-for-all for some of us. The problem I always had with the holiday binge was the self-loathing that followed. I never liked my body that much to begin with, and the extra seven or eight pounds I put on each winter made me feel even worse. So I would follow up the holidays with a January resolution to, in 30 days, take all the weight off that I had gained. When that didn't happen and the dieting didn't work, I would give up for awhile.

This kind of all-or-nothing thinking kept me stuck in a bad cycle for a long time. When I felt bad about my weight and wanted to do something about it, it had to happen NOW or else it wasn't worth my time. I didn't get it—that's not how this works.

We all know this pattern. Resolve to eat right on Monday morning. Restrict calories on Monday through Thursday. Start to lose a grip on Friday. Eat like a madwoman on Friday night. Keep it going on Saturday and Sunday. Feel totally disgusted and resolve to start again on Monday morning.

I believe in a different approach that relies upon looking at the long-term process and developing consistency in our daily behavior. The key for me is the word "add." This week, what am I willing to add? Maybe it's drink more water every day. If I am able to keep that up, what am I willing to add the next week? Perhaps it's one 30 minute cardio workout. Week 3? More veggies. Week 4? Strength training workout. Week 5? More protein with breakfast. Week 6? Wear a pedometer and try for 10,000 steps. Week 7? Switch to skinny latte (that one's for me next week).

Can you begin to see where you might be in a year? 52 things added to your life in support of your health and fitness. Deprivation is nowhere to be found.

I lived the other way for too long. I went through the weekly restriction/binge/self-loathing cycle. I went through the holiday binge/self-loathing/New Year restriction cycle. I had enough. See these cycles for the self- destructive things that they are and don't go there. Spend your energy on adding satisfying things to your life that support your health and fitness. Once you experience the peace and stability of consistency, you will never go back.

★★★

You do not have to go on another diet to lose weight.

Do you believe that? I do. In fact, I believe diets are one of the reasons we have such a terribly hard time losing weight. Diets give food all the power. It has all the power, and we are supposed to work up enough will power of our own to deprive ourselves of just enough to lose weight.

You may be thinking: "but what about calories in calories out?" Well, the energy equation is how our bodies are made; that's biology and physiology. But starvation and chronic dieting cannot be the answer. Neither can living on food-like substances that remove most of the calories (and nutrition and joy) from food and are marketed to us as "lite." The cycle is destructive.

It starts with feeling unhappy with my body. I decide to start Monday and count calories. I decide I need to get to 1200 calories (or 1400 or whatever it is) to lose weight. I find lots of diet foods so I can stay within that range but feel completely unsatisfied and the minute I have the chance, lose control completely and eat like a ravenous madwomen. What comes next is that feeling of guilt, self-hatred, and disgust at my own lack of ability to control this. I just blew the whole week. I feel worse about myself than I did before. Might as well eat like crap the rest of the weekend and start again on Monday. Ugh.

There is another way and it's not being at war with food, it's making peace with food. Food is our life-sustaining force. Food is at the center of our community and family. Food is enjoyable and abundant.

If you want to get healthier and drop excess weight, stop restricting. It is not working! Eat more mindfully, eat at home instead of out, eat with thanks that someone grew and picked this food, cook every meal that you can, and load up your plate with nutrition-packed food.

Take a week and eat mostly plants. All the fruits, veggies, beans, nuts, and oats you can. Add small portions of very lean protein (fish, chicken, turkey). Add some high quality, high fiber carbohydrates (brown rice, robust bread). Cook at home. Check out some Eat Clean recipes.

If you want to count calories to be aware of how many you are eating, I can understand that. I still do that around the holidays to keep my awareness. But you won't have to do it obsessively to try to control the amount of food you consume. When you give yourself the gift of being full, fed, and satisfied, you don't crave quick-fix junk because you have energy. You are much more in control of your choices because your body has what it needs to feel strong and healthy.

Give yourself the gift of high quality, high nutrition foods. Fuel your body; then get going on your cardiovascular exercise. You can't lose excess weight without daily exercise. If you have been trying to make up for lack of consistent exercise with dieting, turn around. That's a bad path that leads to feeling bad about yourself, hungry and deprived. There is a better way that leads to health for the whole person: body, mind, spirit.

★★★

"Maybe you have done this before, but would you mind sharing what you eat in a given day?" I received this in an email and it really got me thinking.

One of my first thoughts was along the lines of "Why would you want to know what I eat?" I don't exactly have this down to a science. I am the woman, if you remember from my past newsletters, who has meltdowns and still goes to McDonald's and KFC in one day. And this year on Trick or Treat night, I had two sloppy joes and five candy bars and felt sick because I was so full. It wasn't pretty.

I am just like so many of you. I still have to remind myself that I have had some victory in this area. Sometimes all I can see is what I don't do well, instead of how far I have come. I have downfalls and temptations. Ice cream, pizza, French fries, Oreos. I have days that I feel in control and days I am so disappointed in myself.

As I thought about how to answer this question, I looked back at my weight loss. I ate a lot then, and I eat a lot now. Somehow, I managed to lose 45 pounds, though, and feel a whole lot better about myself. I don't ever feel deprived, and I enjoy food more than I ever have. Here are my thoughts on what changed over the last ten years:

I move a lot more than I did back then. And I exercise in my heart rate zone consistently now.

I got healed of a lot of the junk I was carrying around from my past, which helped changed how I relate to food (and everything else).

I made changes one at a time because I am very resistant to changing everything at once. A few examples come to mind. I used to eat a high sugar, low fiber cereal for breakfast. Now I eat a low sugar, high fiber cereal for breakfast. It took me awhile to switch. I started by adding just a little of the high fiber cereal to my regular cereal, and over time, I increased the ratio until one day, I just stopped buying the first cereal. I don't miss it at all because I feel so much better. Another example; I used to get a 1200 calorie burrito when I went to Chipotle (rice, beans, chicken, sour cream, cheese, guac...) Now I get a burrito bowl with 1/2 rice, black beans, 2 salsas and cheese (~380 calories). I still have Chipotle, just within reason.

I make something on Sunday for the week. It could be grilled chicken, veggie egg white frittata, turkey chili, or veggie pasta, but I know if I have a batch of something healthy prepared, when I walk into the kitchen hungry, I will choose that because it only needs to be reheated. I have gotten better over the years at adding lots and lots of veggies to my creations, and I enjoy cooking them now. The more I cook, the healthier the meal and the easier it is to stay within a healthy calorie range.

I take food with me. On the days I take my lunch, I eat fewer calories than on the days I run to Chipotle, Panera, etc. I can get a good salad at Panera now for under 500 calories, but that doesn't include the 200-calorie baguette, and I'm not good at saying no to the baguette. Add one of their cookies, and just like that, lunch is 1200 calories. I try not to eat more than 500 calories at once.

Now, don't get me wrong. I eat birthday cake, French fries, 1,000 calorie meals, etc. I just don't do those things consistently anymore. Now they are the exception. Before that was my lifestyle. Now I eat healthy, filling, satisfying, veggie-packed foods most of the time and save the treats as just that- treats.

I don't know if that really answered the question. In truth, it would really depend on whether I was having a good day of being mindful, planning things out, and feeling good about myself or whether I was not organized, eating on the run, feeling crappy and struggling. But it's not about what I eat. It's about what *you* eat. Take the food you like and find ways to make it healthier, less calories, and delicious. Make it your own. Take time to prepare for the week. Give yourself what you need to feel good about yourself. Make the healthy choices most of the time. Then you can have treats and crazy days occasionally but still remain on the path and heading in the right direction.

★★★

I received an email from a client this week that I think we can all relate to. She allowed me to share it with you:

"I know that I can get stressed out (who doesn't?) by all that I have to accomplish in any given week. It's so very easy to abandon healthy habits because it's just one more thing you have to do. I still struggle with this, but what I am quickly realizing is that when I "wake up" on the other side of having abandoned what is good for me (exercise, eating well, etc.) I don't feel good. My belly aches. I have wicked intestinal issues. And I don't look good. My skin is puffy. I have bags under my eyes. I could just chalk it up to being over 40, but if I do that then I'm not being honest with myself. When I go "off program" I'm like a computer who's been feed bad code: Garbage in, garbage out. I'm suffering from that very thing this morning. I had a bad weekend. I mean BAD. From Saturday evening through Sunday I was on a sodium binge, did no exercise and I awoke to a scary swollen-looking face this morning. I'm trying really hard not to beat myself up too much over this (as I am prone to do) and move through the day making better choices. I had a healthy breakfast. I had a healthy snack. I have to eat out for lunch and dinner, but already made my choices for tasty, healthy items, so there's no need to look at the menu later. And I've had a ton of water already. I can't yet erase what I did to myself this weekend, but I rejoice in the fact that I am making better choices today. And I hope my face will soon respond to the change in my programming direction!"

I'm sure that most of us know what she is going through. What happens that causes us to go "off program"?

I believe the answer lies in our defaults. When I have had a long day and am exhausted, the last thing I want to do is work. Thinking about and getting organized to prepare something healthy feels like work. So my automatic tendency is to reach into my brain for my list of default easy meals.

My default meals are pizza, Mexican food, Chinese food take out, any fast food value meal, chips and dip, Pop Tarts or macaroni 'n cheese. I didn't exactly choose these as my defaults, they are just what I gravitated towards before I had any idea about nutrition. These are the foods I ate when I first lived on my own. It's all I knew; it was easy and cheap.

My default foods are not very healthy though, and they are high in fat, sugar and salt, which lead to weight gain over the years. Yet, when I am hanging out at home wiped out after a long week, it's the easiest thing to get. I know I like it, I know where to get it, and I don't have to think about it. I don't *want* to have to think about it.

Tonight I made whole wheat pasta marinara with turkey sausage and lots of veggies. Enough for the week. When I get home at

8:00 Monday evening too tired to think about food choices, I can walk to the fridge, take out the container, scoop it into a bowl, and microwave it for three minutes. A new item on my default list for the week! Since I make it often, I know the ingredients I need at the grocery store, so that doesn't require extra thought, either. And it tastes amazing.

If I add one new item to my arsenal of healthy, easy, don't-need-to-think-about it-at-all choices a week, pretty soon I have so many items to choose from that I will never get bored. If I get sick of something, I make way for something new. Do this consistently, and pretty soon, you have a whole new set of default items. You've created or chosen them, so they are the stuff you like. But you've made these choices now with your health and nutrition in mind, not the old criteria you used when you were 22.

From the same client's follow-up email:

"I have successfully made it through three days of better eating, and I am in a much better state of mind about my fitness. Onward I go!"

If living a healthy life seems like another project that you just don't have time or energy for, I understand that. Keep it simple. Make a list of five meals under 500 calories that you can have ready without any thought or time or energy. That will be a good place to start.

★★★

Obstacles are mighty forces, especially around the holidays.

I personally find it almost impossible to stand in a kitchen where chips and dips are laid out in front of me without munching endlessly. Especially if I have a cocktail in my hand. I find it equally difficult to have one plate of food on Thanksgiving. It's just so good!

It is a challenge for me to get my workouts in consistently when there are other things I am being invited to attend that conflict with my usual workout times.

When my time is pressed by shopping, cooking, baking, wrapping, decorating, and all the other things that need done around this time of year, it seems reasonable to just put everything fitness- and health-related on hold and put all my energy into the to-dos of the season. There is only so much time in each day and so much energy left to conjure up the will power needed to resist cookies that are everywhere. Cookies are everywhere!

But I know what happens if I do this. The reason I know what happens is that this is what I did for many years. I decided it took too much energy to keep up fitness over the holidays, so I gave myself a free pass and took a mental break from it all.

If only our bodies took the break with us, but they don't. What I learned was if I took the holiday free pass, I woke up out of a sugar coma in early January feeling absolutely horrible about myself. There is a reason marketing of fitness services and products goes crazy at the beginning of the year. They know how we feel and are exploiting us because we are so desperate to feel better that we will try anything.

I believe commitment is stronger than obstacles.

I can make a commitment to keep up my healthy lifestyle right through the holidays. I can stay motivated and inspired to do so because I know the resulting pain and self-loathing when I don't. I refuse to do that to myself ever again. Can you say that with me? I refuse to do that to myself ever again.

I know it takes extra planning and being very organized. I know we're all tired and overwhelmed. But close your eyes and take a deep breath. Remember what it felt like to gain five, six, seven pounds over the holidays. Remember what it did to your spirit. Remember how you felt about yourself.

Now take another deep breath and envision yourself stronger and healthier than ever this January. Picture how you will feel about yourself. Allow yourself to feel that strength, that confidence, the joy of sticking with this even when it got really difficult. Then make the commitment. Then make it again. And make it again every hour of every day if you have to, so none of us ever has to feel that bad about ourselves again.

★★★

No one was ever criticized into changing. It doesn't work. What works is encouragement, commitment, and a vision of something better.

There is often a "theme of the week" at the studio. I don't know why that is, but the energy somehow focuses on specific issues. This week was about beating ourselves up. Maybe it was the post-Thanksgiving holiday feeling. It's hard not to feel fat when you purposefully overeat like we all do. It is a feast!

It is tempting to believe that if we feel disgusted enough with ourselves, we'll change. So we stare at the parts of our bodies we don't like in the mirror and think the most unkind words. Gross, disgusting, fat, cottage cheese, jiggly, saggy, rolls. Or we avoid mirrors and cameras entirely and just give in to the fact that we don't want to see ourselves.

We all must make a commitment to love ourselves.

When I hear those words, I think back to my years in counseling. I used to think that I had to somehow conjure up loving feelings towards myself or my body even though I didn't really feel that way. I've come to learn that loving yourself is meant to be an action, not a feeling.

Part of loving yourself is knowing who you are. To me this means knowing I am unique, that I belong, am of value, am worthy of love, and no one else has the combination of gifts and talents that I do. I make a difference. If you feel empty in this area, your spirit may need attention. Let me remind you that you are unique, you belong, you are worthy of love, and no one else has the combination of gifts and talents that you do. You make a difference!

The other part of loving yourself is giving yourself what you need to thrive. It is the choices you make. Something may taste good but is it loving? In other words, does it contribute to your long-term health and happiness? Or is it self-destructive? My definition of this would be feels good in the moment but causes long-term pain and suffering.

When I smoked, each cigarette sure was pleasurable. But it was destructive. There may be some immediate comfort in eating foods high in fat, sugar, and salt, but is it loving? Does it contribute to my long-term well-being? I know that it doesn't, and I remember well what being at an unhealthy weight felt like physically and emotionally. I was not a happy person and beat myself up constantly.

But how to get there from here; from instant gratification to long-term well-being? One loving choice at a time, forgiveness when you blow it, and a commitment to your future self that you will never, ever give up. We have all heard stories of people who have overcome their habits and past to become healthy and happy. These stories allow us to envision ourselves the same way. If they can do it, maybe we can do it.

I know it is easy to allow critical thoughts to creep in and even to take over. But they are destructive, and so we must not feed them. When they arise, cut them off. They are lies!

Here is the biggest lie of all: I will never be good enough.

Here is its fitness translation: I will be happy (good enough) as soon as I lose x pounds.

Here is the truth: I am unique, I belong, am of value, and am worthy of love exactly as I am right at this very moment!

If you want to make positive changes in your life, that's great. Exercise consistently. Make healthy food choices. Rest. Stretch. Walk. Lift. Just make a commitment to do it out of love and not from a place of criticism or judgment. Don't allow a lie that you aren't good enough as you are at this moment rob you of one more day of joy in this life.

★★★

The holiday to-do lists are in full swing. How are you doing managing it all? Are you finding time for your fitness? Are you keeping your health a priority?

It's not easy to do. We all have such busy, hectic lives that it's a challenge to fit in time to exercise, cook, check calorie contents, and all the other things associated with living an active, healthy life. Add Christmas on top of that, and it can feel like too much.

There are a couple truths I hang onto during the holidays. The first is: if I keep exercising, everything is going to be OK. Exercise seems to be a stabilizing factor for me when it comes to stress and eating. I tend to have much more control over my food choices if I get in a good workout that day. Maybe it is because I feel the effects of that hard work and don't want to wipe it out by overeating party food.

The second is: exercise makes me feel less stressed. It may feel like there just isn't 30 minutes in your day for a workout, but I find it is worth getting up earlier or saying no to something else to get that time to myself. It's only two weeks, not forever. Set the alarm clock a little earlier. Get up and get it over with. Trust me, you will be amazed at how much more you get done if you start your day like that.

Third and most important: I remember how I feel about myself when I eat badly over the holidays. I have done it enough times for the memory to be very clear. I refuse to ever go through another first week of January feeling like I need to go on a diet, start drinking shakes, taking pills, counting points, get liposuction or try anything else to feel better. I know how to feel better. I just have to do it.

In a few short weeks, the holidays will be over, and we will be hit with an onslaught of diet marketing that will be hard to resist. 30 pounds in 30 days! The new invention that burns fat without any work at all! Eat chocolate, lose weight! If we let ourselves go with a free pass to eat anything and skip workouts, we're going to end up in a vulnerable place emotionally where these lies sound good.

What I want for us is to stay strong and focused through the rest of the year. Remember the truth. Health and fitness require hard work, perseverance, patience, and commitment. There is no quick fix. Diets don't work or we'd all be thin by now! (How many diets have you gone on in your lifetime?) It is important to come out of the holiday season physically and mentally strong, so we don't give in to lies. Haven't we all done enough of that? I know I have. I believe we can all break the destructive cycle and do things differently this year.

Remember the truth.

★★★

Last week I was in Body Pump class when one of the instructors said "If nothing changes, nothing changes."

I thought to myself, how true! Funny that I need reminded of that, since it sounds like common sense. But the reality is that even though I may really want to change something about my life, I may not be doing anything about it except thinking about it. I call that being stuck in my head. I have found that I can spend quite a lot of time thinking about doing something without ever getting it done.

It takes a lot of courage to make a change. You have to get out of your comfort zone. Since we talk about fitness, getting out of your comfort zone may mean getting your heart rate up higher, sweating more, feeling those muscles burn, or being sore. But I think what's even tougher is getting out of my mental comfort zone. Once I am out of my comfort zone in that way, I am vulnerable to failure, feeling stupid, or feeling insecure.

There has to be something stronger to override the desire to quit and crawl back into the very safe place of where you are right now. There has to be a well of hope, inspiration, motivation and desire for something better. There has to be a vision of what is possible. Don't we all love stories of people who have overcome obstacles and changed their lives? It is inspiring to see possibility in others, and it allows us to see that same possibility in ourselves.

I believe change is possible. I believe we are all capable of being at a healthy weight. I believe we all have the right to feel good about ourselves. I believe we each have the courage it takes to make a different choice this week.

If you feel like you've been stuck in your head, thinking about making a change but not taking the action needed to make it happen, take a look at what you believe. So many women walk through my door having lost the belief that being at a healthy weight is even possible for them. That is a lie. You may have obstacles to overcome. Don't we all. You may have old ways of thinking to dig through and false beliefs to expose. But it can be done!

It is scary. It is hard work. Those of us who beat ourselves up regularly may want to avoid ever trying again because the self-esteem crash is just too painful to endure one more time. I get it. But quitting is not the answer. Believing is the answer. Remember who you are—a strong, inspired person capable of achieving anything you set your mind to.

★★★

ZAP FAT FAST! New Year, New You. Get sexy legs in 6 easy moves. SLIM DOWN SECRETS.

I took these from the cover of one magazine. Not four, one. Do you believe them? I don't. Let me challenge these claims.

If you are like me, you've been battling weight in one way or another for a long time, and you have tried lots of different approaches. Do you think there really is a way to "zap fat fast"? Does fat loss happen quickly? It sure didn't for me.

New Year, New you? Is the New Year's resolution really that powerful? Has it worked in the past or has it just been another source of pressure that says you should be doing more? You should be thinner. You should be not like you are now. Is that healthy?

OK, six easy moves? Really? Have they actually done a leg workout? Have they felt the burn that only a good set of lunges and squats can provide? I'm sorry, but creating lean legs, arms, or any other body part is hard work and definitely not easy.

Hmm, I wonder what the secret is? So someone knows the secret to the "slim down" but is just sharing it with readers of this magazine. Ugh, whatever. This stuff really bugs me. I hope it bugs you, too, because they are lies. I am going to ask you to prepare yourself for the onslaught of lies and temptation that's coming.

You've been doing great. You're working hard, getting in your cardio, strength training, eating cleaner. You are adding positive, healthy steps to your life that feel doable to you. You are learning how to be forgiven and move on when you blow it. You have stopped the insanity of dieting. You are focusing on living life in a healthy, balanced way. You are developing a healthy relationship with food and feeling much better about yourself.

Then the holidays came and you ate. Maybe just a little extra, maybe a lot. And you missed workouts. I sure did. And you can feel the difference. That sluggish, foggy feeling. And the tight waistband. And the sugar cravings. And the thirst. Worst of all, the feeling that you must somehow start over.

This year let's do it differently. No New Year's resolution about your weight, your exercise, or a diet. You don't need it. You are already doing it. If the past week or two has been rough, that's OK. Change direction today. Get a long cardio workout in tomorrow. Sweat your butt off for an hour. Schedule a strength workout this week. Get those muscles working. Stock up on healthy stuff. Don't give into the free pass mentality this week. It's not worth it.

I believe what some of us tend to do, maybe even subconsciously, is start preparing for the big restrictive diet on the 1st, so we go free-pass wild with all kinds of junk in the week leading up to it. Get your motivation in check right now. Set your plan for the week today. Make something yummy and healthy to have available this week whenever your cravings pop up. Make all the work you did last year mean something. Don't throw it away for a two-week binge that will only leave you feeling empty and sad (and vulnerable to the lies that are coming).

What we're going to see and hear for an entire month on the TV, radio, magazines, Internet and everywhere else is that you should be dieting. And the reason we are hearing this again in January is because companies make a lot of money selling diets. And they know they have a lot of repeat customers.

Don't be one. Remember the truth. Being a fit, healthy, happy human takes hard work and dedication. It takes commitment and sweat. It takes eating healthy most of the time and exercising consistently. It is not easy for anyone, it can't be done quickly, there is no secret to it, and you don't get a new you. But what you get is a you that feels good about herself, is motivated and inspired to be her very best, and is willing to do whatever it takes to be what she is meant to be.

★★★

Weight loss is not fun.

It's like quitting smoking. It's emotionally painful and mentally draining. I know with absolute certainty that I will never have to quit smoking again. Hallelujah! Remembering how hard it was to quit reminds me to never, ever go back to my old habit. I don't know if I could conjure up the mental strength to go through that again.

When I finally quit smoking, I had a mantra to keep me going. It was "whatever it takes!" I was so sick of being a smoker that I didn't care what it took—I was going to succeed. It actually took me a lot—way more than most people. I used the nicotine patch, I got the prescription for Zyban, I attended an eight-week smoking cessation support group, I belonged to an online forum for 'quitters', I got a Quit-Meter for my computer which counted how many days I'd gone without a smoke (next Friday it will be 12 years), and I carried a survival kit with me that had suckers, gum, a card on it with my reasons for quitting, and stuff like that.

I had tried all these strategies separately before, but that January I finally put it all together. I don't know exactly why I finally conquered my addiction at that time. I know I was sick of failing, I was ready, and I finally made it the most important thing in my life.

Weight loss can be just as difficult, emotionally painful, and mentally draining. It's so frustrating! You can be exercising your tail off and not lose a pound. You can be practically obsessing over calories or points and be stuck right where you are. What is going on here?

I believe that losing weight is like quitting smoking, in that it takes a drastic change in your life to make it happen. If you've done it, you know you don't just put cigarettes down one day. You quit and relapse and quit and relapse. You think about it. You plan. You run from it. You dream about it.

To lose weight, you have to put it all together. You may have finally gotten the exercise part down, but your pantry is still stocked with the same foods it has always held. Or you may be counting calories, but are not getting daily exercise for the necessary amount of time in the right heart rate zone. If you talk to anyone who has lost a significant amount of weight, I think they would all say one thing. They changed their lives.

You just don't transform your body without transforming your life.

I talk a lot in my newsletter about gradual, gentle change. I believe that is very important. We as humans are resistant to change, so going from one extreme to another and asking our psyches to tolerate that is asking a lot. But we can tolerate step-by-step. I believe if you get enough step-by-steps going, you create transformation.

What are the steps? I believe that's specific to the individual, but there are some common ones. Get enough sleep. Drink your water. Take time for yourself. Pray. Meditate. Get organized. Do things that help you feel good about yourself. Be active. Eat your veggies. Eat lots of fiber. Move your body. Process your feelings. Lift weights. Stretch. Walk. Work your core. Sweat every day.

If you are stuck, look at your life. Does your day look different now that exercise and activity are a daily part of it? Is the food you order at restaurants different than it used to be? What's inside your fridge these days? Where's your water bottle?

If it seems like you are working hard at weight loss but not getting anywhere, maybe it is time to put it all together. Are you sick of thinking about it enough to make it the most important thing in your life? Are you willing to really change? Can you let go of your old ways and make your days look different? If you are ready, then go for it. Do whatever it takes. It is worth all the hard work. And when you succeed, it will transform what you believe to be possible in your life.

★★★

It's Tuesday morning. I just woke up from a great night's sleep, and I feel so good. I feel like I lost five pounds overnight! Love this feeling. I really should get on the scale and see if I actually did lose five pounds overnight. So tempting. I want validation of how I feel. I want to see a number I haven't seen in awhile. I want rewarded for working hard and eating healthy this week.

Luckily, I know better. The scale is not my friend. It would *not* validate how I feel. It would probably say I gained two pounds and my happy day would be ruined. So I'll enjoy Tuesday with pants that fit well and a body that feels strong and is responding to the new workouts I've been trying. Love this feeling!

Now it's Saturday. I overslept, missed my spin class, and I feel like I screwed up the day. I love the way I feel when I get my long workout in on Saturday mornings. I love seeing over a thousand calories burned on my heart rate monitor. So frustrated with myself. I know that missing this one workout won't make me overweight again. I don't know how else to explain it except I wanted today! I wanted the feeling of being proud of myself for getting up and going, of working hard and taking care of myself, of sweating and feeling good.

It was so tempting to blow off the whole day. But the feeling kept at me. I wanted to feel good today. So, at 2:30 in the afternoon on a Saturday, I got my heart rate monitor and my water bottle, and I went to the gym and worked out on my own. Not a lot of people in the gym at that time of day! I hopped on that treadmill and cranked it. My mind started to change from beating myself up to "YEAH"! This is what I needed. By the end of an hour, it had turned into a really good day.

I learned over the last ten years that peace of mind with this whole weight thing does not come from getting to the perfect weight. It comes from having confidence that I will never gain it back and that I have healed. I don't live in fear anymore. I just know what I need to do to maintain and, with support, I do it. Isn't that what we want really? To feel in control of our weight, to do what we tell ourselves we will do, to feel good about ourselves. I do. It's my top motivator. I want to feel good today.

All of us are capable of making changes in our lives. If we feel undisciplined, we can change. If we feel out of control, we can change. If we feel like we're going in the wrong direction, we can change. Cling to the truth about health and fitness. Find all the support you need. Step out of your normal routine and do something different. Think about nutrition, not just calories. Drop the excuses. Find the time. Feel good about yourself. Peace doesn't come from thinking about it, it comes from doing it.

★★★

I've been working out too hard again. Yes, you read correctly. You can work out too hard, at too high intensity. This goes against our intuition, which says if you want to see more results, work harder. That really isn't true; it all comes down to what your goals are and how you are fueling your body.

When I first started losing weight, I was going to Highbanks Metro Park often. I lived right out there, so it was convenient, plus I love it there. I always tried to run that trail, and I would slow down and walk only when I couldn't breathe anymore. I wanted to lose weight so badly. I was sick of feeling bad about myself and was ready to do the work. I tried and tried to get better at running so I wouldn't have to take as many walk breaks. I worked and sweated and didn't lose any weight.

It was so frustrating. I couldn't imagine doing more, but I wasn't getting anywhere. What I didn't know was I was just emptying my body of all its carbohydrate fuel, so as soon as I got home I was out of control and needed sugar. Immediately. I usually got it by sticking my hand into a cereal box multiple times. Then I'd make dinner.

I like biology and I like to read, so I started trying to figure out what was going wrong. I learned about heart rate zones and aerobic versus anaerobic exercise. I bought my first heart rate monitor, and I went back to Highbanks. It turns out that I could barely run 5 minutes without my heart rate shooting right out of my target zone and into carb-burning. What I wanted was a high percentage of my calories burned from fat. What I was doing was burning near 0% of calories from fat.

So, I switched to walking. I kept my heart rate in my target zone for fat loss, except when it went up during the big hills. I lost two pounds that week. Then, another two the week after. For years I had been stuck, and now it was moving. I felt like I had cracked the code. It motivated me to eat healthier because it was so rewarding to see some success. It was also much easier to make good choices because I wasn't operating on low blood sugar. I was well fed from my fat stores that were being broken down into energy during my walks.

For me, that is also when exercise became enjoyable. It was working! I was losing weight. When exercise is effective, it is not nearly as difficult to make yourself get those shoes on and go. It's when it feels like you are spinning your wheels but getting nowhere that it seems so difficult.

I spent the next few years getting almost fifty pounds lighter and enjoying a combination of strength training, walking, and running. Eventually, I could run my slow little run and keep my heart rate in the zone. I walked at Highbanks and anywhere else I could find. Then in 2008 I injured a disc in my back. Walking was good for it, but I could not run without pain. I couldn't ride a bike or use an elliptical. I took it easy for about a year and a half while it healed.

When I started to run again last year, I was so happy. Except I couldn't breathe. My heart rate was way back up where it used to be when I was huffing and puffing through those first Highbanks runs. I worked and worked. I did speed work. I tried to run faster. No improvement. I got my lungs checked. No asthma, x-ray was fine. What was going on?

I finally got a metabolic assessment, which told me exactly what was going on. The heart rate at which I burn the most fat is 128. The heart rate at which I start to lose my endurance due to lactic acid build up is 138. I was running at 168. All carbohydrate fuel. No wonder I wasn't getting anywhere. Same as before.

So, I put on my heart rate monitor, went to Highbanks, and walked. I watched my heart rate the whole time. Never let it get above 138. I tell you what. I burned almost the same number of calories as if I had run as fast as I could, it felt enjoyable and almost easy. I felt good later, not out-of-control hungry. It was wonderful.

This applies to everyone. Runners, walkers, elliptical, Zumba. Find your target zone, measure your heart rate, and go the speed/intensity needed to stay in your zone. I had to back it WAY off in my spin class but I still got an awesome workout. I felt better after, and I am much more confident that it is moving me towards my goal. That is way better than spinning my wheels.

Here's the bottom line on exercise. Strength training is for your metabolism. You need muscles to burn fuel, and they need to be strong to be able to get those miles in. Interval training (hills, speed work) is also for your metabolism. It works by burning lots of calories after your workout. Both of these workouts can be done once or twice a week.

The key to fat burning is consistent aerobic exercise. By consistent I mean almost every day. You know I believe in gently adding, but if you have been at this awhile and are still not exercising consistently, you are moving too gently. Figure out what the obstacles are and kick them out of the way. It will be much easier, I promise, because if you get into your target heart rate range and stay there, the workout will not be so strenuous that you dread it or feel awful afterwards. Plus, you will see results, and what is more motivating than that?

★★★

Interesting information about heart rate, wasn't it? It certainly created lots of discussion at the studio. All good stuff. So if weight loss is your goal, what are the lessons and how do we put it all together?

NUTRITION

1. Eat protein—active women need enough.
2. Eat more often—the standard three square meals doesn't apply to you.
3. Eat leafy greens and whole grains—fiber.
4. Don't cut out fat from your diet—think quality fats.
5. Drink water.

WORKOUTS

1. Aerobic workouts—This is the workout that burns fat for fuel. Stay in your target heart rate zone. Find aerobic workouts that keep you from getting bored. Find a walking partner or go to Zumba with a friend. Sign up for a 10K walk or half marathon and then train for it. The key to this

is getting the most time in zone as possible. An hour a day is your ultimate goal.

2. Intervals—This is the workout that boosts your metabolism. Due to something called EPOC (excess post-exercise oxygen consumption), it burns lot of calories for many hours after you work out. This is speed work, spin class, or hills. The key to intervals is heart rate. Get your heart rate into your anaerobic zone for short intervals, then recover in your fat burning zone (aerobic) repeatedly. Twice a week is plenty for this type of workout.

3. Strength training—This workout builds muscle strength and endurance, improves balance and posture, boosts metabolism, and sculpts and tones the body. This is weight lifting, Pilates, Body Pump type classes. What is important is the workload placed upon the muscles by alternating reps, sets, weight, etc. and working all the major muscle groups safely. Two to three times a week is ideal for strength training.

Circuit classes combine strength training with aerobic exercise to keep the heart rate in your zone while lifting. It is a hybrid workout.

Many clients are consistent with their strength training but haven't gotten the aerobic (fat burning) workouts down yet. You get your strength training done by appointment with your trainer, and so it gets on your schedule and gets done. The cardio tends to get pushed out of the way as things get busy, stressful, exhausting, or overwhelming. We all struggle in our own way with motivation, accountability, and consistency. Especially with the workouts we do on our own.

Many clients are doing lots of workouts, but either in the wrong heart rate zone for their goals, or are sabotaging their training with poor food choices. For those of you working very hard but not getting anywhere because of food, I challenge you this week to do things differently. Create an environment in which it is possible to be successful. Get rid of the junk in your house. Substances such as chips, crackers, cakes, cookies, etc. may be marketed as food, but they are not real, whole food. They are lacking nutritional value, and they wreak havoc on your body. Get organized. Get inspired. Cook healthy meals. Make healthy choices.

The changes to your body aren't immediate. Weight loss takes time. Keep going anyway. Decide to never give up. Be as honest as you can with yourself. What's keeping you stuck? What are you eating? When? In response to what feeling, emotion, trigger? The only way out is through. In other words— if there are things you aren't dealing with, you will probably stay stuck until you deal with them. You have to be willing to look under every rock for clues.

I believe each and every one of you is capable of taking the next step.

★★★

What's the key to weight loss?

Is it Weight Watchers? If you "do" Weight Watchers, you measure food, count points, either track online or attend meetings. I have many clients who claim that Weight Watchers works great. The only problem seems to be as soon as they go off Weight Watchers, the weight comes back on.

Is it Adkins? If you follow the Adkins diet, you cut out almost all carbohydrates. You can eat unlimited protein and fat. People lost weight when they went "on" Adkins, but as soon as they went "off," they gained that weight back. Plus, they had an unhealthy lipid profile to deal with from eating all the unhealthy fats.

Is it calorie counting? To track calories you have to figure out how many you need, how many you burn, and how many you eat. It requires a notebook and a calculator everywhere you go. Many people lose weight at first when they start counting calories but either become obsessed with it to an unhealthy extreme or get burnt out quickly of all the counting, tracking, and calculating.

Is it the Eat Clean Diet? To eat clean you eat from a specific set of whole foods. All the food is natural—straight from the earth. No processed sugar, fats, flour, rice. You eat five to six small meals a day to keep your body from ever feeling hungry. It's wonderful until it's your birthday, and you feel like you can't eat the cake your loved ones made for you or have a slice of pizza at the Superbowl party.

Is it low fat? Low carb? Jenny Craig? Nutrisystem? The Special K challenge? Slim Fast? South Beach? No, it is not. No diet or plan has the answer. What all of these things do is make you eat consciously while you are on them.

Have you ever had a day of mindless eating? You went into a restaurant and ordered whatever you felt like without having any idea how many calories it contained or the nutritional value of it. Or, I've done this many times— went to a social gathering and found myself hanging out by the chips and dip counter for too long chatting away. Next thing I know, my stomach is protesting, and I realize I probably just ate my day's worth of calories just munching away. Mindless eating.

The opposite of mindless eating is conscious eating. It is what Weight Watchers, Adkins, calorie counting, the Eat Clean diet and all the others have in common. As soon as we go "on", we immediately become very conscious of what and how much we are eating. We know it's the only way to lose weight. But we don't believe we have what it takes to be conscious eaters on our own, so we rely on this plan or program to do the work for us.

If only that worked. The reason it doesn't is that at some point, we get sick of the restrictive nature of the program. Whether it's points, carbs, calorie counting, or birthday cake—something triggers us to quit. They just aren't sustainable. I have said this a million times. If you can go on it, you will go off it. It just doesn't work.

You have to change. You have to change, from somewhere deep within you that is sick and tired of this cycle of dieting, into a conscious eater.

You can use Weight Watchers, calorie counting, or Eating Clean as tools to help you. All three have helped me become much more aware of what and how much I eat. But they can't do it for you. And they aren't permanent. Only change from the inside is permanent.

The great news is that anyone can choose to become a conscious eater. And that means no more counting, or restrictions, or the destructive cycle of dieting. You have to be willing to take the time and make a commitment to stick with it. Remember, if you get focused and organized, you only have to lose weight once. Once! If you learn how to eat right for your body and life, you will never have to do it again.

The hard part is realizing how much there is to learn and accepting that this will take time. You have to be willing to look at your habits and challenge them. This is not a diet you are going on; you are creating changes in your life. If you got a new job, you'd make changes. If you moved to a new city, you'd adapt. If you got married, you'd create new habits. We are all capable of this. We change when we need to. We change when it means enough to us. If being overweight is keeping you from living your best life, then the time has come. You deserve more than that, my friend.

★★★

When the guru sat down to worship each evening, the ashram cat would get in the way and distract the worshipers. So he ordered that the cat be tied during evening worship. After the guru died, the cat continued to be tied during evening worship. And when the cat died, another cat was brought to the ashram so that it could be duly tied during evening worship. Centuries later treatises were written by the guru's disciples on the religious and liturgical significance of tying up a cat while worship is performed.
— "The Guru's Cat" from Anthony De Mello, *The Song of the Bird*

I love this little lesson. The first time I read it was in the book *Eat, Pray, Love.* I see how, in my life, I've made misinterpretations of events that led to a long list of false beliefs about how my life works. Some of my false beliefs? I don't have self-discipline. I'm not a morning person. I'm not athletic. I don't like vegetables. I can't make changes in my life. I can't be happy. I'll never be good enough. I don't matter.

The best thing that has ever happened to me was a crisis in my emotional and spiritual life that made me look at all these lies and decide if I was going to continue to live under their power anymore, or if I was ready to break free and live a new way. All I knew was my way didn't work.

From a health perspective, I wanted to be a non-smoker *so* badly. And I wanted to be at a healthy weight.

I realize as much as I wanted to quit smoking for my health, I really wanted what I believed I would feel like if I quit. I believed people would stop judging me. I would no longer be under the control of an addiction. I would feel better about myself. I would feel in charge of my life. I would have self-discipline. I would be happy.

I think losing weight was the same for me. Yes, if I lose 5 pounds or 50 pounds, my cholesterol and blood sugar improve. My clothes fit better. I become healthier. But that wasn't my motivation. Ever. My motivation was internal. I wanted to know what I would feel like if I didn't dislike myself so much for weighing more than I wanted to. I wanted to do what I said I would do instead of always feeling stuck and hopeless.

My true goals: Confidence. Self-discipline. Feeling good about myself. Freedom. Joy.

From one of my favorite authors, Debbie Ford: "What if you discovered that what you are craving is not the outside goodie—the new career, the fit body, the loving family—but the feeling that you think you'll experience when you get it?"

Here's what I learned on my winding, crooked path. Losing 5 pounds or 50 pounds does not create a feeling of confidence or self-discipline. I don't feel better about myself because I'm thinner. The freedom and joy I experience come from the changes I made to get here.

I learned to get up earlier to fit a workout in. It feels so good to plan it the night before and do it the next morning. I get to take that feeling with me all day that I did it.

I learned many strategies to eat healthier, lower calorie versions of the foods I like whether I am on vacation, at a party, out to dinner, with friends, or alone. It feels good to not have the self-loathing meltdown (often) from the free-pass overeating I used to do. Every day that I make slightly better choices, I feel better about myself, and I heal from all that self-judgment.

I believe when we see that we are making progress toward what we want out of our lives, we feel powerful, hopeful, and confident. Each time I experience those feelings, I want more! And it motivates me from the inside out to keep going, keep fighting, make changes, and stick with them. I never want to go back to the days of self-loathing and hopelessness. By pressing onward and never giving up, I believe it is possible for everyone to begin to experience the freedom and joy that comes with knowing that you, and only you, are capable of creating a life that you absolutely love.

★★★

Did you feel the different energy this week? Spring is almost here. How do you feel? Did you make it through a winter without gaining weight? Or are you feeling disappointed because despite all you know, you find yourself up 6, 7, 8 pounds and not feeling so great?

I understand. This is the time of year when we all start thinking about bathing suits, vacation, shorts, and sleeveless tops. But there is new energy and a fresh start as well. What would happen if we let the disappointment of the last year go and focused on moving forward? I'll bet that would feel a lot better than getting beat up over and over about the past. Let's move forward.

"Each of us has the ability to find and nurture new parts of ourselves and become the people we aspire to be."—Debbie Ford

I really believe that. Just because we have done things a certain way doesn't mean we are destined to do it that same way forever. We all have the ability to create new habits and let old ones go that are not serving us well anymore. We all have the ability to learn and grow. So what stops us?

I know for me, I was afraid. I didn't realize it, but fear was like the wizard behind the curtain running the show. I wanted to change, but as soon as I would try I would feel overwhelmed and slip right back to my old, comfortable behaviors and habits. Did you hear the woman on The Biggest Loser say she realized that her comfort zone wasn't really all that comfortable? I loved that and can relate. But it still takes that push to get past stuff that can come up when you try to make a change in your life.

Have you ever tried to make an important change in your life? Wow. The stuff that comes bubbling up can make anyone run back to their comfort zone! For some women this is the fear of failure that comes up when they try to change their eating, because every diet they have gone on has failed. It's hard to work up the courage needed to go through that in case it fails again. For others, it is the fear of succeeding because that might mean leaving loved ones behind. If you and your best friend or spouse have been overweight together for many years, what will happen to your relationship if one of you changes?

These are all valid feelings, but getting healthy and fit is a change worth fighting for. It takes courage, but pull back the curtain and expose your fears. It will be OK. The antidote to fear is love and truth. Remember who you are. Remember the truth. You are unique, you belong, you are worthy of love, and no one else has the combination of gifts and talents that you do. You make a difference!

Then translate that into action. Love yourself— in action. That means feed yourself inspiration, movement, light, love, truth, whole healthy food, water, connection, time for you, and anything else that awakens the part of you that knows what a strong, courageous person you really are.

★★★

Do you need to have your fire of motivation lit? I love feeling the fire. I spent a good part of my life without it, so I am very grateful to feel that burn to work my body and to push myself. I love the way it feels to move, lift, and sweat. It's still hard to believe it's me saying that. I was not always an exerciser.

Sometime back in the late '90s when I was still smoking and overweight, I had a vision—sort of like a daydream. It was so real that it scared me. I saw myself sitting across the desk from a doctor as I listened to a diagnosis. I had not taken care of myself, and now it was too late. I could have prevented this, but I chose to keep going with my unhealthy behaviors. The feeling of regret was overwhelming.

I had been a smoker for 17 years and didn't really believe I could quit but I decided to try again. This time, though, was different. A fire had been lit in me that I'd never experienced before. I had experienced a shift and was now 100% conscious of what I was doing to myself and what the consequences of that would be. This time I didn't care whether I believed I could do it or not, I was going to change. Whatever it took.

After years of trying, that was the time I finally succeeded and quit smoking for good. But that didn't solve all my problems. To quit, I had let myself eat whatever I wanted to take the place of cigarettes. You can imagine the result. Up several sizes and feeling pretty awful despite having conquered this addiction. Thankfully, I still carried the vision with me of that scary conversation with my doctor, so I didn't give in to the temptation to go back to smoking. I had to put this all together.

Then I started moving. After learning the lesson about running, I just started walking. (It takes me awhile, but I do finally get to the point where I am so sick of hearing myself and I just have to do something about it.) So I walked and walked every day. Wow do pounds start to melt off when you walk every day. The feeling of knowing that losing weight was actually within my control was quite amazing to me. It was up to me.

I have a note written by my desk that I wrote back then and saved. It says "no one is going to do this for you." It was an epiphany. I had to do the work. I had to take each step. Even with the help of a personal trainer, it was completely up to me to show up, work hard, and follow up with good choices. Ugh.

I so wanted the magic fix, the easy way out. I really did. I was afraid of taking full responsibility because I just didn't believe in my own ability to follow through. I had blown it so many times before, what made me think this time would be any different? But it was. The light had come on, and I knew there was no other way.

I couldn't pretend anymore that it was anyone or anything else's responsibility but mine.

Since those first walks on the trail, I've learned a lot. I've learned that it is up to me to put myself in places and around people that help me keep the light on and the fire lit. It doesn't just happen on its own. It is up to me to show up and work hard and make good choices. It's up to me to get help when I need it, to say no to the things that don't support my journey, and to always believe that anything is possible.

★★★

You know when you wake up in the morning with a strong commitment to eat healthy and get a workout in? It feels good to be focused and to have things planned. Sometimes those days go well. Then, there are the other times when, although the intent was there, it all seems to fall apart. Those days usually end with eating something really awful late at night as an exclamation point on a mess of a day.

What's going on here? Why doesn't our intent always translate into action? Why does the commitment seem to fall apart and lead to eating a whole sleeve of Thin Mints? I believe that we are in a battle.

We all have a normal desire to feel satisfied, happy, at peace. For me, planning out my workouts and having my healthy foods around is all part of that desire. I want to feel good about myself. I want to feel good physically. I want to feel strong, filled up, and confident. I've learned that to feel that way, I have to plan things out and prepare for my day.

That doesn't mean the day always goes as planned. Things come up all day long. We are needed by our kids, our family, our work, boss, coworkers, house, neighbors, parents, friends, and pets. We say yes and we're there for them. We meet their needs. We fulfill their requests. We try to make as many people as possible happy. And we give up our time.

We do that over and over until we just can't take any more deprivation. Then we sit down with the bag of chips or the ice cream or the wine or the [please insert your favorite "I'm taking some time for me dammit" treat here], and we get that moment or two for ourselves. It's just a few minutes. It's just a snack. We can get so much pleasure from it, and we don't have to say no to anyone to get it. An hour workout takes mega-planning. A Reese's Peanut Butter Egg takes none. Going to the gym means feeling guilty for whatever the thing is you are having to neglect for that hour. Eating 12 cookies after everyone is in bed? Super easy, delicious, delightful, and no one gets hurt.

Or do they? Maybe the instant gratification is really not creating the feeling of satisfaction, happiness, and peace we want in our lives. If the rush only lasts a moment but has long term consequences, is it worth it? When I smoked, every cigarette for me was a nice little break outside from whatever was going on, with the added bonus of a drug rush to my brain's pleasure centers. Who wouldn't want twenty of those a day! But they lie, because they kill you eventually.

If you are deprived of time for you and getting the only bit of pleasure you have from food, I challenge you this week to look for other things to add to your list of gratification—givers. I believe food can be on that list, but it can't be the only thing. Maybe what you need at that time is sleep. Or a shower. Or a walk. Or four deep breaths. Or to lay down and stretch your back. Or a big glass of water. Or some tea. Or a good song. Or a workout. Or a text from a friend. There are other ways to steal a moment for yourself, and they can be very healthy. You choose.

For me, I got into trouble not by depriving myself of time day after day, but by depriving myself of me. I was so lost, that I really wasn't living what I now call authentically. I was walking through life doing what I thought I should, without knowing much about what would make me love my life. I was full of fear, guilt, and regret. I had a lot of "shoulds." But I felt very deprived, so I ate. It was a temporary fix to a very deep problem that food was never able to solve.

If you have been struggling with your weight most of your life and you are sick of thinking about calories, carbs, fat grams, etc., maybe it's time to take the next step. The truth is: it's not about the food. It's about what need is being filled by the extra food and what you can do to feel fulfilled without it. What do you need? Is food really giving it to you or is it fooling you into thinking it is, then robbing you of that very thing over the course of your life.

I believe we can choose differently and at any moment set our lives on a different course no matter how lost we feel right now. That's the truth.

★★★

Let's do an experiment. Stand up with your arms hanging at your sides. Now lift your arms straight out to about shoulder height, then lower them. Repeat that. Feel like a bird?

Now, this time lift your arms straight out to about shoulder height slowly by using your shoulder muscles. Once you get there, hold and squeeze those muscles right on top of your shoulders. Now release slowly. Repeat that. Feel those muscles?

One more time. This time lift your arms straight out to about shoulder height slowly by using your shoulder muscles and squeeze your fists as tightly as you can. Hold. Release slowly. Feel those muscles?

Strength training is interesting. You can do a lot of it and not make much progress, or you can do a little of it and progress by leaps and bounds. The difference is intention.

When we create movement, our bodies have the natural ability to recruit all kinds of different muscles to make that movement as comfortable as possible. When we are strength training, however, the goal is to challenge this comfort and move the body past its natural ability. It is then that we create strength, balance, posture, and flexibility. We can never reach that goal if we're just going through the motions.

When I take BodyPump class, the lunges just kill me. My legs burn and it's very difficult to make it through the song. I know how to make it easier, though. All I have to do is spend more time with my legs straight, and get a nice little rest at the top on each repetition. But I also know that I'll not progress the way I want to by making it easier. It's *supposed* to burn.

I get the most out of my set of lunges when I get in the correct stance, fix my posture, then sink down to just the right level, hold for a second, then push my front heel into the floor powerfully and lift myself up without ever straightening my legs at the top. I connect with my leg muscles, I feel them work, I feel them burn, and I don't give in to the temptation to go all the way up to straight legs and rest.

I feel the same about walking. When I get out there on the trail, I know how to make it easier. Slow down a little, relax my arms, relax my posture, and focus on something else. But if I want to make the most of my workout, I tighten my arms, straighten my posture, engage my core muscles and focus on bringing power, energy, and intention to each step.

This kind of focus is a whole different ball game. It's mental. It's emotional. It's physical. And it's spiritual. It brings all your reasons, your passions, your energy to every movement and every choice you make. It doesn't allow you to disconnect or just go through the motions. It doesn't allow you to take the path of least resistance.

It is hard to stay motivated. Believe me, I know. Very often, just showing up for a walk or a workout is a victory for me. And I celebrate that. But what I really want for myself and for every one of you is to go beyond that. Connect to your dreams. Create intentional movement that you are confident will help you progress toward those dreams. When this happens, your muscles burn and you feel it the next day. You know you did something. And you also realize how important every minute on the bike is. Or every step of your walk is. Or what power every bicep curl has.

I try to bring my reasons with me to every workout because they are so important to me. I work out because I feel so much better about myself when I do. I walk because I watched my mom spend the last ten years of her life in a wheelchair, and I know she would have given anything to take a step. I do my lunges the right way even though they kill me because it teaches me that I can persevere, I can keep going, and that I am stronger than I know. And you are, too.

★★★

Wow, did I eat badly this week. I'm not sure I could have eaten worse if I had tried, and I don't know why. Movie theater popcorn—which I haven't been eating. A Burger King double cheeseburger. Peanut butter eggs. Way too much sodium, not enough water. It wouldn't bother me so much except I feel like crap. I have a headache, I feel bloated, dehydrated, and unhealthy.

The sad part is I worked out really well. I had an excellent week. I guess one way to look at it is, "good thing I had such good workouts or this overeating would quickly affect my weight." But I don't want to feel like this at all. Nothing I ate is worth feeling like this. I want to be healthy, strong, and energized. I want to feel good about myself.

As I think back through my week, I see what some of my mistakes were. First and foremost, I didn't have enough food made up ahead of time because I only made a quick trip to the grocery store. I was out of egg whites, so I didn't have my egg frittata made up. I was out of salmon. I ran out of lettuce for salads. No broccoli. I know better but last weekend I did some other stuff instead of preparing my food, and I paid for it. Since I didn't make time for it Sunday, I really should have done it on Monday. Funny if I don't do it on Sunday, I don't do it at all. That's not very good thinking.

I also didn't have my normal snacks available at work. No yogurt in the fridge. No granola bars in my desk. So when I ran out to grab something, I remembered that I had a Burger King gift card. Why not use it? Yuck, I remember why. Because I don't like Burger King. It's not the taste really, it's the after-effects. I can feel that saturated fat clumping up in my arteries. I get very thirsty from the high salt. It's just not a good feeling.

There is always something more fun to do than go to the grocery store. There are definitely more pressing priorities than spending an hour in the kitchen on a sunny Sunday chopping veggies and making egg white frittatas. But my fitness is important to me. I know this one. If I don't have things organized, I don't do well. I have to have my environment set up for success, not failure.

It only takes three days of eating clean to feel much better. So—guess what I did all afternoon?

1. drank lots of water
2. went grocery shopping
3. cooked broccoli, red pepper, feta, egg white frittata
4. cooked a pound of salmon
5. chopped cucumbers, red peppers, tomatoes, and onions for salad
6. pressed turkey burger patties and froze them individually

These are the things that I know work for me. When these strategies are in place, I make much better choices. Your strategies may not be the same as mine, but I bet if I asked you what strategies have worked for you in the past, you could list several. They are still available to you! They are your arsenal, your toolbox. Bring them back out and put them to use.

If you are like me, you will always be someone who could easily default to junk food. That's just me. If they were low calorie and made me feel awesome, I would live on pizza, French fries, Oreos and ice cream. But they don't, so I choose differently. Not because I am so wildly in love with broccoli. It's good. I like it now (didn't used to). No, I choose differently because I am wildly in love with the feeling of health. And being proud of myself. Of feeling good about myself. And not feeling out of control about my weight.

At any moment, no matter how bad your day or week or month has been, you can choose differently. Your weight will not change overnight. Weight loss is a slow process. But the way you feel about yourself, the feeling of empowerment, the feeling of loving your body and your life can be yours. All it takes is a few simple choices that get you moving in a direction in which you believe that these things are possible for you. And they definitely are possible.

★★★

"Sue, I know I have a problem. When I'm overly stressed I go to food. But I also go to food no matter what kind of day I am having. It was a very stressful week and I wanted comfort food, but even after I would grab something, I would continue to eat. Am I hungry?

Nope...I just want to eat. I wait for my husband to go to bed, so I can sneak in the kitchen to get something. Since I can't sleep, I find myself getting a bowl of cereal, snack bar, sandwiches, sometimes all of the above. I know I'm not hungry. I look back on just about my entire adulthood, and this has been my problem. How do I fix this addiction? Go to meetings? Seek counseling? I know what I want to do. I want to have my mouth wired shut! I've done Weight Watchers meetings for years to seek help from others in the meetings, but it's not a permanent fix. I love your newsletters, I always feel energized and think I'm ready to face the week. Then a couple good days go by and I lose control again. You've got me motivated to begin moving again. I'm enjoying my workouts and I look forward to a new goal each week. I'm looking for help to put this addiction to rest."

Thank you for writing to me so openly about your struggles with food. You have no idea how much you just helped someone else by sharing your story. I know there are other women out there who are struggling just like you, and there is comfort in knowing we're not alone.

I am proud of you for having the courage to say "I have a problem." You didn't maneuver or shift the blame somewhere. You said this is me. This is where I am and I don't know what to do. That is a very tough thing to do, so I want you to be proud of that.

Here is what I believe. I believe that the struggle you described in your email is common to every single one of us to some extent or another. The hold or addiction isn't always food. It could be shopping, alcohol, approval, prescription drugs, sex, eating disorders, anger, gambling, work, people pleasing or anything else that can get hold of us and leave us feeling out of control and desperate.

The first time I read the Apostle Paul's letter to the Romans in the Bible, I knew that this was a struggle common to all of humanity. If Paul was writing about it 2,000 years ago, it must be a humanity problem and not a defect in me. From The Message Remix: "I obviously need help. I realize that I don't have what it takes. I can will it, but I can't do it. I decide to do good, but I don't really do it. I decide not to do bad, but then I do it anyway. My decisions, such as they are, don't result in actions. Something has gone wrong deep within me and gets the better of me every time. It happens so regularly that it's predictable."

Take comfort in that. It's not just you. It truly is all of us and we each have to find our way to freedom from the things that have kept us from living our lives the way we were meant to live. With freedom, joy, passion, and love.

I will name the things that were keeping me stuck: Shame. Fear. Regret. Feeling worthless. I don't know what pain or shame you may be dragging around with you from your past. But I know if you have gone through all the layers in weight loss such as becoming aware of calories in/calories out, scheduling your workouts, getting yourself organized, finding support, creating an environment in which you can succeed, and you are still stuck and suffering, then I believe it's something deeper.

You asked about meetings or counseling. I went to several different therapists over the years. The problem was that I was too afraid to share all my junk, so I would go to my counseling appointments and not be totally honest. There were some things I never talked about. I still cared more about what they thought of me than getting healthy. I didn't have a breakthrough until I found a group that I finally felt comfortable sharing everything. The hardest thing for me to say back then was, "I am afraid." But I learned that as I shared my story and let go of the need to look like I had it together, the junk I had been carrying around lost its power.

As I was preparing this newsletter, I looked up the 12 Steps. I hadn't read them in a long time. They are printed below. Look at what it asks of you. Admit the problem; then hand it over to a power greater than yourself. That's tough for us. We want to fix ourselves, not let go and surrender.

For me, healing came in ways I didn't expect. The first support group I ever attended was a grief support group for people who had recently lost a loved one. I hadn't recently lost a loved one, but I didn't know where else to go, and I was desperate. I was 40 years old. I sat down in a small circle of chairs with the other participants. When my turn came, I started crying and apologizing because I just didn't feel like I had the right to be there. Everyone else was in such pain. They had just lost their loved one. So I said, "I know I am not supposed to be here. My dad died 27 years ago. My mom died 17 years ago. I should be over it by now, but I'm not. I'm sorry." That small recovery group of people made me feel so welcomed and in the absolute right place I couldn't believe it. In my mind, I was convinced they would just think I was a moron because I was still dealing with all of this. In reality, they offered me such grace and love that I was changed forever.

You can change, too. I am very proud of you for sharing your struggles and allowing me to share it with others. I believe there are many readers who will relate and be impacted by it. Keep sharing your story. Don't give in to the lie that we are supposed to look like we have it all together. We don't! I don't! All I have is my own story and the belief that anyone, no matter what they are going through, can be healed of past hurts and regrets and start new. Even you.

THE 12 STEPS

Step 1—We admitted we were powerless over our addiction—that our lives had become unmanageable

Step 2—Came to believe that a Power greater than ourselves could restore us to sanity

Step 3—Made a decision to turn our will and our lives over to the care of God as we understood God

Step 4—Made a searching and fearless moral inventory of ourselves

Step 5—Admitted to God, to ourselves, and to another human being the exact nature of our wrongs

Step 6—Were entirely ready to have God remove all these defects of character

Step 7—Humbly asked God to remove our shortcomings

Step 8—Made a list of all persons we had harmed and became willing to make amends to them all

Step 9—Made direct amends to such people wherever possible, except when to do so would injure them or others

Step 10—Continued to take personal inventory and when we were wrong promptly admitted it

Step 11—Sought through prayer and meditation to improve our conscious contact with God as we understood God, praying only for knowledge of God's will for us and the power to carry that out

Step 12—Having had a spiritual awakening as the result of these steps, we tried to carry this message to other addicts, and to practice these principles in all our affairs

★★★

This is a really good time of year to make some changes. The days are getting longer, we're pulling out the summer clothes, working outside, getting more walks in. There is a positive energy that says if you have been thinking about going for it, why not now.

I have a challenge for May. Let's really examine some of our false beliefs, replace them with the truth, and then take action.

As some of you know, I was really enjoying Starbucks Iced Chai lattes. At 42 grams of sugar per drink (and almost $4) it was getting old, but I was having a hard time quitting. I would decide not to buy them anymore, but then it was like my car was taken over by some other force and I would find myself back at the window getting my treat. Depending on the day, I was either resigned to being hooked on these things and making a deal with myself to work off the extra sugar, or vowing, once and for all, to give them up. It was making me crazy.

I've never done this before, but for Lent I decided to give something up—my iced chai's. The first two days were rough. I really wanted one. I thought about them and missed them. But it felt to me like they were not an option, so I just dealt with not having them. Then by day 3, the craving disappeared. I mean completely. For the next seven weeks, I hardly thought about them at all. When Easter came and Lent was over, I drove through and got one right away. (Smart, I know. Remember, I struggle.) But I just didn't enjoy it. The craving was gone.

I am happy to say I haven't had one since, and I feel much better. I don't miss it and it taught me a big lesson. I still have lots of false beliefs floating around in this head of mine. The false belief was "I am addicted to iced chai and need to buy one when I crave one." The truth is I was creating those cravings by drinking them, and I don't need them at all to be happy.

Here are some of the false beliefs I hear the most. I don't have time. I'm too busy. I'm not motivated. I can't. It won't happen for me. I have other responsibilities. I don't like vegetables. I'm a sugar addict. Can you imagine for a moment what your life would be like if you believed the opposite? I do have time! I'm not too busy! I AM motivated. It will happen for me.

The only way to manifest your heart's desire is to take radical responsibility, which means taking action. None of this happens by thinking about it. A lot of the things I write about are internal, and I ask you to search your motives and the things that keep you stuck. But it can't stop there. It gets exciting when you begin to understand yourself in such a way as to get unstuck and begin to move forward. To choose differently. To take action.

Some of you have a hundred pounds to lose. Some of you want to lose the last five or ten. Both of these scenarios can torment us equally. No matter where you are on your journey or how long you have been there, today is the day to step it up. No more excuses. Take radical responsibility for your choices, and if you don't like the outcome, choose differently.

What lies have their hooks in you? Do you believe that you can't exercise daily? Do you believe that you have to have sugar and crappy carbs? Do you believe that you are too old to experience your healthy weight? Do you believe that being healthy and fit is for other people? That you don't have self-discipline?

I reject all these lies. They are not helping us love life or experience our heart's desire. I want you to expose them for the deception that they are. The only way to do this is to prove them wrong by taking action. Get yourself organized. Take some positive steps. Big ones—big enough for you to see some real results and success. That means buy lots of healthy stuff. Cook. Eat simply when you go out (grilled chicken salads with balsamic). Get off the sugar. Get up early and work out. Take the old "I know what to do, I just don't do it" and turn it on its head.

Close your eyes and take a deep breath. Now imagine that the rest of your summer you are moving in the direction of your dreams. Allow yourself to feel what it will be like to succeed. If fear comes up, that's OK. I am afraid. I've tried before and failed and it was horrible. It is safer to stay stuck and blame it on my excuses. But that is selling yourself so short. Don't give up. It is worth the fight. It really is worth the fight.

★★★

I want to talk about deprivation.

When I used to think about quitting smoking, I would get these horrible fears about being deprived. For example, I thought I could never enjoy vacation again. What would the beach be like without chillin' with a smoke? No smoke breaks at work, how would I ever survive that? Beer wouldn't be any good, coffee wouldn't be the same, dinner wouldn't be as enjoyable without that after-dinner smoke. I just couldn't imagine life without cigarettes.

What a lie that turned out to be. I just could not have been more wrong. Life is so much better as a non-smoker. Vacations are wonderful because it is much easier to travel without worrying about when and where I can smoke and freaking out if I have to wait too long. I'm too busy loving my new career to worry about a smoke break. Beer tastes better. Coffee tastes better. Dinner is much more enjoyable, and I don't have to go stand in the rain afterward to get my fix.

When I talk with clients, many of them have a similar fear of being deprived when we start talking about food. I understand this completely. I once shared the view that healthy eating meant depriving myself of anything really yummy and having to live off cardboard, rabbit food, and no chocolate. I want to tell you that this is a lie.

Eating mostly whole, healthy foods hasn't deprived me of *anything*. I am finding more and more ways to cook so everything tastes wonderful. There are tons of recipes out there with less sugar, no fructose, true whole grains with lots of fiber. Check out *Eating Clean*, for example. We believe that life without all our sugary foods, baked goods, processed foods, snacks, chips, crackers, cookies and the like will leave us feeling empty and missing out on the good stuff. Not true.

How many of us have been deprived of enjoying clothes shopping?

How many of us would give anything for a whole day of feeling good about our bodies?

How many of us have been deprived in social situations because we just didn't feel confident enough to attend or enjoy the party at the pool, beach, etc.?

How many of us have been deprived of our health and lost our freedom to be without medication?

How many of us are selling ourselves short in life, relationships, and career because of our weight?

How many of us are being deprived of the life of our dreams?

That is the deprivation I want you to overcome. Is any tasty treat in the world worth giving up these things? I challenge you to fight back this week. Fight for it. Make your own list of what you have been deprived of by eating the way you have been. Then take one look back, receive forgiveness, and make a different choice. I guarantee that if you cut out the excess sugar and choose whole, health-filled foods, you will quickly feel like a new person. I will never let a snack, drink, drug, substance, person, old belief, or anything else deprive me of those things ever again, and I truly hope the same for you.

★★★

There are a lot of false beliefs out there. I have learned that if you set out to improve your health and fitness but rely on false beliefs, you will stay stuck and become disillusioned with the whole process. The hope that it will work for you will disappear.

This process is a challenge. It requires commitment. It requires courage. You have to be willing to keep digging, to peel back layer after layer and figure out what it is deep within you that is keeping you from treating yourself and your body like the sacred home of your heart and soul.

A diet can never do this. So please stop dieting. I can only imagine if I had lost weight like that, the torment I would live under of trying to keep a grip on that deprivation so as not to gain my weight back. Just a terrible way to live. And it's not how we are meant to eat. We are supposed to eat. A lot! We are supposed to enjoy food and feel satisfied.

Exercise alone can never do this. It is a very good thing to do, but alone it will never be enough. You cannot out-train an unhealthy diet. We are meant to feed our bodies with lots and lots of healthy food. I believe the way to this is not by conjuring up a bunch of self-discipline, but rather by healing the things that got us here in the first place. That way, you don't have to experience deprivation and a lifetime of dieting. Instead, your wants completely change.

Take a look at some of the lies we tell ourselves. Are they really true, or could we find others with the same circumstances that are doing it anyway? You have to do it anyway. Remember the transformation comes by doing. By conquering. By overcoming.

Just a few of the thousands of false beliefs we hold near and dear (all of us):

> I don't have time.
> I don't like healthy food.
> I can't cook.
> I can't change because I have a family.
> I can't change because I live alone.
> I've always failed before.
> I know what to do, I just don't do it.
> I just don't like exercise.
> I need my wine.
> My kids' sports.
> I can't make time for me.
> I'm not a morning person.
> My metabolism.

My genetics.
I'm not beautiful.
I'm too busy at work.
It's stressful right now.
I don't want to be deprived.
I'm not worth it.
I'm too old.
It's too late.
I'm not good enough.
I have no strength.
I have no balance.
I'm too tired.
It's not possible for me to be at my healthy weight.

The way to transformation is to see lies for what they really are. They are what hold you back and keep you stuck. Expose them! Shine as much light as possible on them. Peel back those layers. See if you can get an understanding of where they came from, then say to yourself "That was then, this is now!"

Then from that place of truth, that place inside of you (inside of all of us) where you know you can do anything, be anything, accomplish anything, conquer anything—from that place, begin to make new, extraordinary choices. No more ordinary. No more living out of the wounds we've carried or the lies we told ourselves. Only abundant, radiant, exuberant life.

★★★

How do you lose weight or get healthier? By changing what got you there to begin with. For me, this went very deep. I was not able to make good choices because my choices weren't coming from a place inside of me where I believed that I was worth it or that I could do it.

One of the most common things I hear, from new clients especially, is "I know what to do; I just don't do it." I want to challenge each and every one of you. Why not? What's wrong? What's blocking you? What's holding you back?

You can start by looking at whether you believe you are worth it. Are you able to put yourself first in a healthy way without feeling guilty? Do you give your own body, mind, and spirit the level of time and attention it needs? Do you care for yourself as much as you care for others? If not, find help and support in understanding your worth and learning that taking care of yourself is not selfish, but rather one of the greatest gifts you can give to others.

If you've gotten through that layer and know who you are and how valued you are, do you know what choices to make to move you in the direction of health and wellness? What exercises are best for weight loss, what healthy food choices are, how the body works and the kinds of fuel it needs, etc. There are a lot of lies out there; lobbying, policies, and marketing that are dangerous and can get us off track. We have to be vigilant in finding the truth and being real. You don't lose 50 pounds by just taking the stairs, and whole grain Cheez Its are not healthy. Educate yourself.

Once you are educated and know the truth, then you can really begin to walk this out. It is your job to make exceptional choices that support your best life. I know what I am asking of you is a challenge. I know that the society as a whole is going in the opposite direction. So what! What fun is it to swim with the current anyway? Let's be rebels and go against this wave of obesity, disease, and unhappiness. Let's show the world that there is another way to live. We can make exceptional choices and get to our healthiest weight without ever dieting, taking pills, injections, or anything else. And we can let our joy be our gift to the world.

What I believe happens when we go through these layers, is we heal from the inside out. We all have some wounds or fears or something that gets in our way. If we act bravely and dig a little bit, we can find a new way of being in the world that is so much better than our old way. We know who we are! We know we are valued! We know we are worth it. We know the truth about health and fitness. We know the truth about food. And we take all that knowledge, make one exceptional choice after another, and a miracle happens. Because once we feel better about ourselves and truly let our light shine, not only do our own lives improve, so does the world.

★★★

Everybody's got something. Each of us has our own personal challenges to overcome. No one is perfect and no one has it easy.

One of my challenges is renal disease. I was diagnosed with chronic kidney disease about fifteen years ago and have less than half my kidney function. My doctor assures me that one can live long and prosper off of less than that, but he also encourages me to do everything possible to preserve the healthy tissue that's left.

When I was diagnosed, I was a smoker who ate a lot of junk food, fast food, processed meats, processed sugars, and really didn't think about my health very much. Back then I was so overwhelmed with my emotional issues that my physical health was not on my mind whatsoever. My approach to the disease back then was to figure out what the right medicine was and get on with it.

I was never a person to just make up my mind about improving some aspect of my life and then do it. It has always taken me forever. I must have tried to quit smoking a hundred times before I did it. I resisted, I lived in denial, I gave up, then I tried again. With exercise I started and stopped. Started again and stopped. And nutrition is the same way. I will never be a person who can wake up one morning and declare to the world that I will eat only healthy foods henceforth. Never gonna happen. I am rebellious and resistant, so it takes me a very long time. But I am willing to add things to my life incrementally.

So instead of adopting the "kidney diet" in 1997, I added some fruits and veggies. In 1998 I started to walk at Highbanks. In 1999 I finally quit smoking. In 2000 I added running 5Ks. In 2001 I learned about heart rate monitoring and finished a marathon. In 2002 I went to Utah to hike for the first time and I started working with my personal trainer. 2003 was the year I really lost some weight and made some changes. You get the message. It didn't happen overnight. I know, I'm slow.

Here's my point. You don't have to make changes all at once. They add up! One day after another. Week after week, year after year. They really add up. The problem is if we get so focused on the fact that we're not doing it ALL RIGHT NOW (and if we misinterpret that as failing), that can keep us from progressing. We get stuck. Do something this week for your health that you are proud of and focus on that. Commit to it! Then, keep that up and do something else next week.

I didn't make all the right changes the moment I was diagnosed. It took me years to really understand my disease and get educated on what foods are best. It's still confusing sometimes but I keep pressing on. And you know what? My tentative, slow efforts actually paid off in a major way. I not only lost 45 pounds and joined the world of non-smokers, but my kidney numbers improved, which is not something that my doctor generally sees.

What you eat and drink really matters. Moving your body every day really matters. It makes a difference. Eating lots of vegetables is life changing. But what matters more than anything is never giving up. Don't give in to momentary gratification if it is going to make you compromise your long-term health and happiness. It's not worth it. There is incredible joy that comes with taking care of yourself and overcoming your personal challenges.

★★★

A little physics this week. Inertia is the resistance of any object to a change in its state of motion or rest. Inertia comes from the Latin word *iners*, meaning idle. In common usage the term "inertia" may refer to an object's amount of resistance to change in velocity, or sometimes to its momentum.

What is your momentum right now? Are you moving? And more importantly, are you moving in the direction you want to be going? Because unless you apply a different force to your life, you are going to keep going in that direction, according to the law of inertia.

To get the results we want, we have to do something different than what we've been doing. I know that sounds like common sense, but to put it into practice in our lives seems more like advanced level physics. It is challenging because of the momentum of our lives.

To change, you first have to be willing to change. You have to fight through the resistance and overcome the current momentum of your life. It is one thing to want to lose 50 pounds. It is quite another thing to want to lose 50 pounds bad enough to get out and walk for an hour in your target heart rate zone just about every day. Because choosing to walk for an hour a day means saying no to something else in your life and that takes a very strong force. But it is the only way.

Once you are willing to change, you have to become aware of what it takes to change. So, to lose that 50 pounds, if we read some silly magazine article, all you have to do is take the stairs instead of the elevator and eat dark chocolate while you visualize yourself healthy and fit. The truth is to lose 50 pounds, you need to create a balanced fitness program for yourself that includes whole-foods-based eating, strength training, and aerobic exercise. And you need to take your time and deal with all the old, bad thinking that comes up that got you there to begin with. And trust me, it will come up. You know: the all-or-nothing thinking, or the "if this doesn't work in a week it's too slow I quit" thinking, or the I'll never be at my healthiest weight because of my genes, kids, job, spouse, lack of spouse, lack of job, etc.

Once you understand that your body is a biological machine that burns calories of carbohydrates, protein, and fat for fuel, then you can get to work. That means lifting weights. And getting your walks, runs, bike rides, swims in consistently. Eating mostly whole foods in healthy portions. Drinking your water. Recovering and getting good sleep. The most challenging part of this is inertia. You will need to change direction and do things differently. You simply cannot lose a significant amount of weight or change your health drastically without making some major changes. Throw out the junk food! You don't need it. Shake up your life. Get outside and walk. Take a new class. Your job is to overcome the natural tendency to keep going in the direction you've been going.

This conversation happens frequently:

Client: I haven't lost a pound and I've been training for 6 months. It's frustrating.

Sue: Tell me about your aerobic activity.

Client: I haven't had time. [Insert excuse here.]

Sue: Tell me about how you've been eating.

Client: I was doing pretty good until the weekend came.

This conversation also happens frequently:

Client: I lost another two pounds this week! That's 25 total so far. I feel amazing.

Sue: Tell me about your aerobic activity.

Client: I walked almost every day with my HR monitor. I just made it happen.

Sue: Tell me about how you've been eating.

Client: Great! We've been trying healthy recipes and cooking at home. I love it.

The difference is not that one has more time than the other. The difference is not that one has it easier at home than the other. The difference is not that one has better genes than the other. Those are all lies. What makes the difference is when a woman knows it is going to be a challenge but decides to push against the momentum of her life anyway to go in a new direction. By doing so, she becomes victorious! An overcomer creating a new path. Creating a life she loves. I believe that woman is you.

★★★

Last week I went to an unusual party with about 30 friends. We all dressed in black and white, I wore a sequined top and sparkly earrings, my sports bra and workout shoes. The party was in the spin room and we were all on bikes. For two hours we listened to party music around the disco ball as we laughed and got our heart rates up. I burned over a thousand calories and had a blast.

Later in the week I met clients at Highbanks. The weather was perfect and we walked and talked. One client asked me every question that came to her mind and I told her my story and we ended up having a really amazing talk. Through stories and tears we ended up making a very powerful connection, and it is a walk I will not soon forget. We each burned almost 500 calories but I know we also went home with our hearts filled with gratitude and faith.

Saturday I went to Body Pump class and lifted weights to great music and an awesome instructor who keeps everything fun and challenging. I never leave that class feeling like I could do more. It wipes me out, but in a good way. I feel my muscles the next day and know I did something good for myself. If I'm not there for a week I usually get a Facebook post with a little nudge to get to class. It matters to people if I'm there.

Today was another walk, this time at Sharon Woods. Light drizzle and cool temperatures made it feel like spring. The open-hearted conversations we have on these walks are such a gift. These are not just walks, they are encouragement. Consistency. Accountability. Motivation. Inspiration. Who doesn't need more of that in their life!

One of the great lessons of my fitness journey has been learning the power and importance of relationships. I can't do this on my own. I can't solve this problem with the same mind that created it in the first place. I need others to inspire me, to mirror my thoughts back to me, to keep me from quitting, to call me out on my excuses. Things tend to get twisted up when left inside my head for too long. But if I have a safe place to express my thoughts, fears, and insecurities, they always seem to lose their power.

For the four years I worked with my trainer, he listened and encouraged me to work hard and to keep going. He kept me from quitting when I felt like I was never going to get "there." My life coach helped me remember who I really was and to see past my failures and fears. She inspired me to do things in my life differently and to take chances. It wasn't easy to let down my wall and show people what a mess I was, but I found incredible freedom by doing that.

If you believe that this fitness thing is just about dragging yourself to the basement or the gym to get on a treadmill and force yourself to slog out a few boring miles, I am here to tell you that there is so much more to it! There are people out there doing this with you, who would love nothing more than for you to join them. There are walks, classes, trainers, coaches, and friends. And if you haven't experienced one of those amazing workouts in which your walls come down and you feel your full heart, I want to encourage you to keep going because it is wonderful.

I can't do this on my own. The cravings, the compulsions, the excuses are all bigger than me. But with you by my side, I can do anything. You give me strength, encouragement, and community. You fill my heart in ways I never dreamed of. You allow me to be my authentic self as I lift, spin, walk, laugh, and cry. And all while I am moving my body, getting stronger, feeling every breath and my full heart. If you feel alone in this struggle, whether it is with your weight, your health, or your life—connect. Work out with a group. Walk with someone. There is a safe place to let the wall come down and be the beautiful, wonderful mess that you (that we all) are.

★★★

"I am afraid."

Those are three of my favorite words. Learning to say those words was one of the most empowering moments of my life so far. Before I could say "I am afraid", I spent a great deal of time and energy suppressing all my fear and trying to create the image that I wasn't afraid. I just couldn't own it. I thought that owning it would make me weak, and I had the false belief that I always had to be strong.

Getting to this level of honesty with yourself isn't easy. But it is worth the effort. Changing is scary and stepping out into that vulnerable place of trying again can be really hard. I understand completely. I tried to quit smoking so many times. Hundreds, probably. I would always fail by 2:00 p.m. each Monday I tried, and all the months of building up the courage and thinking about changing would be lost in a self-esteem crash. It was devastating to fail. It became easier to quit trying. Except that feeling of wanting to be healthier and feel better about myself would creep back up, and I would once again spend months getting up the courage to change only to fail again. I experienced the same thing with dieting.

During the times when I would quit quitting, I couldn't really own that, either. I would find excuses. I couldn't change right now, work was too stressful. Vacation was coming up. It was summer. It was winter. The kids' schedules were too busy. My schedule was too busy. I had lots of reasons why I couldn't. Now I know that those were all lies. These things never went away. Life never got less stressful or less busy. I just finally found a way to do it anyway. And the key for me was to stop believing the lies and get radically honest with myself.

The truth was I wasn't happy with myself, my weight, or my smoking but I just didn't believe I could change it. I felt powerless over these things, and I had lots of evidence (past failures) about why they had power over me. The truth was I was using my family, my job and everything else in my life as an excuse not to try again because I was scared to crash and burn.

So how do you get past it? Admit your fears and do the work anyway. It is the only way I know to get unstuck and move forward. I had to learn to say, "I am afraid." I had to learn to honestly express my feelings instead of maneuvering around them with excuses and rationalizations. I had to lace up my shoes and go walk no matter what else was going on. I had to be real about what I was eating and quit blaming everyone else. Radical responsibility.

That might mean calling someone or writing an email next time you find yourself with junk food in front of you that you are about to use to sooth your feelings of stress, loneliness, anger, or fear. Say out loud to someone what you are really feeling. Own it. Own the fact that you are about to use food to feel better. Watch it lose its power once you get that honest about it.

It might mean setting your alarm for 5:00 a.m. and getting your workout in early before all the other responsibilities and busyness set in. And if you aren't willing, then it is up to you to own that and recognize that the only thing that is keeping you from daily exercise is you. None of your excuses are valid. Being that honest and finally letting go of the list of excuses that has kept you stuck all this time is extremely empowering because once they are gone, there's nothing to stop you!

Take your power back. Own your feelings. Admit your fears. And do the work anyway. The only way out is through— and you will get through starting right now. Put your arms up powerfully into the air, smile, and as loud as you can say it with me, "I am afraid!" And just like that, you are free.

★★★

I cannot thank you enough for being part of this dream of mine— to build a community of women who are supporting and encouraging each other to live their very best life. I want to remind you that I am not someone who, according to the world's standards, should be living my dream right now. My parents died when I was young. I dropped out of high school. I've been dirt poor. And at several points in my life, I lost complete and total faith in myself. But for some reason that is beyond me, there has always been this part of me that keeps fighting and refuses to believe that I should give up.

I believe, after working with all of you, that this fighting spirit is in all of us. There is absolutely no reason why you cannot live the life of your dreams. You can accomplish anything. You can overcome anything. And yes, you can even be at your goal weight and love your body.

It is common to have a deep false belief about ourselves that we build everything else around. Lies such as *I'm not good enough, I will never succeed,* or *I'm not worth it.* If you don't believe you will ever succeed at your goals, keep fighting. Keep searching. The answer lies within you. The key is to shine as much light as possible on the lies that keep you stuck, so much light that eventually they have no power at all and the truth shines instead.

The truth is that you are a beautiful, capable overcomer. You have everything you need to succeed no matter what your past or your circumstances. You can change, transform, be freed. You can take radical responsibility for your health and your life. You can make extraordinary choices that support your dreams.

I want you to envision your future. You've done the hard work and uncovered the root of your struggle. You allowed light to shine on the lies you've been carrying with you your entire life. Once the power of those lies was broken, junk food lost its appeal. It became much easier to prioritize exercise and activity in your life and say no to things that no longer matter to you. Your weight drops slowly but without dieting. Your relationship with food is healed. Exercise is now enjoyable because the results show up consistently. You feel good about yourself and your body. You have confidence and joy in your life. I'm so happy for you. I want to be there to say, "See?? You had it in you all along!"

★★★

When I think about a balanced, effective fitness plan I include the following components: nutrition, hydration, cardio (aerobic exercise), strength training, flexibility, and healthy ways of dealing with stress and sleep.

I didn't get enough sleep last night. I got caught up in what I was doing and stayed up too late. When my alarm rang at 6:45 a.m., I did not hit the ground ready to tackle the day. I had to drag myself out of bed and work really hard to get moving. If I had not had a scheduled walk at 8:00 a.m., I am quite certain I would have skipped my work out entirely and slept in instead.

It is tough enough to stay motivated and make extraordinary choices consistently. Being tired makes it even more difficult. Here are some of the things I noticed today:

— I wanted more caffeine than usual, and I craved sugar because my energy was low, which made it tougher to choose my normal healthy foods. I wanted something sweet all afternoon for a boost of energy.

— I felt bloated and sluggish. Not the way to feel my best. I always make better choices when I feel better about myself, so to have the waist of my jeans digging into my belly all day was not a good way to support making great choices.

— My legs felt achy and tired. I don't think I got the right amount of recovery time, and I felt it. The problem that created was I really didn't feel like getting up and moving. The inertia was to spend the day on the couch, not outside being active.

— I felt slightly detached and not super clear on my goals and what I wanted to do today to support those goals. Not the way I like to think.

I used to be a night owl, stayed up late watching Letterman or whatever was on at night. I would sacrifice sleep in order to get some "me time." No wonder it was always difficult for me to get consistent with exercise. It is so much harder when I'm tired! No wonder I didn't get organized with my food. It wasn't my priority— finding things to ingest to get my energy up was my goal.

I know the temptation to stay up late and get stuff done or just finally relax in front of the computer or the TV. I understand it completely. But if you want to go to the next level in your fitness, and especially if you want to lose weight, you have to get more disciplined about going to bed earlier. The more active you are, the more recovery your body needs. Sleep is crucial in the weight loss process.

If you feel stuck in your weight loss, try something different. Whatever your nightly habits, try changing them so you can get eight hours sleep. Even if you have trouble sleeping, try creating a new pattern and see if it helps. Change how you eat and drink in the evening so it supports getting to sleep on time. Pack your gym bag, have your clothes ready for your workout. Experience a different level of motivation when you are well rested and not sleep-deprived. It is a wonderful thing to be clear on your goals and not feel like it is a constant fight. Sleep really does support that. So get to bed early and connect that choice to your overall goal of living and feeling your best.

★★★

Refuse to let the past define your present.

That's a tough one, I know. But it's the only way to get unstuck and move in the right direction. What if you believed with all your heart that you would be at your healthy body weight this time next year? What if you knew absolutely that you would never gain the weight back? Would that motivate you? Would you be inspired to get outside and walk this week? What would your food choices look like?

The problem, if you are stuck, is a false belief that you will not succeed at weight loss. I understand that this false belief was created because of past failures, but I am here to tell you that doesn't make it true. The truth is, for every single one of you, that you can be at your healthy body weight. You just have to be ready.

"But I am afraid to believe, because if I believe and then fail again, I don't think I can handle the feeling of failure." I understand completely. But all we really do when we let that thought keep us stuck is live under the rule and reign of fear. I don't know about you, but I am sick of letting fear rule my life. I am ready for another way. You can use the word that feels best to you, but I want belief, faith, love, freedom, joy, and peace to rule and reign in my life.

But how?

I believe the first step is about forgiveness. If I tell you that you are completely and totally forgiven for all your past failures at weight loss, and you are also forgiven for allowing yourself to get fat or out of shape, can you receive that? Do you believe me? If not, why not? It's true. No one is holding any of that against you except you.

The second step is about knowing who you are. You are not your past mistakes or failures. You are not your body fat percentage or the number on the scale. When you die, no one is going to talk about what size you wore or what your body fat was, they will talk about how you lived and how you shared your heart.

Then, I think you have to believe. You have to let go of your fear and believe that you can be at any body weight you want. You have to surrender your compulsions and addictions to something bigger than yourself and believe that they will be healed. You have to believe that there is power to restore your body, your health, your thinking, your emotions—everything. It's all just waiting right there for you to be ready to see it. It's quite a miracle.

There is not a lot in my past that would lead anyone to think that

I would succeed at much. I dropped out of high school. I made bad choices. I smoked and tried to quit for years, failing miserably every time. I gained weight. My marriage failed. I gave up on myself and wanted to quit. Then I saw the light. That's not who I am. I am a girl who loves music, books, art. I have a heart that feels deeply. I have a soul that loves nature and being with God. I am not my failures, and I am no longer going to let my past define my present. I am a whole soul in a wounded human and I believe I can do anything. It's time we all stopped seeing ourselves through the lens of our past. See yourself through the lens of truth, of love. You are a beautiful and whole soul in a wounded human, and I think you are incredible.

Our Deepest Fear

"Our deepest fear is not that we are inadequate. Our deepest fear is that we are powerful beyond measure. It is our light, not our darkness that most frightens us. We ask ourselves, Who am I to be brilliant, gorgeous, talented, fabulous? Actually, who are you not to be? You are a child of God. Your playing small does not serve the world. There is nothing enlightened about shrinking so that other people won't feel insecure around you. We are all meant to shine, as children do. We were born to make manifest the glory of God that is within us. It's not just in some of us; it's in everyone. And as we let our own light shine, we unconsciously give other people permission to do the same. As we are liberated from our own fear, our presence automatically liberates others."

—---from A Return to Love, by Marianne Williamson.

Healing Old Wounds and False Beliefs

I love the energy this time of year. The kids have gone back to school, it's finally cooling off outside, fall is coming and people are motivated. I noticed last week that my weight lifting class was packed full of people. It was hard to park in the Sharon Woods parking lot this morning, because there were so many walkers and runners. And I have lots of new women in the studio just getting started. This time of year seems to be similar to the energy of the New Year; a fresh start, new goals, a new routine.

How many of you are geared up for a fresh start this week? I got organized this weekend. I cleaned out the food pantry, went grocery shopping and stocked up on foods for this season. I cannot look at another tomato or cucumber thanks to a very hearty garden this year, and I'm ready for some new foods. I got a little bit excited today at Kroger because I bought ingredients for soup! I really love fall.

I know some of you are going to wake up tomorrow morning feeling like you are starting from scratch. Others will see your progress so far and will be ready to go to the next level. Where are you today? If you were to make an honest assessment, do you feel good about the way things are going? Are you progressing the way you want? Are you scared, frustrated, excited, hopeful, confident?

It takes strong commitment to develop a balanced fitness program for your life. You would think the most important pieces of that fitness plan would be about lifting weights, cardio, heart rate zones, and calories. But it's not. The most important pieces go much deeper than that. The most common sentence I hear in the studio is "I know what to do, I just don't do it." So it cannot be a lack of knowledge about lifting weights or heart rate zones or food that is the issue. The issue is: why do we continue to make choices that we know are not good for our long-term well-being?

For me, there were many reasons I did not make extraordinary choices for myself. I didn't think I was worth it. I thought I was broken and defective. I didn't believe I would ever be whole and happy anyway, so why bother? I had no idea how to think past the momentary pleasure of sugar or junk food to see the long term effects it all had on my soul. And I was brokenhearted and scared, which created all kinds of obstacles to taking good care of myself.

This was one of the hardest lessons for me to learn, but I had to take radical responsibility for all these things before I could ever get anywhere. That meant no more blaming others. No more resentment of the past. No more excuses about not having time, money, parents, a husband, children, whatever. That meant looking in the mirror and realizing that no one had gotten me to where I was but me. My choices got me here. I did this. Ouch.

But the miraculous thing about that, I realized, was if I had gotten me there, then, I was empowered to choose differently. I could be free. I did not have to wait on anyone or anything to line up just right for me to get healthy, quit smoking, lose weight, or be happy. I had everything that I needed within me. I just had to deal with my excuses honestly. What I like to call bringing them into the light. Because having all that fear hiding in the dark and running the show was no fun. I didn't feel capable of choosing my path at all. But in the light that fear loses power and suddenly my choices came from a place of spirit, truth and love. Believe me; choices from that place inside you are much better than the ones from the dark.

If you are energized and motivated, I want to encourage you to learn all you can about lifting weights, aerobic exercise, heart rate zones, calories, and nutrition. But I don't want you to stop there. Keep going. Keep digging. The only way you will be able to get to the place where, once you are educated on all things fitness, you make choices that support your long-term well-being is by bringing everything into the light. Leave no stone unturned. Be brave. Why go on a diet and lose a few pounds when you can experience this miracle and be free from all the junk that has been holding you back? Love is the only way to freedom because it casts out fear. And once fear is not in control, being your healthiest just comes naturally.

★★★

Why is weight loss so difficult? I decide to lose 20 pounds. I write down everything I eat and count every calorie or point. I track the calories burned during my workouts. I get weighed every week. And although I may follow this regimen, at some point I say, "Heck with it," and splurge because "I deserve it" and blow the progress I made. Why does this happen?

I believe this happens because tracking food, whether it is by points or calories, does not change me. All it can ever do is teach me to be aware of how much food is the appropriate amount. We do live in a country where we need to be taught that, since we are often served portions that are much larger than what is healthy for our bodies. But that's all food tracking does is teach and bring awareness. It is our responsibility to be aware of how much to eat and what to eat. That's the only way to make extraordinary choices. But tracking food is not the answer to a lifetime battle with being overweight.

The only way to end the battle is to get to the root. As I'm sure you know, the battle is exhausting. It feels obsessive, self-destructive, and often ends in feeling like a total failure. That's because we are determined to manage all the symptoms that are the result of what is at the root. Get to the root and the symptoms dissolve away. How can I find what the root of my battle with weight is? Be brave, look inward, and start asking yourself some tough questions. Don't let things get off track by looking outside yourself for the answer. It is all within you.

For me, I thought for a long time if I could drum up enough will power and self-discipline, I could lose weight and quit smoking. I tried every program out there and spent a small fortune. It never worked. I always self-destructed rapidly and almost got to the place where it felt safer to never try again. I hated feeling like such a failure. Thankfully, I got to a very bad place in my life where I was giving up on everything when I found a grief support group. I felt like an idiot because it was for people who had just lost a loved one, but I went anyway.

That was the beginning of a new path for me. I learned in that group that I had determined my worth and value to be less as a person because of my losses and my responses to those losses. I had been allowing them to define me. What I didn't realize is there is a place in my soul that is untouched by any circumstances, losses, or bad decisions. My authentic self.

When I allowed my losses to define me, I made decisions from a wounded, broken place in my heart. So when I wanted ice cream, it wasn't just an "Ooh, ice cream sounds yummy" thought. It was a compulsion to have ice cream or suffer in pain at that moment. The pain would start to creep in or a memory would be triggered, and it needed to be medicated, soothed, and comforted right away. There was no resisting it.

Then there was the resulting self-hatred of course, because I had convinced myself that happiness and being thin were one and the same and would never be mine to experience. What a lie! Wounds can be healed. Bad decisions can be forgiven. Your true self can be discovered at any age, in any circumstances. You just have to be brave enough to uncover her.

It is still something I must remind myself of every day. Human transformation of any kind doesn't happen from the outside. It doesn't come from programs or points or the scale. It comes from knowing who you are and the peace that comes with that. It is truly a miracle. The most exciting thing about this is that it is available to everyone. No exceptions. You have your true self within you, underneath the layers of your past. She is patiently waiting for you and I believe when you connect with her, your choices will no longer come from a place of separation or wounds or compulsion, but rather from love and peace and joy. Imagine that!

★★★

What difference does today make? It is just one day—right? That's what I used to think, and still do on my bad days. What difference does it make if I eat this pizza—it's just one indulgence. What difference will it make? I deserve it! I worked hard today. I worked out today. I deserve it.

When I was a smoker, I never thought of one cigarette as making a difference in any way. I mean, I was smoking about 20 of them a day, day after day. At 365 days a year for 17 years, that's about 124,000 cigarettes. What I didn't realize was that each time I lit another one, whether consciously or subconsciously, I was choosing to do so. Any one of those 124,000 cigarettes could have been my last, but I chose to keep it up one more day, day after day.

I remember my last one very clearly. I actually didn't know it would be my last. I was sitting in Bob Evans. I had just finished my dinner and I lit up. This was before the indoor smoking ban. (I am so sorry to everyone whose meal I ruined by smoking in restaurants. I was an addict.) Anyway, I was sitting there smoking, waiting to leave to go to my third group meeting for smoking cessation. I knew I wanted to quit, but I didn't know how, and I didn't believe I could. I had failed too many times.

I finished that cigarette, put it out, and left the restaurant. At the smoking cessation group that night, they had a guest speaker who was an ex-smoker talk to us. He told us his story about going to the doctor for a checkup and ending up in surgery the following morning for an emergency quadruple bypass. He talked about how smoking had been part of who he was for 40 years, but the moment they cut his chest open he knew he had smoked his last cigarette. It had been a year since his surgery, and he was getting healthy. The thing I remember most was him saying he didn't miss it. He didn't miss it!

WOW. If it was possible for a guy like that, after smoking for 40 years, to just be done and not miss it, then maybe it was possible for me. And that night, all the preparation I had been doing, all the thinking about quitting smoking and hoping to be free of this addiction, clicked, and I never smoked another one. The pack sat in my car for two weeks before my support group friends convinced me to throw them out. And despite all my fears that life would never be as good without cigarettes, well we all know that was a lie.

Here's the thing. Any one of the 124,000 cigarettes could have been my last. It only takes one time of choosing differently to change direction. But there has to be that beginning. The first step must happen. Then the second step, and so on. And for those of you who have never smoked, you don't instantly become a non-smoker. It is a process and a battle that you fight every day until you are free.

We all want so badly to take a giant pole vault from where we are now to where we long to be. I understand the temptation. If I can't have the result right now, how can I keep going? By putting one foot in front of the other day after day and believing that those steps will get you to where you long to be. Here are some truths to hold onto on this journey:

Walking every day is one of the key components to long-term fitness.

Strength training consistently can change your body.

What you eat every time you eat matters.

Any day can be the day that you make a different choice and change direction.

There are lots of ways to get moving.

It is your challenge to find ways to keep moving.

There is absolutely no shortcut, and fitness takes work.

Let's make a new commitment this week. Let's get out of the fantasy world of "30 pounds in 30 days" fast weight loss and promise ourselves we'll get real about it. Today could very easily be your last day of life as you know it, and tomorrow could be the beginning of your new life in a totally different direction. This is possible for every single one of you. All you have to do is make a healthy choice next time you eat. Just one time, right now. Worry about next time when it comes and step-by-step, you will move into the life you have always dreamed of.

★★★

Are you a rebel?

I believe to lose weight and stay fit, you have to be one. To ride along with the rest of society just doesn't work. Have you seen the line at the McDonald's drive-through? It's packed! Steak & Shake now has all you can eat pancakes for $3.99. Yipee. The culture in general is not a great supporter of radical responsibility or extraordinary choices—both which are necessary to be fit and healthy. It's time we had a revolution and rebelled against all the choices that are leading to us not feeling good about ourselves.

What does it take to be a rebel?

I believe it takes making a different choice, one choice after the next. We are not overweight or out of shape because of genetics or hormones or menopause or age. We are overweight and out of shape because of the foods we eat and don't eat, and the amount of exercise we get. This may sound bad, but really it is great news because we can't change our genetics or hormones or menopause or age, but we can completely change our nutrition and our exercise. We are all empowered and capable of being at our healthy body weight. All of us.

Rebellion Step 1: Shut off autopilot. There comes a time when you have to take responsibility and choose differently. Even when I am eating compulsively— and I would define that as eating something while telling myself not to and feeling totally powerless to stop—I recognize the need to say, " I choose to eat this." It is the only way I know how to choose differently next time. If I believe I have no ability to choose, change is impossible. Own your choices.

Rebellion Step 2: Quit making excuses. I absolutely have time to work out and so do you. Some days I choose to exercise and some days I don't, but it is always an option. I know athletes that get up before 5:00 a.m. to make sure they get their training in. It is important to them so they find a way. It's not that I can't get up at 5:00 a.m. and exercise, it's that I DON'T WANT TO. Who does? It's not that I can't exercise at 8:00 p.m., I just am tired and would rather watch Dancing with the Stars. There are actually people at the gym at 8:00 p.m., though. Recognize that if it is important to you, you will find a way. The excuses have to go.

Rebellion step 3: Shop and cook. Make your own food. Pack a cooler. Take your lunch. Think of your little cooler that you have with you every day as a survival kit. If only I had half a PB&J every time I got crazy hungry when out and about, I would never end up in the drive-through. And when you end up out to dinner, be part of the healthy revolution and order off that part of the menu.

I was at a restaurant over the weekend that has an "Enlightened Menu" now with several yummy entrees less than 575 calories. Cheesecake Factory has an entire page of their menu book with entrees under 590. I believe if we order off these menus en mass, then the restaurants will keep offering healthy choices, and we'll be part of the revolution. Try it and see how good you feel about yourself for making that kind of choice.

It's not easy. Eating healthy and exercising as a lifestyle does not always feel like the norm. It's against the grain and takes a rebellious spirit to push against it and do something different. But who wants to be the norm anyway? I have gotten to know many of you, and you are truly amazing women who have experienced life, loss, and pain, yet you have found ways to overcome and conquer. I think you are exceptional and I hate to see anyone with so much heart give in to a society where the lifestyle is not leading to your best possible life. All of us deserve to feel great about ourselves and to live our lives as an expression of that.

So, go do it. You have to do it—you can't just think about it. You can't think change. But you can join the revolution.

★★★

Sometimes it is uncomfortable to look at your past, but if you want to lose weight, you have to. Here's why.

Let's start with the biology. If you are overweight, at some point in your life, for whatever reason, you spent day after day eating more calories than your body burned for fuel. That leftover fuel was then stored as fat, because that's how our bodies are made. They are programmed to store all extra calories as fat. The reason for consuming the extra calories may have been due to pregnancy. It may have been that an injury or illness kept you from being as active as you needed to be. It may have been your way of dealing with a relationship problem or a boss who made your work life miserable. Maybe we put everything else first before our own health. The list goes on. Our bodies don't care why we ate extra. It gets stored no matter what.

When I tell people that I lost weight, I get the same question almost every time. Can you guess what that question is? It's "How long did it take?" I usually answer with something like seven years because that's the truth. And I usually get a look of horror. Something happens once we wake up and realize we've gained weight and are in a pretty deep hole. We want out immediately. I understand that, I really do. Once I had the courage to really look at myself and own how I was treating myself, I wanted to change it all at that exact moment.

But we have to go back to biology. All those months or years of storing fat are the choices of your past. Here you are carrying them around, and all you want to do is to be able to put them down. But your body is made to lose weight one pound at a time. And it is not possible to lose all your pounds at once; it must be one, then another, then another.

It is quite easy to get so hung up on the fact that you got yourself into this hole in the first place that you never make the extraordinary choices that will get you out of it. When I would look in the mirror, I got *so* angry and ask myself, "Why did I do this??? I don't want to have to lose weight." It was overwhelming. I felt like I'd never succeed. It's a terrible feeling of defeat and resignation. And it's easy to feel disgusted.

Repeat after me. "I am forgiven completely for getting myself into this hole." No one is perfect and we all fall short. For whatever reason, I ate too much or didn't exercise enough (or both) at some point in my past. But just for today, I am going to let it go and look ahead. Today is a new day. And I believe that anything is possible. Then, just for today, I am going to choose differently. I will exercise today. I will choose my food wisely today. And I realize I won't see the changes I want to see so badly today.

So I will commit to waking up tomorrow and saying, "I am forgiven completely for getting myself into this hole." And once again, just for tomorrow, I will let it go and look ahead. I will exercise. I will choose my food wisely. I won't see changes yet. But I won't give up either because I believe in the process. I believe that daily exercise and eating wisely will lead me to the changes I want. That is the truth and the only way out of the hole.

The change does come. It really does, but only if you don't get hung up on the past. If you continue to punish yourself for being in this place, or keep beating yourself up for falling short, you can't move ahead. Every day must be a new day. Even if you have to see your past in the mirror for right now, you can learn to override all the negative feelings and experience forgiveness and a second chance any time you are willing to receive it.

★★★

After you read something inspiring, do you get moving?

I believe it is really important to understand why we ended up where we did. Without shining the light on all the things that we talk about, like learning to make time for you, saying no when you want to, saying yes when you need to, and taking one day at a time, it is difficult to change. But just understanding why doesn't actually create the change we want. We must take action.

In fitness, I believe the three most important actions to take are relating to nutrition, heart, and muscle.

When I say get moving, I want you to think about your nutrition and take action. This means making wise choices when it comes to what you eat. Become a mindful eater. Find healthy ways of dealing with your stress and emotions. Plan and prepare. Get organized. Learn what foods are high and low in calories. Look your foods up. Look your restaurants up. Get radically honest about your food and make as many extraordinary choices as you can. This means choosing healthy, nutritious foods to support your healing and your progress.

When I say get moving, I want you to think about your heart. To lose weight and stay fit, it is important to get your heart rate into your aerobic zone almost every day. If you do not know what your heart rate zones are, learn. Then challenge yourself to arrange your schedule so that you can get a walk in. Take an aerobics or Zumba or swim or spin class. Mix it up, but find a way to fit it into your day, every day. You will burn calories, strengthen your heart and lungs, boost your metabolism, and improve your mental health. Guaranteed.

When I say get moving, I want you to think about your muscles. That means strength training at least twice a week. There are so many good things that happen to your body when you lift weights. Tone, strengthen, boost, and burn. The more muscle you have, the higher your metabolism. The more muscle you have, the more calories you burn. The stronger your core, the better your posture. The stronger your core, the less chance of back pain. The more triceps exercises you do, the less flap you have under your arms when you wave. That's good stuff.

There is always time to look at why we got to where we did, what went wrong, what old wounds still play a role in our choices. However, the only way to progress is to follow up every bit of looking inward with action forward. We've got to move forward. That means doing. That means making different choices. That means overriding the old way of doing things and being brave enough to create a new path. It is scary but it's so very worth it. You'll see.

★★★

Have you ever heard the quote by Eleanor Roosevelt, "Do one thing every day that scares you."? I am starting to understand it for myself. I think what she means is to get out of your comfort zone every day. I don't think she means go paragliding or run a marathon unless that is something that pulls at your heart. What is important is to find little challenges to meet so that your inner voice can sing "Yes, I can" more often than "No, I can't."

You can't change yourself. In other words, you can't sit around thinking about changing and have it be so. Changing comes by doing. A walk can change you, a healthy choice at dinner can change you, saying no to something you don't want to do can change you. But it is in the action that something happens.

If I spend each day of the next week thinking about going for a walk, but not doing it, I wear away at my "Yes, I can." If this happens week after week, I can get stuck in an unhealthy way of thinking. Excuses and rationalizations creep in, and it never gets me to where I want to go. The only way to get there is to walk, whether I feel like it or not. Then I get to celebrate with "I did it."

To me, there is nothing better than "I did it." I used to live in the world of "I can't." I can't lose weight, I can't quit smoking, I can't leave my job, I can't be happy. I had a long list of excuses that I was quite attached to, and a victim's outlook on life that kept me stuck. But then I did something different and broke through some of those lies. I quit smoking! And if I could do that, maybe I can work out with a trainer. I did it! I worked out with a trainer. Maybe if I did that, I can walk a half marathon. I did it! Maybe if I did that...

You get it. It is the opposite of the downward spiral. It is the antidote to being stuck. It changes you and opens up your life to all kinds of possibility. All it takes is the first step. Do something different. Do something uncomfortable that you know is good for you. Celebrate the 'I did it!' Allow it to change you from the inside out. Then build on that. You may not end up strapped to a parachute or in the crowd of 17,000 doing the marathon, but you never know.

★★★

In September of 2008, I was very excited to be registered for the Air Force Marathon in Dayton. In early August, I joined a few running club friends for a 20-mile training run. It turned out be get quite hot, but the run went well; I felt confident that if I could complete those 20, I could do the 26.2 miles in a month.

Later that day, I started having some tightness and pain in my right hip. I stretched, iced it, took some Advil and didn't think much more about it. After all, I was in training and didn't have time to deal with a cranky hip. I took a few days off, and later that week I went to Sharon Woods. I parked, got out of the car, walked for a few minutes, then started a nice, easy run. BAM.! Shooting pain in my right hip.

I had to stop running immediately and walk. I turned around and limped back to the car. What the heck! This is not good. I am four weeks away from my event and suddenly my hip doesn't work. A wave of panic swept through me. I had to get this fixed within two weeks so I could complete my marathon. Who could fix this for me...today?

It was in this state of fear that I made a series of bad decisions. I rushed from one health care professional to another, regardless of cost, trying to find the quick fix. The pain got worse and ended up shooting down my right leg to my foot. It started having an impact on my sleep and my ability to work. Each day seemed to get a little worse.

I ended up walking the Air Force Half Marathon, having to downgrade my entry from full to half. How could I skip it? I had trained for it, I had paid for it, I was going to do it. It reminds me of the recent story about the woman who finished the Chicago Marathon then had a baby later that day. She was going to do that marathon no matter what.

Here's what I learned through my injury, besides more than I ever wanted to know about bulging discs, herniated discs, sciatic pain, and SI joints.

If you are involved in athletic activities including fitness walking or strength training, at some point there is a good chance you will get an injury. There are several chronic injuries that are very common. Plantar fasciitis, shin splints, IT Band syndrome, tendonitis (knee, elbow, shoulder, Achilles), bulging or herniated disc, and piriformis syndrome.

The best thing for these injuries is resting the affected body part. That may mean cross-training or modifying your workout, or it may mean taking some time off completely.

R-I-C-E is very good wisdom. Rest. Ice. Compression. Elevation.

Not every injury can be diagnosed accurately by every health care professional. If you see someone, choose carefully and try to choose someone who approaches your injury holistically. If they don't listen to you, they are probably the wrong doctor.

Working through it is not always the way to go. It is difficult to do, but there is great value in taking time to heal. There are always other ways to get your workout done. Did you see the Biggest Loser episode where the woman with the stress fracture in her leg lost 14 pounds? Everything was done in the pool or from a seated position.

When I got injured, fear was what really drove me at first. I have to get this fixed quickly. I can't miss the marathon. I can't not run. I'll gain weight, get fat again, lose my dream job, lose my house BLAH BLAH BLAH...fear can get quickly out of hand. When I finally realized that it was going to take a lot longer to heal than I hoped, I changed my strategy. I switched to fitness walking, and I didn't lose anything by doing so. I may not be able to run at the pace I once could, but my back healed! I can sleep again. I am not in pain at work. And I formed a walking group that has been very rewarding and fun. We've power walked three half-marathons!

I know many of you are dealing with chronic pain right now. Take a few deep breaths. Trust me, decisions made from that place of panic are not good ones. You will not lose all the progress you've made. You've learned too much along the way to ever go back. You may have to get creative with your exercise, but it can be done. Rest the injured body part and give it time to heal. Breathe. Focus on some other part of your process. Get educated on how to take care of your back, your knees, and your feet. But have faith that your body will heal and you will be back to your exercise when the time is right.

When I was SCUBA diving earlier this month, when I first jumped into the water with all that gear on and tried to descend to the ocean floor, I could not remember what any of the buttons on my equipment did. I went completely blank. Because I was anxious, I just couldn't think clearly. It was frustrating and made me more anxious. I got out of the water, sat down on the boat, and thought about quitting. Then one of the dive instructors encouraged me to relax. So I did some deep breathing, acknowledged my fear (I am afraid!), and tried again. The second time it was wonderful. The fear subsided and I had an amazing dive. What it taught me, though, was my thinking skills are impaired in a major way when I am afraid. And it reminded me of my Air Force Marathon experience and everything I have learned since then.

So, for all of you struggling with an injury, I encourage you to relax. Your health and fitness is a long-term journey, and there is a way to get through these things without doing more harm. Believe in the overall process, find a way to either modify or cross-train, rest, and know that your body is an amazing machine that will heal if you give it the opportunity to do so.

★★★

Taking care of yourself is one of the highest expressions of a healthy soul. If you are not taking good care of yourself, I believe you need to look inward and find what is keeping you stuck. Being overweight, being inactive, compulsive eating and self-destructive habits are symptoms. Find the root cause and bring it to the light. Your soul will thank you by making healthy choices.

Fitness can be a joyful journey. I don't believe we are meant to drag ourselves to a gym we hate. Connect with how you feel when your body moves. Remember with gratitude that not everyone's can. Everything is connected. While lifting weights, learning to push and complete those last few reps can teach us to be stronger mentally. Going beyond what you think you are capable of is a good skill to have.

Diets don't work. Please stop dieting. Diets will never work. It's just not the way our bodies are made. We are meant to eat lots of healthy food. Whole food from the earth. We are meant to move our bodies and burn through that fuel before we eat again. If you can go on a program, system, pill, drug, whatever— then you can go off it, and when you do, if you gain the weight back, then you haven't learned yet. Diets don't work. Please stop torturing yourself.

You can't go back. If you lost weight in the past, it is easy to idolize that time but remember; if you gained the weight back, you aren't there yet. Move forward. You are meant to be at your healthy weight for the rest of your life because you healed and changed. I know many of you don't believe this is possible because you have spent a lifetime so far losing and gaining the same 10, 20, 50 pounds, but it is possible. Don't give up.

You must have a noble goal, a higher goal. Wanting to look good, wanting to be a certain number or size, these goals just aren't deep enough for when the going gets tough. This takes a lot of work. So why do it? What do you really want? To finally, once and for all feel good about yourself? To feel confident after a long struggle with self-esteem? To know that you are doing everything in your power to spend as much time as possible with your grandchildren? Find your heart's deepest desire and connect every choice you make to that, and there will be no stopping you.

★★★

It takes a lot of courage to walk into a weight room, a gym, a class or even the personal training studio. So if you are working out with weights, I want to congratulate you for overcoming that feeling of intimidation and doing something that is really good for yourself. It may have been a while ago, or it may have been very recently that you started. Either way, you are doing something really good for yourself.

I believe that a fitness program is personal and each of us has to find our own formula that works with our lives, our schedules, our work, and our physical limitations. But within that formula we have to find a way to keep our muscles balanced and strong, get our cardiovascular exercise for our heart and for fat burn, and to find the foods that support our very best life.

How on earth are we supposed to do that and get everything else done? Especially this time of year! Here's my view. We build it—slowly over time.

A common scenario is this: a woman comes to Clear Rock and begins strength training once or twice a week. She hasn't been doing much exercise on her own and it's gotten to the point where she feels like she has to do something. Maybe she went up another size, maybe she's heard bad news from her doctor, or maybe she was inspired by someone in her life that is getting healthy and feeling better. But something has tipped her motivation enough to get started. There's an excitement and a hope at the first meeting. There is actually a way out of this hole she's dug for herself.

She schedules her first week of workouts, comes to the studio and gets through her very first strength training sessions. Her body feels like she's done something, and it feels exciting to be making a good choice. She gets another two or three weeks under her belt, starts to know the difference between a row and a press, and looks forward to her workouts. Then the honeymoon is over. This is hard work! It is hard work to get to the gym, it is hard work when you're there, and the scale hasn't even moved.

That scenario is very common. The reason the scale hasn't moved is because strength training is just the beginning. It is the foundation. It is metabolism-boosting muscle tissue. It is leg strength so that you can start walking consistently. It is balance. It is posture. It is core. But it is not the only piece. You have to build on it.

It can seem so overwhelming to talk about everything that needs to happen to lose weight the right way so that it stays off; strength training, cardio, nutrition, hydration, sleep, stretching, and finding healthy ways to deal with stress to name a few. It really doesn't work well to try to do everything at once. That's why diets and resolutions fail. (Starting January 2nd after my six week binge, I am going to count calories or points, walk six days a week, lift weights twice a week, do yoga, get to bed on time, drink eight glasses of water a day, and try not to shoot anyone.) It's not the right approach.

Master one thing. Get consistent with your strength training. Twice a week is great. Learn proper form, bring your best to every workout, and give it your all. Learn what to eat and drink that works for you. Feel the confidence that comes with mastery, then build on that. If you are lifting twice a week but aren't doing any aerobic exercise, can you add one cardio workout? Add one. Then for the next however many weeks, do your two strength training workouts and your walk (or run/bike/swim/Zumba/elliptical). You just went from two to three. That's awesome!

Now build on that. Once you've got those three scheduled consistently, can you add another aerobic workout? Now this is starting to be fierce; two strength training sessions, and two cardio

I KNOW WHAT TO DO, I JUST DON'T DO IT

workouts. Can you make the commitment to stick with this? Can you overcome the old obstacles that always tripped you up in the past? Schedules, stress, work, holidays, vacation—same old same old, right? It's always the same stuff. So how do your pants fit now? Is the scale moving yet? It might be, but it might not.

If not, build on what you are doing. Look at your food choices. Are bad food choices undoing everything you are doing at the gym and on your walks? This is a common place to get stuck. Old food patterns die hard, but they do die if you are willing to work on them. Remember to build on what you are doing. You have four workouts a week now that you are invested in. If you are still not progressing the way you want, make some different choices.

I believe a good place to start is by adding. Add vegetables. Add grilled fish. Add egg whites. Add apples. Add water. Pick one and see how that goes. Then once you master it, build on that and add some more. Add things that you are willing to stick with. Make them part of your new healthy lifestyle. Keep building.

We are gaining weight, losing weight, or staying the same weight at any given time. It's really a direction. If you don't like the direction you are going in, you have to change something. Change one piece at a time, master that, and then build on it. Make the commitment to stick with it, and eventually you will have implemented so many changes you will have basically changed your life. Do it in your own time, but do it.

I remember the day I came to the realization that no one was going to do this for me, and if I wanted to be moving in a different direction, I'd have to make a different choice. It was not an easy thing at the time, but ever since I got really honest about it, I've felt empowered in ways I never thought possible. It may sound like bad news. No one is going to do this for you. But really, it is the best news possible. You don't have to wait for a single thing outside of yourself, you are completely empowered to change any time you're ready.

★★★

Making fitness a priority can be tough.

Why is your health and fitness important to you? I know why mine is important to me. A few things helped me realize how important. The first I'll call a vision of the future. I was a smoker for 17 years and as you know, I had just about given up trying to quit. But then I had this vision. I was sitting across a large desk from an intimidating doctor, who was telling me some very bad news. I could feel the emotions pulsing through me as though I was really having this experience. I knew for certain the deep regret I would feel if I didn't stop smoking and had to hear that devastating news. The regret of that moment was very clear. I had had the chance to do something about this, but now it was too late. Knowing that vision could become reality moved quitting smoking from the bottom to the top of my list.

The second reason is how I feel about myself. I was a girl who struggled with never feeling good enough. On this long and winding path, one of the things I've learned is that my life works better when I am exercising. It levels out my thoughts and my emotions. Whatever those "feel good" chemicals are, I am someone who needs them, and they really make a difference for me. They bring me to a place where I can make good decisions. I also experience the benefit of feeling stronger and more empowered with each workout. I feel good about myself when I exercise consistently. Knowing that this one choice has that much direct impact on my self-esteem keeps exercise at the top of my priority list.

The third reason is about my health. I have chronic kidney disease, and my food choices have a direct impact on how long my kidneys will last. When I am 90 years old, I want to be out in Arizona or Utah hiking around all my favorite red rocks or SCUBA diving in Maui, not sitting somewhere tied to a machine. I have some say in that! Knowing that, I am going to make the best food choices I can, and when I don't, I am going to receive forgiveness and move on because quitting isn't an option. Giving up isn't the answer; I am going to fight. I know which foods are good for me and which ones aren't. (Don't we all!) That's not the issue. Keeping good food choices at the top of my priority list is the issue.

There seems to be a constant battle for the top spots on my priority list, and I've learned that it takes a great deal of clarity and commitment to define my core values and then support them with the best choices. Without acute, urgent health issues, it is not as easy to see. For example, if I break a bone and am in pain, I know to take care of it right away. No matter what else I am doing, I need to attend to that right now. Or if I have severe chest pain, my health will suddenly become a priority, and I get to the hospital to get checked. But with chronic health issues like diabetes, heart disease, and high blood pressure that take years to materialize, there may not be symptoms that need to be dealt with *urgently*. We think, "as soon as things settle down, I will make my health and fitness a priority." But "as soon as" never comes, and each day we get a little bit closer to the symptoms becoming urgent.

Did you know that two 45 minute workouts a week equate to less than 1% of all your time? That really shocked me. Walking one hour a day every single day is still only 4% of your total time. When I say I don't have time, I see that what I really mean is that it isn't a priority to me. If it were at the top of my list, I would do it instead of something else. We must own our choices. It is not that we don't have time. That excuse must go away, and we have to replace it with the truth: I have it low on the list today; other things are more important. The beauty about the truth is that if we are willing to own that, then we are able to make a different choice. As long as we are living under the lie of "I don't have time," we are powerless. When we tell the truth, we can look at our list and decide. Does this choice really support my core values? Or am I putting something first that is not as important to me? I am free at any moment to move something to the top of the list.

I believe that every single one of us is capable of living our best life which includes health and fitness near the top of the list, not the bottom. The only things that stand in our way are our excuses and all those are really lies. Remember the truth. It is possible to have a family or a job or a business or friends or a dog or all of the above and still take really good care of yourself. In fact, you deserve exactly that. You were never intended to put all your energy into these things at the expense of your health. You matter. Your family needs you. Your business needs you. Your friends need you. Your dog needs you. You matter.

★★★

Your body is not separate from your mind so much as it is a reflection of it. As you change your mind, you change every cell in your body. Such thoughts as I am. fat, I am ugly, and I hate my body are like commands given to your body to materialize accordingly. If you think negatively about your body, your body will reflect your negativity. If you think lovingly about your body, then your body will reflect your love. And there is no such thing as a neutral thought. What is not love, is an attack. And what is love, is a miracle.
—*A Course in Weight Loss* by Marianne Williamson

I used to be at war with my body. I hated it, and I never spoke kindly to it. It took me a very long time to realize that it was not my body's fault I felt the way I did, it was mine. I abused it with bad food, lack of movement, and a whole long list of things that were anything but loving. To diet from a place of self- control is no different to me than looking at a child and saying "No, you may not have that cookie. You are fat and ugly and you must be deprived of treats." That type of deprivation will never work for long, and even if it did, it is abusive. There is another way.

Imagine if you loved and respected your body so much that it was hard to imagine ever putting junk into it. Every choice, whether it was dinner or a cookie, was not an act of war against it but was an act of self-care. What would that look like? I think it would be different for everyone, but I know what it feels like. It is peaceful. It is fulfilling. It's not a battle. It is not self-sabotaging. The problem is how to get there when you are stuck feeling bad about the body you have right now. Here are a few small things you can start with and then watch as your mind begins to change.

Learn to accept every single compliment you get. Smile and say, "Thank you." That's it. Do not argue, do not go on and on about what a long way you have to go, just receive. Learning to receive is a very important step in changing the way we think. And we must change the way we think to make changes that last.

Find one thing that you like about your physical body and focus on that every day. If you like the color of your eyes, then when you are getting ready in the morning, look in the mirror and acknowledge those beautiful eyes. Say, "Thank you," out loud for them. Flutter your eyelashes and make a big deal about them for just a few moments. If you start to hear things like "those eyes would sure look better if I lost 50 pounds" or something cruel like that, stop! Do not allow it.

Find one thing about your body that is responding to your fitness and celebrate it. I notice that some of you have developed amazing arms. I mean, your arms and shoulders look incredible to me. Muscular, lean, strong. Find words of victory to describe them and use them often. Say to yourself as you are working out, or getting dressed, or driving to work, "my arms are strong."

Stop cursing the parts of you that you don't like. These parts of you are PARTS OF YOU. They don't respond well to bullying, name calling, or humiliation. They are a reflection of something that is hurting inside you. They are a reflection of choices you've made in the past that were not rooted in love. Being judgmental and critical of these parts of you will only keep you stuck. Freedom is found in finding ways to receive love for every part of you.

When you catch yourself bullying any part of yourself, picture the most adorable but dorky or different kid that you can imagine. Maybe it is someone you love, maybe it is your younger self. But picture this child being spoken to that way and see his or her little heart breaking under those words. And immediately, as soon as you catch it, change those words to loving words of truth. "You are beautiful just the way you are!" "You are an amazing creation." "You are perfect in every way!" Then watch that little smile just light up. That's your heart.

I believe that these small changes can have a huge impact on our hearts and minds. We don't deserve to be punished for the rest of our lives for having struggled. We've all struggled. Accept forgiveness and begin to live a life rooted in love, especially when dealing with yourself. There is nothing you've done that your body won't forgive you for. It has an amazing ability to heal, to renew. It is constantly reaching for health, despite our best efforts to damage it. Take a leap of faith and begin to work on your mind instead of your body. Accept every compliment, develop gratitude for something about your body that you like, celebrate your fitness accomplishments, and stop being a bully. Once your mind is healed, your body will reflect that peacefully and the war will be over. You will be free.

Dear Body,

Thank you so much for everything you allowed me to do this past year. Thank you for legs that allow me to walk miles and miles—my walks bring me so much joy. Thank you for the miraculous way you function even when I don't take good care of you. I am *so* grateful.

I realize that without you, my life would end. I realize that without you, I could not have experienced the paragliding flight, or SCUBA diving with the turtles, or the Zion hikes, or hugging my sister, or dancing. I am so sorry I treated you the way I did for so long. I am sorry I yell at you and call you names. I am so sorry I never show you unconditional love. Ever. You deserve better from me.

I am not going to make a New Year's resolution. I am not going to make any stupid promises about losing weight or dieting. I am going to stop putting you through that. What I am going to do is start taking great care of you—starting today. You are part of me and you matter.

I will take responsibility for what I have been making excuses for. I will choose radically healthy foods even when I don't feel like it. I promise to work on the right things so that my compulsions to eat poorly and to skip exercise are finally healed. I will stop taking you for granted and then abusing you with judgment and criticism.

Finally, I am going to love you, my body, and I am going to show you my love by how I treat you. You'll see. I believe I can stop being cruel and neglectful to you and start being supportive, encouraging, and loving. You deserve it, and I'm sorry it took me all this time to see that it wasn't you that did this to me, but it was me that did this to you.

You house my heart, you hold my soul. I am going to start acting like it.

Love Always,
Sue

★★★

I want my routine back!

Wow, this last two weeks has been a big reminder to not take my routine for granted; especially with my fitness. I felt lost, like I was wandering around trying to figure out where to go and what to do. I realize part of the reason for that was the gym I was attending closed at the end of November, so I no longer had my scheduled classes to rely upon. Throw in the holidays and I didn't even know what day it was.

I tried to stay consistent. I scheduled a Highbanks hike, I printed out a 3-day trial pass to take a spin class at a new gym, I took yoga twice, and I even got together with friends to lift. But it wasn't the same consistency that I need to feel good. It's amazing. I could tell after just a few days that I didn't feel right. First, I felt sluggish and tired, then I started feeling down and dark. Anxious.

I had to have a conversation with myself to remind myself what was going on. It sounded something like this in my head:

"I'm depressed today."

"No you're not; you've just eaten a bunch of crap and didn't work out. This is how life feels when you do that."

How did I ever live that way? I don't know.

"I need a nap."

"No you don't, get your ass up and do something."

"No I don't want to."

"I don't care what you want, remember? This is what happens when you eat too much food, too much sugar and too much salt. Not enough water."

"I need a nap."

"No you don't, drink your water. Go for a walk. Do something."

"I don't want to."

Ugh! Here's what I am really grateful for: I know this one! And I know the remedy. All it takes is three days to turn it around: three days of eating clean (no sugar, no salty foods, no alcohol) and a few really good, tough workouts. So I did that! In fact, I burned 1,430 calories on Saturday morning doing an hour of spin and an hour of circuit. Sweat like crazy. Then ate my veggie bowl for lunch and drank a ton of water. Yes!

Here's what it's like inside my head when I'm eating right, exercising consistently, drinking my water and taking very good care of myself:

"Life is good."

"I know it."

"You did a great job today working out."

"Thank you, it was awesome. I can't wait to do that again. It feels so good to move."

"Good choice at lunch today."

"Thank you, love that veggie bowl. It makes me feel wide awake and alive. Great feeling. What should I do with all this energy and life?"

Whatever you want! The world is wide open and waiting. You're doing great. Keep going."

Exercise matters. What you eat matters. Drinking lots of water matters. Good sleep matters. If you don't believe me, check in with the conversation in your head next time you get away from taking care of yourself. There is a voice in there that will let you know when you're off track. So how can you get on track and stay on track? Here's how I've been thinking about it.

When you are hiking, every so often a trail marker lets you know where the trail is. You may hike for a long while, but sooner or later you come to a sign that tells you that you are on the right path. Or another way to see it: when you are driving on a long trip, every so often a sign along the road says "destination 150 miles" tells you that you are going the right way.

Those signs are your scheduled weekly workouts. They are your trail markers that keep you on the right path. You should expect to see them at regular intervals. Have you ever been hiking (or driving on the highway) and gone for too long without seeing one of those signs? Uh, oh. Are we off the trail? Did we take a wrong turn? Do we need to go back? We're lost.

The way to get on track and stay on track is to schedule your workouts. Write them down. Get them on your calendar. Look at that calendar like it's a trail map to the very best you possible. Get going and make sure you see these markers at the intervals necessary to meet your goals. Get things scheduled, whether it is a walk with your spouse, a fitness class, your personal training session, or your 45 minutes on the elliptical. The very best version of each of us is right here, right now. Exercise is one of those things that helps bring it out in us. Commit to doing everything possible to live your best life right now. You are worth the time and effort. We all are.

★★★

We all need to breathe.

Have you ever been in a situation where you couldn't get your breath? Maybe you were underwater making your way to the surface but taking longer than you expected. Or, you had a respiratory problem and couldn't get a good breath in. Have you ever choked? In those moments, your need to breathe becomes the only thing in the world. It moves to the top in importance and urgency.

Does anyone remember the 1982 movie *An Officer and a Gentleman*? There is a scene where the two main characters are in a simulated aircraft that loses pressure and they have to take their masks off and perform a simple exercise with a deck of cards. Recall how difficult it got for Sid? He panicked and flipped out and started clawing away desperately for some air. The character played by Richard Gere, Zack, takes his own mask and puts it over Sid's face and gets him to calm down and breathe.

When any of us fly, we are trained over and over to put our own oxygen mask on first before helping our loved one. Imagine trying to help the people you love the most while clawing away desperately like Sid. But that is what we all do. We put others first over and over and forget our own need for oxygen. At some point we will reach desperation. It is not selfish to take care of ourselves. It is our primary responsibility. If we consistently show up in our relationships, our parenting, our marriages, and our friendships as less than our best selves, we are cheating others and we are cheating us.

There is a strong current within each of us to care for others and to put importance on our relationships and roles. I believe we are made that way. It becomes upside down when we subconsciously decide to put others first and never get around to taking care of us. There are many reasons this can happen. Some of us were taught when we were young that being selfish is the worst thing you can be, and we filed that away. Good people aren't selfish (and I want to be a good person), so I can't take time for myself, I can't change my lifestyle, I can't go after my dream job, I can't be healthy. "Who am I to be brilliant, gorgeous, talented, fabulous?" (Right, Marianne Williamson?)

Excuses can also get in the way. These are really just false beliefs; things like "'I don't have time" or "I am too busy/tired." If you believe you can take exceptionally good care of your body, your mind, your soul and your spirit...that is what you will do. Until you believe it, you will continue to live out your false belief that you can't. You have to change your heart and mind to change the way you live.

What does it look like when you put everyone else's oxygen mask on before your own? Not quite the same as Sid's response; it is not a physical clawing away in desperation. It is more a quiet, internal desperation. Giving up. What difference does it make if I just eat and eat? What difference does it make if I spend another evening in front of the computer or television with food? Who cares if I don't exercise? It doesn't matter anymore. I don't matter anymore...

I want to tell you there is no bigger lie than this. You do matter more than you know. You have a purpose in this world, and you are here to make a difference. Every day that you live in a way that is reaching toward your best self, you are sending a ripple out into your family and the world. When you live as though you matter, you are telling the people you love that they matter. At the same time you are teaching them how to live a healthy life of their own. What better gift to give the ones you love?

How does this translate into daily life? How do I implement "believing"? I do a few things that keep me believing. You will need to find ones that work for you.

Body: I keep moving like my life depends on it. Although there may be strong inertia to *be* still once you *are* still, I feel that moving is a much more authentic way of being. I seek out ways over and over to move my body. It does so many things for me. It gets my heart beating. It produces good brain chemistry. It teaches me that I am capable of more than I thought. It teaches me to be brave. It gets me outside with nature. It seems to encourage better food choices. All these things contribute to feeling my best and reinforcing that I do matter.

Mind: I seek out teachers that I trust and respect to teach me how to live authentically in a world that wants nothing more than my false self; my mask. I read, I study, I practice. It is my responsibility to keep feeding my mind things that support and encourage my journey, not fill it with lies from the media and marketing. Watch what you read.

Soul: My heart and soul require constant care. As many of you know, I lived with a broken heart for many years. It expressed itself in self-destructive life choices, and I am a perfect example of someone who had just about given up. Then there was this little whisper from inside that said, "Please don't forget about me, I'm still here." I found some support groups to deal with my losses and my pain, and it's been pretty amazing ever since. Anything can be healed. Don't ever give up.

Spirit: I believe we all are spirits that need nurturing. I also believe it is your personal journey to find that which will nurture you. All I know from my own life is that I need God. A spirit ignored is a life that feels lost and without purpose and a spirit that is acknowledged and loved is a life filled with joy and peace that's hard to understand.

You matter. You are important. Make time for yourself, put

your oxygen mask on first, and then help everyone else around you. Let your light shine, and you will make the world a brighter place.

★★★

I got an interesting call from a friend of mine this week. She was watching one of the talk shows, and it had been focusing on juicing all week. She wanted to know, "Is this something I need to do to lose weight?"

It is hard to sift through all the information and figure out what will work for you. Much of this journey is personal. I have been saying for years that the key to weight loss is finding your personal formula (not someone else's). You have to be able to build a healthy lifestyle around foods you like and can eat, exercise your body can do, and things you will be able to stick with for the long haul. For me, just any weight loss "plan" won't work because I am a kidney patient and have specific restrictions and needs. I had to create my own. You can, too. The key is to remember the truth; there is no quick fix, weight loss requires hard work, and maintenance requires dedication. So what is the truth? Do we all need to buy juicers? Or cleanses? Jump starts? Colonics? No, none of that is necessary. What is necessary is a solid understanding of the truth when it comes to health, fitness, exercise, and nutrition.

Truth: Natural food is healthier than manufactured or processed food. Nature knows what it is doing. High quality whole foods contain essential amino acids (complete protein), lots of fiber and all the vitamins and minerals we need. You know how all the nutritionists say to shop the perimeter of the grocery store? That is where the healthy food is—the foods that support your health. You can choose to snack on things that come from a box or bag, but remember that these foods aren't healthy food no matter how they are marketed. They are stripped down, processed pieces of stuff that used to be food. They strip out the healthy stuff, so you are left with sugar, flour, fat, and salt. Any time you have that combination—no protein, no fiber—you are eating low quality food (empty calories, low nutrition). Unless you are running ten miles a day, it's tough for your body to burn all these low quality carbohydrates.

Truth: Foods like meat and cheese are often heavily processed. Read your package of chicken breasts, for example. "Up to 15% salt solution added." This is to make it last longer on the shelf and to kill bacteria. I worked in a milk plant when I was in college. The milk trucks that came from farms that were rejected for having too high bacteria counts were sent down the road to the cheese factory where lots of salt was added to the milk to create cheese. If processed meat and dairy are part of your life, nutritionists recommend eating them in limited quantities. And, it is worth the extra effort to seek out preservative-free meats. The link between processed meats and certain cancers is as strong as cigarettes and lung cancer.

Truth: Unhealthy foods have screwed up our metabolism, and healthy foods will reset it. When the complex processes that control hunger and metabolism get out of whack, the result is diabetes, heart disease, and obesity, as well as the feeling of never being satisfied. The way to reset this is by eliminating the cause (over-processed junk food, especially sugar) and replacing it with the cure (plant-based whole foods, especially fiber). Sugar is the poison, and fiber is the antidote. If you have been stuck for years counting calories or points but have never really looked at the quality of your food choices, try it. Ten crackers may have the same number of calories as an apple, but the body responds to them very differently. Calories in/calories out is only one small part of the equation. What do those calories do to your metabolism, your insulin, and your circulation? How are those calories treated once they enter your body? These are just as important.

Truth: Commercial diets have a long-term success rate of 5-20%, depending on the program. That means that 80–95% of people who lose weight do not keep it off. How many of us tried program after program, and may even have had short-term weight loss success while on the restriction, but then reverted to our default habits as soon as we went off? If you can go on something, you can go off it. You have to change and commit to those changes for life. That is the lifestyle change you keep hearing about. It is the truth. At no time in this weight loss and fitness journey have I been able to revert to the way I used to live. I still work out 5 times a week, I still lift, I still walk, I still eat lots of vegetables, I still drink my water, I still eat as much fiber as humanly possible, I still limit processed sugar, I still avoid the deadly fats, I still watch my sodium intake. If I think I can give up any of those and maintain what I have worked for, I am lying to myself. I am committed to these changes for the rest of my life because I'm not ever going back.

Truth: The answer is not outside of you. You can have lots of teachers. Weight Watchers can teach you portion control. Going vegan can teach you that plant-based whole foods make you feel amazing. P90X can teach you exercise consistency or intensity. Yoga can teach you mindfulness and connection to your body. Pilates can teach you how to activate core strength to originate your movements. You can have as many teachers as you need. But the bottom line is eventually you have to say "thank you for the great information; I am now going to take radical responsibility for every choice I make, get unstuck and change." It is all up to you.

Truth: Exercise is the foundation of a healthy life. There are so many options. Walking, running, Zumba, hip-hop dance, BodyPump, spinning, strength training, swimming, elliptical work, kickboxing, yoga, Pilates, old-school aerobics class, boxing, working with a trainer, total body conditioning class at the community center, Tai Chi...there are as many ways to exercise as there are likes and dislikes. You have to find what you like that you can do. If your knees say no to running, no problem; swim! If you hate the water, no problem; get on the elliptical, etc. If you don't like any of it, too bad! Do it anyway because the truth is you cannot lose weight and keep it off without exercise. And in addition to looking and feeling better, you will change the health of your arteries, your heart, your brain, your insulin system, your sleep, and many other processes that have a direct impact on your blood pressure, cholesterol level, diabetes, heart disease, strength, stamina and quality of life. It is worth making the time.

Truth: One hour of exercise is exactly 0.59% of your week's total time. Think about that and get real about what's actually going on when you say you don't have time. If you can't be radically honest with yourself, it will be almost impossible to make changes that last. Here's the truth for most of us: We are not willing to give up the time we spend (insert your thing here)...watching TV, on Facebook, online, ironing, reading, shopping, sleeping, drinking wine...because we are stressed and tired and need to do these things to check out for a while. I get it! But what I want you to get is if you take just one of those hours to work out instead of chill out, your energy will be boosted. Two hours a week and you'll really start to notice. The truth is you will feel so much better.

It is hard to get to the truth. There are a lot of magazine articles, a lot of TV commercials and shows, and a lot of books written about health and fitness. You can probably find a study to support almost any personal opinion about what to eat and the importance of exercise. We have to be very careful about looking at things that will never help us change. Let's commit to keeping our gaze upon that which will support our journey and our dreams. Remember, what you focus on grows. Focus on healthy eating—plant-based, whole foods in healthy portions—and consistent daily exercise. Make it a priority and deal with old ways of relating that get in the way. Ask for help. Say no to things that you don't want to do. Say yes to things that are good for you. Make the time. Get honest and watch what happens. The truth is you will feel better about yourself than you ever dreamed possible, and that is something well worth the effort.

★★★

Which of these are truer for you?
I do exactly what I say I will do.
or
I really want to lose weight and I really want to get healthy but I never seem to stick with it long enough to get there. Something in me rebels.

It is very hard to meet goals that require long term commitment and dedication. We tend to sabotage ourselves over and over. Why is that?

I believe the battle is between feeling good right now versus feeling good in the long run. Financial health is a good example. It requires smart investments and responsible handling of your money right? But then we see an awesome pair of shoes and although we can't afford them, we buy them on credit. It's a wonderful quick hit, right? Those new shoes. But then the bill comes, and the payment is high. There is interest to pay and along with it comes the feeling of being trapped. Not enough money to pay, the balance carries forward. Enslavement to credit card debt can lead to feeling bad about ourselves, we long to feel better, we long for freedom, and then we see that beautiful new coat on sale. You see the cycle.

Physical health and wellness is the same. I want to be at my healthy body weight. I don't want any of the metabolic diseases. But it requires smart investments and responsible handing of your body, right? But then there is temptation; something I know is not good for me and doesn't contribute to my best life but it feels so good to eat it. I can't resist so I do. Yum! Then the bill comes and the payment is high. Too much high-calorie food, not enough clean whole food; I feel trapped. The balance carries forward. Enslavement to high-calorie processed foods leads to feeling bad about myself. I want to feel better, I long for freedom but I really need some comfort so I eat something else. Yum!

I didn't begin to get free until I saw a radical image. I would see myself take a rubber tube, tie it around my upper arm, get my needle out, get my drug out, fill the syringe then inject it into my vein with an ahhh of relief. I have never injected heroin, but I could see how I was using. I was using food to sooth a feeling. I was using food to fill a void in my life. I have (over)used a lot of things for comfort and to fill the big empty space. Food. Alcohol. Drugs. Men. Shopping. Work. Internet. It is an experience we all share. What I had to learn was that I could stop using for temporary relief and start digging for the root of the problem.

There is a battle in us all; our desire for instant gratification versus our dream of long term health and wholeness. Just knowing that this battle is going on and recognizing that it is common to all of us is an important breakthrough. We somehow then have to learn to walk this fine line between the need to live for today while at the same time investing in and planning for our future. I don't know about you but this is a tough one for me.

Have you ever heard this quote?

"Life is not a journey to the grave with intentions of arriving safely in a pretty well-preserved body, but rather to skid in broadside, thoroughly used up, totally worn out and loudly proclaiming ... WOW! What a ride."

That is much more my tendency so I have to be careful or I can end up living totally for the moment without giving enough thought to the long term consequences. I've gotten myself in bondage more than once in my life this way. Smoking, debt, being overweight, bad relationships; all these things are outcomes of preferring the quick hit over the long term freedom that comes with taking care of yourself and making responsible decisions. It's easy to see it in smokers or women that date bad boys. It's easy to understand what you are doing to yourself if you run up unmanageable debt. Eating is the tough one to really see because the consequences are slow and insidious. But there is a slow loss of freedom and if you have experienced it you know exactly what I am talking about. You don't have as much fun shopping for clothes. You lose feeling good about yourself in that sparkly way women should get to feel. You lose confidence. Then you lose physical abilities. You wish for and long for the freedom and peace that comes with losing weight but it just never comes.

Ready for the truth? The quick hits are lies. They are the counterfeit fillers for the real deal. You want happiness; it doesn't come from eating something yummy. It comes from making smart investments and taking good care of yourself. It comes from finding balance in living for today while investing in tomorrow. I finally saw that all my drug hits with that imaginary needle in my arm were just making me an addict, not making me happy. I was doing whatever felt good, but I had little joy. I wasn't satisfied, I wasn't at peace, and I wasn't healthy. You can make a different choice.

I really like pizza. But I like having a good report from the kidney doctor better.

I love ice cream. But I love feeling good about myself even more.

I enjoy steak. But watching my cholesterol drop 46 points was much more fulfilling.

I liked smoking. But I love that I conquered an addiction.

Donuts and bagels are really good. But losing 45 pounds and keeping it off is way better.

Wine is very relaxing. However, peace of mind is life changing.

Pasta and bread are tasty. But being able to wear whatever I want feels amazing.

Once you decide what is really important to you, the choices get easier. Once I was clear on my deepest reason for wanting to be at a healthier weight, I was able to stick with good choices more often. Once I knew deep in my heart that feeling good about myself was one of life's most precious gifts, I became much less likely to sabotage everything I was working on with a binge or a string of bad days. Nothing tastes nearly as good as feeling good about yourself feels. Nothing. And I promise, if I can make these changes, then you can, too. I really, truly believe that you can. You will just have to trust me for now when I tell you I don't miss a thing and every change I've made was worth it. Then one day you will see for yourself and I hope I am there to see you smile, all lit up, in your full glory.

★★★

There is too much information out there. T.M.I.!

"Take blood pressure in both arms" a study says. "Caffeine alters estrogen levels in women" a study says. "Fatty foods may cause brain damage" a study says. "Chew more, eat less" a study says. "Cut calories by eating the same food every day" a study says. "Consumers eat trans fats despite concern" a study says. "We are three times more likely to eat the first thing we see" a study says. "People that live near fast food restaurants are more likely to eat at them" a study says.

These are all real headlines that I just got by googling "top health studies." New ones come out every week. Some of them are helpful but most of them conflict with another study and only create confusion. Over the years I have read about the benefits and risks of a glass of wine a day. I have read the controversy about how much protein we need. I have heard that dark chocolate is an antioxidant. I have read conflicting reports on coffee's impact on our health. I've read studies about how important heart rate zone is during exercise and studies that discount zone training entirely.

I believe we have to be very careful about what we read, listen to, and otherwise allow into our library of information. There is a point at which we have so much information floating around in our heads that we really have no idea how to proceed, and that doesn't do anything to encourage belief in this process. And that is the most important goal—to change your belief and to have complete faith that if you make healthy choices and move your body consistently, you will be rewarded with improved health, your goal weight, more energy, and feeling better about yourself.

Bouncing from one solution to another does not help, it hurts. That is because the solution is holistic, involving the physical, emotional, psychological, and spiritual aspects of our being. Therefore, strength training is excellent, but it is not the answer. Yoga is wonderful, but it is not the key. Eliminating processed carbohydrates is very wise, but it is not the secret. Cardiovascular exercise is important, but alone it's not enough. Vegetables are super-healthy but are only one piece of the whole. Eventually you have to put it all together.

Everything is also relative. So, when a study says green beans are good, I find I have to run that through a common sense filter. Good for what? There are many different goals out there. Good for weight loss? Good for overall health? Good for digestion? Good for heart patients? Good for kidney patients? Good for runners? Good for body builders? When an article or study is written, it is helpful to know who the writer is and who they are writing to. Another question I like to ask is: Who is this information helping? If it does not support and encourage people to make healthy choices, I don't see the point.

Then, just because a study says green beans are to be encouraged, we are all in a different place with respect to our green beans. Here's what I mean. Back in the day, green beans to me meant French fries. I had a way of spinning the truth to meet my desire for junk food, so I could do some pretty interesting math. Something like green beans = vegetable = potatoes. If A = B and B = C then A = C. Have potatoes instead and don't worry about the fact that they are fried. Then I moved to baked potato (loaded). Next came a baked potato with light sour cream, lowfat butter, and salt. Then I finally got around to the green beans on the plate with the baked potato. Those green beans had some kind of cheesy sauce on them. Eventually I worked my way to canned green beans with just butter and salt and hung out there for a while. Next came frozen green beans. No butter, no salt! While still using the frozen beans, I also discovered how good fresh green beans were steamed or sautéed. Then I found fresh beans that were organic, with nothing sprayed on them to make them look shiny or last longer—steamed or sautéed with a splash of lemon and a dash of pepper. I may keep going on this road and find a healthier green bean but that's where I am now and I love 'em.

I can tell you the same story for many foods in my life. I am just not a person to abruptly change. I do things incrementally so as not to freak out that part of me that I know will rebel if I change too quickly. I've learned this one. Make small changes that I can live with and commit to keep going. So I have this same story for my coffee, which started with lots of added sugar, then flavored sweetened creamer, and now has vanilla almond milk. My breakfast used to be McDonald's big breakfast, then became a NutriGrain cereal bar, and is now homemade oat granola, walnuts, and flax. My lunch used to be Burger King, then a Lean Cuisine, and is now my veggie bowl. And my snack started as M&Ms, then went to processed energy bars, and is now my whole-food, plant- strong, homemade protein bars. These are changes that work for me and keep me committed to the process that I believe in: whole foods, plant-strong, move my body, lift some weights.

There is nothing perfect or magical about the changes I have made, they are just things I'm trying. If something doesn't work, I let it go. Remember my goals are not your goals; you probably aren't a kidney patient; you may have a health issue of your own you are dealing with. You need to find your own changes. It is important to keep an open mind about trying to improve. For example, I realized that the canned ingredients in my veggie bowl add some extra sodium that I really don't need with my kidney problem. And I want to be the fun, crazy old great aunt at my nieces' and nephew's kids' weddings 50 years from now, so why not try to make it a little better? Today I used black beans from the bag instead of the can. No sodium! Saved over 1000 mg for the whole recipe by doing so, and it still tastes great.

Baby steps always work better than giant leaps. Do me a favor. Stop reading and stand up at the very edge of the room you are in. Now in one giant leap get to the other side. Did you make it? Now get up and cross the room taking small steps. Did you get there? Which took longer? Oh wait, one of the strategies didn't get you there at all! The only way to move forward is right foot, left foot, right foot, left foot. If you catch yourself searching for that one thing, the key, the secret to all this, remember your attempt to take a flying leap across the room. Then get over it, go to your kitchen and start making small changes that you are willing to live with forever. Say goodbye, have a ceremony if you have to, grieve it leaving your life, then embrace the new. Turn your French fries into fresh steamed organic green beans and keep doing that until your changes add up to a transformed life.

★★★

We all work *so* hard. Family, jobs, our own business, housework, grocery shopping, volunteer work, school functions, sports events, yard work, remodeling projects, errands, aging parents, church events. Our days are packed! There is a moment on Friday when I don't have anything else to do for the day that I take a deep breath and feel myself decompress from the week. I love that feeling. I also understand the last thing I want to do is ruin that feeling with the thought "what should I cook for dinner tonight?" Who wants to think about that after a long week? Solution: pizza delivery or out to dinner.

There is absolutely nothing wrong with that. I think we need that time to relax. It only becomes a problem if those choices aren't supporting your weight loss or health goals. Here's the risk: I work hard, take care of everyone, and put many others' needs ahead of my own. I feel the stress of trying to do too much and not getting enough time for myself. I need a moment of peace and stress-free quiet, so like the commercials tell me, I get my chocolate (or insert your favorite me-treat here) and sink into the couch and relax. Ahh! Me time.

Once in a while, that kind of me time is very therapeutic. Every day, though, can lead to being overweight depending on what choices you are making and how loud you are screaming in your head "I worked hard today; I deserve this!" Usually the louder the yell, the less healthy the food choice. That place inside of you that rebels no matter how much mental energy you have been devoting to your new "diet" is trying to tell you something. I am going to suggest that you slow down for a moment and listen. She's actually trying to tell you something very important.

One of my clients said to me today during her workout, "I love coming here." I asked her if this was her me time. She said yes it was and what made it great was she didn't have to think about or decide anything when she was working out. No decisions needed to be made. She was being directed. Don't we all crave that? I do; I love the classes that I take. I just get to show up at the starting time, and the instructor guides me though the workout. No thinking needed except to focus on my form, my breath, the music, and how I feel. It's wonderful. I am a personal trainer, and I could certainly come to my studio every day and work out on my own, but I don't. I go elsewhere to be with others and to be instructed because it feels good.

I understand that the same thing applies to meals. It is fabulous to go out and be waited on, not have to decide what to cook, and not have to clean up. It's good for the soul. It only becomes a problem when we bring the free-pass mentality to the restaurant and order high-calorie meals that don't support our fitness or weight loss. And it's easy to do. I can go out to eat with the best intentions but when I order, something takes over. Next thing I know, "pancakes" or "pasta" is coming out of my mouth, or I'm eating a basket of chips and salsa. We all do it. I started to realize I've eaten these things

attend her home jewelry party, tells you she understands completely and loves you just the same. Grace is the boss that encourages you to go home and spend time with your family or get your workout in when you share with her that you are feeling out of balance. Grace is the husband who is so happy that you told him exactly what you need that he makes a habit of meeting that need. Grace is the friend that encourages and supports your healthy eating. Grace is the person in your life that you can be completely you with and know you are accepted just for being you, not for what you do. Once you start looking, I believe you will find it in your own life. If there is one thing I know, grace in infinitely abundant. It never, ever runs out. Now that's what I call me time.

★★★

Walking is such a great symbol for life.

You can't really know someone until you walk a mile in his or her shoes. Left foot, right foot, left foot, right foot. One step at a time, one day at a time.

Now shall I walk
or shall I ride?
"Ride," Pleasure said:
"Walk," Joy replied. ~W.H. Davies

If you have walked many miles with someone, you know what I mean. You are not just working out. There is a connection that is made in a profound way. I've often wondered if it is because we are walking side-by-side instead of facing each other. Shoulder-to-shoulder we share our lives, we share our struggles. We open our hearts and begin to heal. We listen and we connect.

It doesn't just happen walking. My running friends share this experience. I've connected with people at a level I didn't think possible while lifting barbells together. And I've seen the friendships that form within groups of women I train. Last year, two women in one of my groups both lost their mothers and to see how they began to heal with the help of exercise and the love of the women around them was beautiful.

We lost a member of our fitness family this week to cancer. Lena inspired everyone she met to get moving by losing over 100 pounds and spreading her love of exercise to all. Her trainer told me she was still lifting weights two weeks ago. There is an important lesson here. Moving your body is not only about a goal, it is about the joy of the moment. It's about right here, right now.

There is an evil thought that can take root when we lose someone who loves exercise so much and worked hard to lose weight. Things like "what's the point...why even bother?" That is a lie. Every second counts and the time you invest in movement and connection is worth it! If you feel sad or lonely or anxious or stressed, I want you to find an exercise class or a walking group and show up to it this week. Be brave and open up to someone about who you are and why you are there. Make a meaningful connection. You'll be amazed.

Lifting weights doesn't change your life; what happens inside you as a result of lifting weights changes your life for the better. A walk is a walk until you walk with someone, drop your guard, and let them see the real you, whom perhaps you've been hiding away for a very long time. A fitness class is just that until you let your fellow students know you and care about you. This tribe is a strong one. We encourage, support, and motivate each other. We walk together and we reflect back the beauty and truth inside each of us.

★★★

It's time to get back to basics.

It's been an interesting month or two. I've had some struggles, and I know a lot of you have, too. Respiratory illnesses, the never-ending cough, stomach flu, plantar fasciitis, elbow and shoulder pain, knee and ankle flare-ups, back pain, stress at work and home, and the basic winter blahs. The good news is there are about three weeks left of winter, and we spring ahead to daylight saving time in March. I don't feel terribly off track but I could use a little extra focus right now, so here's my plan.

I can't remember the last time I was outside with my iPod on and my heart rate up! I miss it so much. Thanks to the never-ending cough, it has been several weeks since I've had my favorite workout—outside. I was able to find other cardio to do and I love the classes that I take, but I need my time outside. It's not just a physical need. My mind doesn't function right without that kind of movement. It doesn't matter if it is walking or running, I just know that to keep my emotions balanced I need my cardio. So this week, I'm going to make sure I schedule two sessions at Sharon Woods and get those good chemicals going in my brain again.

Since I didn't have my good brain chemicals going, I've been eating more sugar than usual to compensate. It doesn't work. I do not feel good when I'm eating too much sugar. Ugh. I had a McDonald's milkshake! What the heck?? It affects my energy, my food choices, my mood, and my workouts. It's funny how it creeps back in. I've realized having been on this journey for many years now that getting off the sugar is not a one-time thing. Although I think I am making good choices that I'm committed to, relapse can happen any time. I believe this time my trigger was the lack of cardio. One really impacts the other for me. I get my cardio in, my energy is up, I feel good about myself, so I don't use sugar. I don't get my cardio in, I start to drag, I don't feel so great about myself, and I start using it for that little temporary boost. It's time to knock it off and choose the true way to feeling good, not the counterfeit. Sugar is the counterfeit and the consequences are no fun. So, this week, out with the processed sugar (except for one little piece of birthday cake) which I promise I'll burn off that night in spin.

I must drink my water every day. This is such a basic but sometimes I forget, especially when it is cold out. I crave coffee to warm me up, but the effects of coffee make me dehydrated and nothing works as well when I'm not hydrated. Same goes for soda, tea, juice, and milkshakes. A little in moderation, but the majority of my fluid intake must be water. I know I feel better when I keep a bottle with me all day at work. I know that change alone will make me feel stronger, leaner, and more energetic. If you see me at the studio tomorrow, you'll see my water bottle right there as well.

I must prepare beforehand if I'll be going out to eat. I made the mistake twice this week of not doing so, and ended up ordering poorly and paying for it later. I just don't feel good when I eat like that, but sometimes when I look at a menu, my old self orders for me, and she usually orders fish and chips, a cheeseburger and fries, or something like that. I know that if I think about it beforehand and remember the basics I follow at restaurants, I will feel much better. Deciding what I'll order before I get there and sticking to it is a key for me because it helps me feel confident that I will do what I say I will do. This keeps me on the right track.

I hope you are on the right track, moving in the direction that you want to be moving. If you are not, decide right now to do things differently. Go back to the basics. No need to look any further than that for the answer. Cardio! Limit sugar. Drink water. Choose mindfully. You know the basics and what works for you. If the past weeks or month or year was off track, let it go. Make a different choice and move forward in a powerful, mindful way. I know that I can feel better about myself with three days of eating clean and consistent cardio. That's it! The world is filled with people searching high and low for the answer, but it is no more complicated than that. The key is to actually do it, do it mindfully, and do it consistently. Then enjoy the rewards of your hard work and dedication. Enjoy feeling healthy in body, mind, and spirit. Enjoy energy, confidence, and the knowledge that nothing magical needs to happen to feel better about yourself, it is available to all of us any time.

★★★

Funny how things change.

When I turned 16, I was able to drive to school. What freedom! Turns out, I could skip first period and go to McDonald's on Boardman-Canfield Road, order a Big Breakfast and eat it in the parking lot. Later the same day I could skip regular lunch and go through the snack line getting two Little Debbie Peanut Butter Bars and chocolate milk. To me that felt like liberation, total freedom. I could do what I wanted and no one was going to deprive me. So there. If I was driving around and wanted to feel happy, I could stop at Fast Check for a big bag of Peanut M&Ms and a Dr.Pepper. Open up the bag of M&Ms, put them in the center console, and munch away. Wash each yummy bite down with my Dr. Pepper. It seemed like a harmless bit of happiness.

Now here I am at age 47. I do everything in my power to avoid McDonald's Big Breakfast, and I would be very worried about myself if I was sitting in the parking lot eating one. Dr. Pepper is now Diet Dr. Pepper or water. M&Ms are a rare treat that I stopped buying when I started to get serious about losing weight. But I don't feel like I'm giving up my freedom, I feel like I'm regaining it. What's going on?

I am a user. I use food to feel pleasure, freedom, and independence. Somewhere between sitting at the Boardman McDonald's eating breakfast and topping out my max weight, whatever that was, I lost my freedom (to choose) and became enslaved by the very behavior that made me feel so good at the beginning. It doesn't feel good to lose control of your will, your self-discipline, or your freedom to choose.

I know from working with so many women that there is a big fear of feeling constantly deprived if you commit to eating healthy. I understand that completely. What will I do if I want to feel a bit of pleasure but feel like I can't have my M&Ms (chips, cookies, bagels, ice cream, insert your happy pill here)? How will I live without these things? It's scary to think about. But answer honestly; are they worth what you give up in the long run? Are they worth feeling like you aren't in control of your choices, that you aren't free to be at any weight you choose?

They weren't worth it to me. Neither were cigarettes. Once I became very aware that I had given up my freedom—through addiction to cigarettes and using food—I knew I had to change. But I also knew that just swearing off these things didn't work for me. I had tried all kinds of diets. I had tried to quit smoking. I was not in control of my choices. Something kept taking over, and I had to fight back.

So I started to look within. What did I really want...a snack or to feel happy? What was I really feeling...physical hunger or heart/soul hunger? What I found out, I found out from that 16-year-old girl sitting in her Plymouth Horizon eating instead of going to orchestra class. I had a long talk with her, and, wow, had she been dying to be heard. Turns out all this food wasn't what she really needed at all. She needed help, healing, and someone to talk to honestly who would hear her and understand her feelings.

Once I realized I had not been giving myself those things, I set out to do so. I started asking for help in many ways; from support groups, from my friends, from my family, from my church. I started seeking healing instead of sugar and nicotine. Healing is available for these old wounds, no matter how they came to be or how long ago. Don't give up. I started talking more honestly about who I really was and what I was feeling instead of wearing my this-is-what-I'm-supposed-to-be-and-how-I'm-supposed-to-act mask. It still amazes me that true connection is made with another person by being real not by being perfect.

I love the responses that I get when I write about indulging in a milkshake or eating cake three days in a row. I understand that a real connection is made when you and I talk for real, not by me giving you weight loss or exercise instructions. All I have is my story, and for me nothing worked until I dealt with some stuff on the inside. When I did, even just being honest about what was in there and saying it out loud to someone, everything started to change. What was compulsion eased its grip. What was addiction fell away. And I was left with my authentic self that was able to actually make choices in line with my true desires. And a healthy body weight followed with much less effort than I ever thought possible.

If you have tried everything to control your eating (or your drinking, your spending, your smoking, whatever) and you still struggle, be brave and look within. Look with compassion and understanding for wounds, unmet needs, or fears. Treat them honestly and lovingly but don't ignore them. I talked to a client this week about changing some unhealthy food patterns, and I asked her to read the 12 steps. I think it is extremely important to understand that the 12 steps do not say step (1) stay out of bars, step (2) substitute pop for alcohol, step (3) have a cheat day where you drink all you want. No. The 12 steps say we admitted we were powerless over our addiction, our lives had become unmanageable, and only a power greater than ourselves can restore us to sanity.

I don't know about you, but that speaks to me. I tried to manage my food. I tried to control my smoking. None of that ever worked! I don't have what it takes to manage these things, they are bigger than me. If you look at Weight Watchers and feel like crying that you would ever have to make another attempt to control your eating, I get it. I totally get it. That never, ever would have worked for me. But crazy, radical healing of my heart worked. And all it took was to be brave, open up, and share my crazy, messed up, wonderful life with others and watch as their love and acceptance changed me, inside and out.

★★★

I am really excited this week; we are scheduled to start the Break Free seminar. The class is full. What I envision for this group is weight loss myth busters. You know that set of false beliefs we all have? By the time we're done, we are going to know the truth and be able to act on the truth with confidence instead of being at the mercy of a set of false beliefs that get triggered every time we attempt to take steps forward.

The trigger I heard the most about last week is vacation. Do you believe it is possible to plan a vacation and not suddenly panic and start to diet right away to lose as much weight as possible? What is that doing to us, the false belief that if I don't lose weight: I won't look good enough to enjoy my vacation, I won't be able to wear what I want, I don't get to feel good about myself?

I think those things are dangerous, and we don't know how to fight back. You can take three steps this week to learn to fight back.

Step 1: Become very aware of your triggers. Whether it is going on vacation or out to dinner; attending a class reunion or wedding; or some other special occasion, try to see when you start searching for the magic answer outside yourself. Remember, it is an inside job, so any time you are looking *out there,* you are on the wrong path.

Step 2: Understand what your false beliefs are. If I don't lose twenty pounds by spring break, I won't enjoy my vacation. I have to lose thirty pounds this month or else I won't even bother trying. I can't lose weight without a jump start. I eat healthy but never lose weight. I must eat when I'm stressed. I don't have time to walk every day. All these things are lies that are guaranteed to keep you stuck. Shine a big, bright light on them and expose them for what they are. No-good lies.

Step 3: Override the false beliefs. Make a different choice. It is possible to just stay on the slow, steady path you are on and go on vacation. Incorporate your new strategies while at the beach, but don't switch things up. Stay on the path. Slow and steady wins the race. Make a difference choice. If you feel stressed at work, go for a walk instead of heading for the snacks. Do some yoga or deep breathing in your office. Do something different and reinforce the truth, which is there are many other ways to deal with stress besides eating.

Once you put these steps together and start doing them consistently, you will learn that it was a problem of thinking, and the false beliefs we all create and hold dear are really what keep us stuck. The good news is all it takes to succeed is to start going through them one by one and proving them wrong. That may take some courage, but I believe you are brave.

★★★

Walk every day.
Eat lots of vegetables.
Drink water.
Watch portions.
Food journal consistently until eating mindfully is a way of life.
Lift weights twice a week.
Train with intensity and focus.
Train in your proper heart rate zone.
Minimize sugar.

Avoid bad fats.

Eat whole, plant-based food.

Look for food naturally high in fiber.

Stretch.

Get good sleep.

Use food for fuel, not comfort.

Find healthy ways to deal with stress.

Walk every day.

Eat lots of vegetables...

It is a list of basics. This is what it takes to be at your goal weight and to live your best life. Nothing more complicated than this list, repeated over and over and over.

But what's the typical list?

Oversleep.

Skip the vegetables.

Drink lattes or Coke.

Forget about portions.

Eat mindlessly.

Lift weights maybe once a week.

Train without intensity or focus.

Be unaware of proper heart rate zones.

Crave sugar, eat sugar.

Crave fatty foods, eat unhealthy fats.

Skip whole, plant-based foods.

Forget to stretch.

Stay up too late.

Use food for comfort.

Deal with stress by eating.

Too busy and tired to walk.

Oversleep...

It's what we all do to some degree or another. And that's just one day. Then we hit replay and do it again and again and again.

May I suggest you hit the pause button and make sure you are working off the list you really want to use? If you are operating from the typical list, no wonder you feel crappy. No wonder you are tired. No wonder you don't feel fabulous about yourself. There is no way for the second list to support you in that. No way.

"But it's so hard. How do I change? I really don't want to change my behavior; I just want the result to change." Of course, that will never happen. The way to move forward is to find strategies for overcoming the obstacles that are getting in the way of your changing. These are daily practices that are personal, that work for you.

Here are a few that seem common to women who have had success at changing their lives:

1. Keep as much of the junk out of the house as possible. Just stop buying it. You aren't forbidding those who live with you from having it, they are welcome to have junk anytime they are out and about, but you are asking for their encouragement and support. And that will require a junk-free pantry and refrigerator. Set up an environment that supports making exceptional choices time after time.

2. Find healthy recipes that you like. There are so many resources. *The 400 Calorie Fix* cookbook, *Forks Over Knives* recipe book, the *Eat Clean Diet* cookbooks, *Cooking Light*, Weight Watchers recipes online, and many more. Just slowly build your repertoire to include whole food, plant-based recipes that you really enjoy. As you do, you will feel so much better about yourself that it will be easy to kick the old, high-calorie "easy" recipes to the curb.

3. Have strategies for going out and don't deviate. Write out on paper or a card five meals that you can go out to eat and really enjoy that are less than 500 calories. Look up the calories online if you need to. Become hyper-aware of the pitfalls that you keep choosing over and over. Then make a different choice. Maybe next time when you go out to eat, you really need the experience and the energy of the restaurant more than you need the high-calorie meal. Look

for places with great low-calorie menus. Make them your new favorite places, and have fun trying out their new lower calorie meals.

4. Walk almost every day. It's just not an option. Schedule it on your calendar and do not let anyone have that time unless they are bleeding. That might mean getting up when the alarm rings at 5:30 a.m. so you get 30 minutes to yourself on the treadmill before everyone is up. That might mean taking your shoes to work and going for a walk around your workplace every day at lunch. Who cares if you get a little sweaty—you are changing your life! That might mean a lot of things, but it can't mean finding excuses day after day and never getting into the wonderful, spiritual, peaceful, blissful habit of walking.

5. Understand your body. What heart rate zone is best for your goal? How hard should you push yourself when you are strength training? You have to become mindful of what's going on for every step, rep, set, mile. Each and every one matters. You can work out in too low of a heart rate zone or too high of a heart rate zone and never lose weight. You can go through the motions while strength training and never create the muscles you want. If you have checked out, check back in!

6. Stay healthy. By this I mean mentally, physically, spiritually, and emotionally. Develop a yoga or Pilates practice. Set aside time every day to stretch, meditate, pray. Make exceptional food choices when you are physically hungry. When you have emotional or spiritual hunger, feed your soul something beautiful instead of something to eat. Give yourself the gift of love if you are sad, scared, or lonely. It is such a better life now that I turn to my encouragers instead of food when I am in need of love. It truly is. If you haven't shared your true self with anyone in a while, do so. We all need encouragement.

These strategies are meant to be guidelines or ideas. Make them your own daily practices. Use your creativity and your skills. But be clear on what your strategies are and stick to them. This is a commitment; a promise. You are being asked to make choices from your highest self, the best version of you that exists. It is the only way to change. We can't change from that place of the ego or from our broken hearts. We change from the sparkling place that exists inside us all; the goddess, the warrior, the one that never gives up and always keeps believing.

★★★

The process of change is so fascinating.

I have an example in my own life. Gas prices are really high right now, and the thought of walking to work has been bubbling up in me. I live about 1.5 miles from the studio via the bike path. I have several reasons for wanting to walk to work. One is to save money on gas. Two is to model a fit lifestyle to my clients. Three is because I love to walk. The problem is I am having difficulty making this change.

It is so easy to drive to work; much easier than walking. It is quicker and more convenient. I think it is safe to call it comfortable for me. Driving to work is in my comfort zone.

Walking to work requires me to step out of my comfort zone and do something different. But every time I make an attempt to walk to the studio or even think about doing it, I get hit with a whole bunch of irrational fears. What if there is an emergency, and I don't have my car? What if it pours rain? What if I forget something? What if I get mugged on the bike path? What about my hair? And I'll have to wake up earlier.

I hope you can see how irrational these all are. I have never had an emergency where I needed my car, and if I did, I know I could call someone. I have an umbrella. I've walked in the rain before. I don't forget things when I drive to work, why would I if I walk? I have walked a thousand miles on these paths and never gotten mugged. And since when do I care about my hair at work or 30 minutes less sleep!

These are all fears and lies. The truth is I feel strangely dependent on my car and my attempt to introduce this new aspect of my healthy lifestyle has shined a big, bright light on it. I am afraid to be without my car. Now, I could spend the next few years in therapy trying to figure out exactly why this is, or I can just decide to bring out the antidote to this fear. That antidote is truth.

The truth is I will be fine. But the only way for me to really, truly know that is to do it. I can't just sit here all day trying and trying to believe it. I have to set the alarm a little bit earlier, grab my umbrella and just go. And when I do, these fears start to lose all their power. Every step on that bike path will bring me one step closer to freedom from them. That is the way to move forward instead of staying stuck.

I know what this means. Now that I have all of you to hold me accountable, I have to finish this up and get to bed because the alarm is going to ring a little bit earlier tomorrow. And although I may lay in bed tonight with a hundred crazy lies spinning through my head about the worst case scenario that might happen when I don't have my car tomorrow, I know that if I can find the strength and courage to do this, I will be a changed person. I will experience more freedom in my life than ever. I will be one step closer to the best version of myself I think I can be. And it will spill over into all other aspects of my life.

Uh oh, I just checked the weather. It's going to be cold tomorrow. Maybe I should wait until Tuesday. I have a shorter day on Tuesday so it will make more sense. Or maybe I should wait until the next warm Monday so I can start the week off right. Or maybe April is a better month to start this kind of thing. What if water on the bike path freezes? What if I fall? I see you, fears! I will not allow you to run my life any longer. You had me in your grip for far too long. I will not give in to you anymore. I know what I want. I want to be a woman who walks to work. I want to be victorious over fear, I want to live by truth and walk by faith, and I want to be free. Won't you join me?

★★★

Unstuck feels wonderful.

Last week I shared with you that I'd been thinking about walking to work but hadn't done it yet. Well, I am happy to report that I did walk to work, twice last week, and it was wonderful. No car! Jacket on, backpack on. It turned out to be about a 25 minute walk each way. Not a single bad thing happened. I wasn't needed for an emergency, it didn't storm, I didn't forget anything, and I didn't fall into Alum Creek. I did see turtles sunning themselves on a log in the creek, got some Vitamin D, felt the cool air on my skin, and worked up a sweat. It's my new favorite thing to do.

I couldn't have done that a few years ago. I was one of those people who knew what to do, but just didn't do it.

I had to dig way down deep to figure out why I couldn't consistently make healthy choices. It wasn't like I didn't know smoking was harmful. I did know; I just couldn't quit. It wasn't like I thought pizza for dinner or my nightly dish of ice cream with Hershey's syrup was low calorie; I knew it wasn't. But I seemed incapable of overriding my want for it and making a different choice. It had to do with who I thought I was.

On a cold February night when I was thirteen, my 49-year-old dad started walking around the living room trying to catch his breath. He kept saying he thought he had heartburn and he didn't feel well. It got worse quickly, so an ambulance was called and he left on a stretcher. We found out a short time later that he died of a heart attack on his way to the hospital. I can clearly remember lying in bed that night feeling utterly alone with no one there to comfort me or help me understand what I was feeling. As a thirteen year old, I wasn't capable of processing all that was going on around me. Instead of understanding that what I was feeling was normal for someone who just experienced a devastating loss, I translated it to mean this: I don't matter.

My new identity became I Don't Matter. And I started turning to food for comfort.

The next ten years were spent being a teenager while living at home and helping to care for Mom, who had MS. When she died, I didn't need convincing that I was a worthless, damaged, and insignificant 23-year-old. I was already convinced. I lived out of that place for the next 17 years, certain my identity was that of the girl I remember being on the day I went back to 8th grade after my dad's funeral. They all looked at me differently now and treated me differently. I was no longer me.

During these years, I fought and fought. I fought to quit smoking, I fought to become active, I fought to get healthy and I fought to lose weight. But I could never make good decisions consistently. Every time I decided to make a change, all the crazy fears would come up just like they did about my attempt to walk to work. I would decide to try to quit smoking, and I would be pounded with fears about life not being as enjoyable. Drinking a beer wouldn't be as good, a cup of coffee wouldn't be as good, vacation would be no fun, and I would never be able to go on a road trip again. To override all these fears, I would have to dig down and remember the truth, so I could make the right choice. The problem was I didn't know the truth. I still thought I was I Don't Matter.

Making an extraordinary choice about your health and well-being in the face of your fears when your core belief is I Don't Matter is impossible.

or I'll Never Be Good Enough.

or I'm Worthless.

or I'm Unlovable.

or I'm Wrong.

Another diet will never solve this. The right program will never heal you. This is why so many bariatric surgeries fail and why most people who lose weight on a program or diet gain it back. None of it goes deep enough. None of it changes the false beliefs about who we are.

The truth is we all have a story but we are not our story. We are so much more than that. We are not what has happened to us. We are not our past mistakes. We are not our body fat percentage or our body weight. We are beautiful. We reflect the Spirit of Love. We are the exact same person in the deepest part of our soul as we were the moment we were born. We are whole and perfect.

I believe that we all experience trauma in our lives and, in our weak moments, we can translate these traumas into meaning something about our identity and who we are. This is not the truth. These wounds can be healed and we can learn who we really are in our wholeness and worth. And imagine deciding to make a healthy change in your life. You step out of that comfort zone and get hit with those crazy fears again. Who is more likely to make an extraordinary choice?

I Don't Matter Girl

or

I am a woman of incredible worth. Even though I have been through many things in my life and I have a story, I am not my story. I am not damaged. I am perfect, beautiful, healed, and whole. I deserve to be healthy and happy. I am worth treating with love and respect. I believe we all are.

★★★

FEAR versus LOVE
Fear: I always fail so why try?
Love: I care about myself and I matter deeply to others, so it's time to get to work.
Fear: I will feel deprived.
Love: I will feel amazing.
Fear: I can't.
Love: With help, I will.
Fear: Why bother?
Love: I am doing this for myself and my loved ones.
Fear: I will fail.
Love: I will overcome.
Fear: I will never lose weight.
Love: I will be freed from compulsion and heal.
Fear: I don't have time.
Love: I matter so I will make the time.
Fear: My genetics.
Love: I can conquer anything.
Fear: I will start tomorrow.

Love: I will start today.

Fear: Getting thin will make me worth more as a person.

Love: Understanding my worth as a person will heal the reasons I overeat.

Fear: As soon as I lose weight, I will live my life fully.

Love: My life is now, and I choose to live every second of it wide awake.

Fear: I can't deal with my past or my pain.

Love: I am ready to deal with anything that is keeping me stuck.

Fear: I'm afraid.

Love: I believe.

★★★

We spend a lot of time talking about what keeps us stuck. We have to. Without the willingness to look within, we're stuck repeating the same behaviors, compulsions, and addictions over and over. We never get to move forward out of our old wounds and our old story into the life we were meant to live. I don't believe any of us were meant to be overweight or unhappy with our bodies. Or to be controlled by food. We were meant to live extraordinary lives with purpose and joy despite the culture of food around us. We were meant to be free from self-destructive patterns, compulsions and addictions.

If you are still struggling with these things, take heart. There are many layers of false beliefs to get through before you are living a life rooted in freedom and truth. Things click when they are meant to click. Layers are peeled away as we are ready for them to be peeled away. Don't give up. Stay immersed in the truth and when the lies come at you (it's Monday, so I need to go on a diet; I need to join a program; I need to control my eating; I need the next quick fix) you have the ability to keep them from pulling you off track. Let's be honest, if dieting worked, everyone would be at their healthy body weight by now. Everyone. If diet drugs worked, we would all be done with this. If programs worked, they wouldn't try so hard to sell you on them. Diets, programs and pills don't work long term.

Once we admit that the problem lies within, and therefore, the transformation and healing will happen within, we can begin to work on choices. All this examination, awareness, and introspection is useless if we can't become our best selves, and then make the very best choice every time. Think of how many small choices we make every day. When left to my defaults, I never made very good choices. My default decision making always seemed to come from the most wounded or fearful part of myself. What's for dinner? Comfort food. Am I going to walk today? No, too tired. Not enough time. Am I going to bed on time? No, this is the only time I have to myself. Water or wine tonight? Wine, I'm stressed! Am I getting up early to work out? No, I'm too sleepy. Who cares anyway? It doesn't make any difference. I'm destined to fail. Why bother?

We have to be our best self, our whole-hearted self to be able to make extraordinary choices. When my heart began to heal, what I wanted to eat changed, and the choices to support my healthy body weight started to come naturally. What's for dinner? Plant-strong whole foods. Am I going to walk today? Yes, I can't wait! It's what I do. Am I going to bed on time? Of course, because I take care of myself. Water or wine? Water, I'm at peace. Am I getting up early to work out? Of course, it's how I get healthy and strong, and this matters to me. I matter.

Keep working to get to the place in your heart where you can make extraordinary choices. I believe this is what some of those extraordinary choices look like:

Nutrition matters (a lot!). Keep learning; keep progressing towards mostly whole foods, plant-strong nutrition. I limit crappy carbs, sugar, unhealthy fats, and salt because I feel so much better when I do. A few strategies I use to accomplish this consistently:

— Be very mindful about what to eat when dining out.
— Find several very simple recipes for clean, nutritious meals that you really like.
— Cook in bulk one day a week. Take time to chop, cook, and prepare for the week, so when the busyness comes, you are ready.
— Add vegetables to almost everything.

Exercise matters. Walk almost every day, whether it is one mile or five. Get into your target heart rate range for extended periods of time. Lift weights consistently at least twice every week. Find people to work out with who make it fun and motivating. Schedule your workouts. Even when you don't see any outer changes, exercise is working to change your circulation system, the walls of your arteries, your insulin/sugar system, your heart, your lungs, and your metabolism. Keep moving.

Awareness matters. Incorporate practices into your day that create mindfulness. Try breath work. Yoga. Prayer. Meditation. Walk outside. Join a support group. Seek healing. Seek truth. Read something inspiring. Connect what's going on inside of you to the choices you are making. Find what speaks to you but keep learning.

Here's the heart of the matter. If you don't know what to do, learn! The truth is out there, just choose your resources wisely. Then put your new knowledge into practice every day, with every choice. You will see dramatic changes as soon as you eat properly for your body and exercise correctly.

But if you know what to do but don't do it, that is a different matter entirely. Keep peeling away the layers, and you will eventually understand what has kept you stuck all along. I guarantee that what has been keeping you stuck isn't that you have yet to find the right diet. That's not it. Or that you haven't discovered the right drug, supplement, shake, or meal yet. We have things backwards. We think that if only we would find the secret to weight loss and get thin, we will suddenly and magically feel good about ourselves and know our true worth. The truth is once we know who we really are and our true worth, we are healed and become our ideal weight without much fight at all.

★★★

What does fear have to do with fitness? Quite a lot, it turns out.

Have you ever thought about trying to lose weight but are stopped by the fear of failing again? How about how scary it is to try a new class or type of exercise. Will I look stupid? Will I get hurt?

165

Will I be able to do it? Will I be the oldest? Will I be the heaviest? Will I be judged? Will I be criticized? It takes such courage to step out of your comfort zone and try. I want to celebrate every single one of you who have been courageous enough to work out with a personal trainer, lift weights, try core class, try strength class, try yoga class, walk at one of the parks or any other fitness adventure you have been brave enough to take. You are what I call a fitness warrior.

A fitness warrior is still afraid. A fitness warrior feels the same things and fights the same lies that everyone does.

I'm not good enough.

I look fat.

I will fail.

I'll look stupid.

I won't know what to do.

I'll be laughed at.

I will be judged.

I won't fit in.

But the fitness warrior acknowledges that voice—the voice of fear—and makes the extraordinary choice. She does it anyway! The only place that fear has power to stop us is when it's buried deep in our hearts. When we hide it and pretend it's not there, it can rule our choices and sabotage our lives. But in the light, it is powerless. We have the strength to look it in the eye and step right over it.

I am afraid!

Such freedom in claiming it. Such freedom in facing a fear and overcoming it. The first time I took Body Pump class was one of the scariest fitness things I had ever done. I had to set up a barbell with plates on it and change the weights between songs. Everyone knew each other! And everyone knew the songs! I wanted to set that bar down and run out of there ten times during that first class. But I knew it was just fear, so I decided to acknowledge it and do the class anyway. Well, those of you who know me know it's now my very favorite class—so there! (Take that, Fear!)

I have a client that does coaching sessions with me. I asked her to write up her experience with fear. Remember when the blue tape was on the floor of the studio for the Break Free from Dieting seminar? We used that graphic for several coaching sessions and here is her story:

"We have had some great coaching sessions on fear! I never knew how much fear ruled me until the "box, box, arrow" session. Actually standing in the small "stuck box" drove home the point of how uncomfortable, scary, frustrating, and paralyzing it is when you are confined in fear. The center box is just one small step away; "just lift up your foot and step over!! It's like standing on a diving board, at the pool when you are six years old, absolutely frozen in fear to jump. You want to so badly, but you just can't take the step. After what seems like hours, something in you makes you move forward and into the water. From that moment on, you can't stop jumping; it's so much fun! Moving to the center "change" box feels just like that for me. My moment of stepping forward (or stepping off the diving board) was when I wanted to do a boxing class. My friend had invited me, but I wasn't sure I could do it. Would I look dumb? Would I be the oldest one there or the fattest? Could my body do it? I don't have boxing gloves—these were all the false beliefs and lies that Fear was throwing at me to keep me in the small stuck box. Thanks to your challenge "Why not?" and your loan of some boxing gloves, I had no excuses left. I called my friend and said, "I'm all set for Saturday boxing class; I'll meet you there!" I was so excited; this center box is not so bad. It actually feels empowering. The Saturday I chose to go boxing, my friend was in Florida. OMG, now what? New workout place, new class, don't know anyone, not sure I can do it, never boxed before; how could my friend do this to me? Not wanting to go back or give in to the small box thinking (and afraid of telling Sue I didn't go), I went anyway. Not only did I do it, I could keep up, I could do all the moves, I never quit! I wasn't the oldest and there were five other new people that day, too. I burned over 600 calories and was on a high all day. TAKE THAT, FEAR!"

Indeed! Take that fear! Now she is a fitness warrior and well on her way to meeting all her goals. I know this to be true because she now has the ability to see her fears, acknowledge them, then make a different choice. Every choice; every time. She has found freedom.

Another Clear Rock client wrote in to tell her story about what it was like to start strength training and the difference it has made in her (and her husband's) life.

"I want to thank you for making such a difference in my life. I left the class on Thursday with such a feeling of deep gratitude and with a warm glow that I wanted to share it with you. It is a small class and it compliments my walking and gives me the extra push that I need. Also, it focuses on my core and my strength while helping my waistline! I feel I have come a long way since I first came to Clear Rock Fitness and started training. I remember the first few times I took the classes. I would drive home tearful and mad, feeling these classes were more than I could handle and who wants to lift weights and be strong? I had never lifted a weight in my life and never thought I could do a plank. I now look forward to my sessions. Even though I still whine at times! You also opened my eyes with the movie afternoon when we met and watched *Forks Over Knives*. Little did I know at the time that my husband would be diagnosed a few months later with high cholesterol and severe plaque in his coronary arteries. Since October of last year, we have followed a 90% plant- based diet, and he has been able to cut his total cholesterol in half. He has incredible HDL and LDL numbers all without medication. He has lost all his belly fat too!"

Way to go, fitness warrior! Doing planks now all week long and looking fabulous. Changing her life and her husband's life. And doing it even though fear said no. Don't do it. Quit. It's too much. But she did it anyway and look how it changed from tearful and mad to deep gratitude and a warm glow. Ah, precious confidence how I love when you arrive and change lives.

It may be fear of joining a new class, it may be fear of failing at a diet, or it may be fear of showing your true self. But it is one of the things that connect us all. We all in some way struggle with fear. Unacknowledged fear can leave you hidden behind a mask. It can keep you stuck in your comfort zone. It can keep you from living the life you were intended to live. But the good news is we do not have to listen to the voice of fear. Acknowledge it, yes. Follow it, no. But to do so takes courage. So get ready. It is time to battle for the truth. Truth says you can do anything you set out to do. Truth says you will overcome.

★★★

Encourage: To inspire with hope, courage, or confidence; hearten.

I talked about courage last week. I believe that there is a battle to be fought if we are going to reach our weight loss and fitness goals. We have to battle against a long list of false beliefs that conspire to keep us stuck. Beliefs such as:

I've always had a weight problem so I always will.

I can't lose weight because of my age.

My genetics dictate my life and my health.

I don't like salads. I don't like vegetables.

If I eat healthy, I will constantly feel deprived.

I'll have to starve myself to lose weight.

I've failed at weight loss every time, so I'll fail again.

I don't have time to do strength training and cardio every week.

The truth is we are all completely capable of being at our healthy body weight and almost everyone can reach that goal or at least be well on their way by the end of the year.

What? What just went through your mind? All the doubt? The objections? Is it possible for you to believe that? Why is that so hard to believe when it is absolutely the truth?

I think we've established that the issue isn't knowing what to do. We know what to do, we just don't do it. Why not? What's missing? As I was thinking about that this week I got to thinking about the word *courage* and I realized that it was also found in the word *encourage*.

To have the courage to fight for what you want out of life takes confidence and a belief that it can be done. So where do we get courage if we need it? How does one become encouraged?

For me it started to come when I started to be more authentic, taking risks and sharing my true self with others. I had no courage at all when my life was lived hidden behind a mask. My mask was that of a strong woman, independent, a survivor. But because it was outer and not from within, I lacked the confidence to pull it off when it mattered. That strength never showed up when I had to make extraordinary choices. Therefore I was overweight, addicted, unhappy at work, unhappy in my relationships.

Then I had some life changing experiences. One of the most radical for me was my experience in grief support where, despite all their own pain, every person in the group was able to encourage me and let me know that I, indeed, was supposed to be there. They didn't judge me or criticize me like I expected, but they really just accepted me right where I was and allowed me to express myself. It was such a gift and it changed me. I stopped hiding as much and became more willing to talk to others about my real life, not just my mask.

For me, that was the start of true confidence. All the other mechanisms I had in place before that showed outer confidence. Yes, I could lead a project. Yes, I could get a degree. But they were covering up an inside filled with pain and unbelief. It wasn't until I risked opening up and letting someone, even strangers in a support group, know who I really was and what I was really experiencing did I start building a true confidence from the inside out.

I began to ask for and seek more opportunities to share my experience, and as I did, I received more and more encouragement in my walk. My encouragers came in many forms; a personal trainer, a coach, authors, friends, family, a pastor, speakers, and musicians. They all met me right where I was and were able to help me understand that I could heal and change my life. Having people know the real me, the authentic me, and accepting me as is gave me the strength to start fighting for what I wanted in life, and it gave me the belief that it can be done.

If you don't believe that you can reach your goals and live the life you have always dreamed of, I want you to know you have encouragers. I want you to know it is OK to try again. I want you to know that you can do this. I want you to know that weight does not have to be your issue for the rest of your life. You can be free. But you have to take the steps. You have to walk it out. I believe that you can do it, and I believe that you will change your life for the better in the process by overcoming your fears, eradicating your doubts and living the life you were meant to live. I'm cheering for authentic you all the way!

> I will not die an unlived life
> I will not live in fear
> Of falling or catching fire.
> I choose to inhabit my days,
> To allow my living to open me
> To make me less afraid,
> More accessible
> To loosen my heart
> Until it becomes a wing,
> A torch, a promise.
> I choose to risk my significance;
> To live
> So that which came to me as seed
> Goes to the next as blossom
> And that which came
> to me as blossom,
> Goes on as fruit
> —Dawna Markova

★★★

I've been talking a lot about the reasons we get stuck in old wounds and old patterns of behavior. It is important to understand what is underneath compulsive eating or lack of exercise in order to start healing and changing. If you know what to do but just aren't doing it, your inner world is in need of attention. But once you've started to deal with these things—things like putting everyone before yourself or struggling to say no to things that don't support your health—it's time to put the rubber to the road. It's time to get moving.

None of this hard internal work does any good unless you start making different choices.

We all know what it is like to be stuck. It feels heavy, hopeless, and frustrating. We've learned that when we work up the courage to step out of that comfort zone, we can get hit by a wave of fears and lies. Those fears and lies can really pack a punch. I will be deprived. Life will never be as fun. I won't be able to enjoy food. I'll have to be obsessed with exercise. I'll fail. These lies are deadly and they push us right back into our comfort zone where we stay stuck (heavy, hopeless, frustrating).

Once we are aware of the change process, we can courageously step out of the comfort zone again. This time, however, we are dressed as warriors for battle. We know we'll get hit with the wave of fear, but we wield our sword and shield and we fight; one choice at a time. So, when someone upsets us and we feel like eating, we go for a walk instead. When someone orders pizza, we make a salad. When we're tired or busy, we make time to exercise anyway. The battle is fought and won in the small choices, day after day. Peace and freedom is what awaits us all, and it is well worth the fight.

One of the best choices you can make for yourself is walking.

You can create a calorie deficit by decreasing the amount of food you eat. You might lose weight temporarily when you do that, but you will not fire up your metabolism. If anything, restricting calories may slow it down. My recommendation to anyone that wants to lose weight is to walk because it not only burns fat directly, but it fires up your fat burning processes. I like to picture my metabolism as a row of light switches. Some of them are on/off switches and some of them are dimmers. I know that certain choices turn on or turn up certain switches. I know that besides making me toned and strong, strength training fires up my resting metabolism and muscle building (anabolism). I know that high intensity intervals fire up all kinds of fuel burning including the afterburn (EPOC). But guess what fires up the fat burning switches? Walking does. The reason walking does this better than anything else is because our heart rates tend to be in the perfect range for burning off fat and keeping it off.

There are two really difficult things about learning to walk for weight loss. One is learning to find the appropriate walking intensity (speed) that puts you into your perfect heart rate zone. Two is doing it consistently enough to see results.

If you know your heart rate zones, put on your monitor and get walking! This is something that you can do for the rest of your life that will help you get to and stay at your ideal body weight. If you don't know your target, now is the time to learn.

Look, we are all busy. I understand. But there is never going to come a time when we're not, so stop thinking about it, stop talking about it, stop beating yourself up about it, and just do it. This is your year. Close your eyes and take a deep breath. Now imagine that it is several months from now and you are down three sizes and feel so much better about yourself. Imagine yourself with more energy and more clarity. That is what awaits you if you start walking consistently. Do it on your own, do it with a friend, with a walking group, but do it. Yes, I am passionate about it. I know the potential it holds for you. I know the life changing self-esteem that came with conquering my weight issues. I want that for you if you're ready.

★★★

You ready for some tough love?

I'm going to ask something of you. I want you to stop holding onto all the unhealthy things that are keeping you stuck. I want you to lay them all down and instead, I want you to hold onto the truth. And I want you to hold onto it passionately.

What is the truth?

You have to exercise daily and make healthy eating a habit for life if you want to meet your weight loss goals. Ask anyone who has done it. They will tell you they stopped overeating sugar. They stopped overeating unhealthy fat. They cut back on wine. They cut back on salt. They will tell you that vegetables became very important. They will tell you about fruit. Black beans. Pecans. Almonds. Smoothies. Egg whites. Avocados. Chicken breast. Salads.

When you talk to these people, notice that they are smiling (big time!). They do not have a scowl on their face because they feel so deprived of their old "treats." Turns out, those treats were liars and killers. They were imposters acting like pleasure that really robbed us of our health and our self-esteem.

Yes, sugar, fat, and salt set off our brain's pleasure centers. That is why the line at McDonald's at lunchtime is always long. We like pleasure. But the momentary pleasure of cookies, crackers, chips, cake, bread, muffins, bagels, etc. is an imposter. It doesn't last. If you have ever had a self-esteem meltdown after a food binge, you know what I'm talking about.

A client of mine asked me last week if I still crave those old foods. Here's how it has worked for me. In 2000 after my one-year quit-smoking anniversary, I got fitted for a dress and was asked to pay extra since it was a plus size. Something about that day jolted me into reality. I was so sick of feeling bad and wishing I was different. The first thing I did was try to start running. I would huff and puff my way around the trail at Highbanks pushing as hard as I could. Nothing happened. I was confused, so I started reading about weight loss in the science journals. I learned about target heart rate zones and bought a heart rate monitor. Turns out, my heart rate was way too high for burning fat, so I switched to walking. As soon as I switched, I started to lose some weight. I lost the first twenty or so pounds in the first two years, but I was still 30 pounds overweight; I hadn't really dealt with my nutrition yet. I was still a dieter. I was still looking for the quick and easy way out of this, but a way that allowed my bowl of ice cream every night.

Then something clicked. I started taking real responsibility for my food intake. The reason I wasn't losing more weight was not because of some circumstance in my life. It wasn't stress, or my genes, or my job, or my boss, or my travel, or my family. The reason I wasn't losing weight was because I was still holding onto my pleasure foods as if my life depended on them. I believed that without them, my life would lack pleasure and would no longer be enjoyable. It reminded me of what it felt like to try to quit smoking—the thinking that I would never enjoy coffee, beer, vacation, and road trips again. That's addiction speaking. And it's lying! Every person who was hooked on heroin has thought the same thing. Every smoker who has thought about quitting has thought the same thing. And, if you are hooked on pleasure foods, it can be very scary to picture life without.

But let me ask you this. Have they delivered? Have they delivered what they promise? Or are they lame substitutes for the real thing? I know the answer. Sugar does not deliver. Unhealthy food does not deliver. How many cookies did I eat and I never got to where I wanted to go. How many do you need to eat to see they aren't getting you what you really want? They don't work.

It took me some time to figure out what I like and what works for me. Now, I eat mostly fruits, vegetables, chicken, fish, black beans, egg whites, and salad with a few treats and cheats thrown in. I don't miss the old way of eating any more than a heroin addict misses being addicted to heroin. I'm free of it. I'm free! The promises those foods held weren't true. Feeling good and loving life, myself and my body came when I let them go and embraced the good stuff. There will never, ever be any food that feels as good as my weight loss. I know it's hard. There are things to overcome. I promise not to enable you and if you ask me, I'll tell you the truth even if it's hard to hear. Remember, I understand completely.

★★★

I like to use heroin.

Not like you think, although back in my dark, dark days of self-destruction I don't doubt that if someone had put it in front of me, I may have used.

What I mean is I like to use heroin as an example. I believe a lot of the things we say about the foods and behaviors we hang onto that keep us stuck are the same things a heroin user would say about her heroin.

"I could quit if I wanted to."
"But I like it."
"How would I handle stress?"
"I've tried to quit before and failed, why bother?"
"I'll just control the amount."
"I can't imagine life without it."

Heroin is made in several different ways but they all come back to a single base—morphine. Morphine comes from opium, the substance found inside the fruit of the opium poppy. So heroin is all natural, comes from a plant grown from the earth, and then extracted by some laboratory process to concentrate it. Once it is in that form, it lights up the pleasure centers of the brain in such a way that it is highly addictive.

Stay with me. I have a point.

What do all these substances have in common?

High-fructose corn syrup is produced by milling corn to produce corn starch, then processing that starch to yield corn syrup, which is almost entirely glucose, and then adding enzymes that change some of the glucose into fructose.

Gluten is extracted from flour by kneading the flour, agglomerating the gluten into dough, and then washing out the starch.

Vegetable oils first need to be removed from the oil-bearing plants, typically seeds or legumes. This can be done by mechanical or chemical extraction. The extracted oil can then be purified and, if required, refined or chemically altered.

Sugarcane is a tropical, perennial grass that forms lateral shoots at the base to produce multiple stems. Traditionally, sugarcane processing requires two stages. Mills extract raw sugar from freshly harvested cane, and sometimes bleach it to make "mill white" sugar for local consumption. Sugar refining further purifies the raw sugar.

Trans fats are created by the processed food industry as a side effect of partially hydrogenating unsaturated plant fats (generally vegetable oils). These partially hydrogenated fats are used in fast food, snack food, fried food, and baked goods industries to increase shelf life.

Now if you mixed these five ingredients together, you would have many of the products you find on the shelves at the grocery store. Bread, for example.

We're taking plants and finding the most potent chemical in that plant. We're concentrating it, putting it through a chemical process, then ingesting it frequently. When we feel tired. When we feel anxious. When we feel depressed. When we crave it. Remind you of anything?

All five of these chemicals light up the pleasure centers of the brain. Same place that heroin does. All of them have a kick, then a dopamine surge (feel good chemical), then a crash. If you ever wondered why you might actually be addicted to what you are eating, this is why.

Here's the good news. We have fruits, vegetables, fish and chicken, grains and nuts in their whole food natural form to give us all the energy and nutrition we will ever need.

I had lunch a few weeks ago with a friend of mine who I had not seen in a while. She was down 25 pounds and told me that she followed the 17 Day Diet. My conversation with her got me thinking. What do effective food plans have in common...so I looked. Turns out the Eat Clean Diet, the 17 Day Diet, South Beach, Forks Over Knives, Best Life, and all the other healthy-food-based diet plans have a nearly identical list of foods on their shopping list with the exception of whether meat and dairy are included.

— Fruits
— Vegetables
— Lean meat in small quantities
— Walnuts, almonds, pecans
— Beans and whole grains
— Low fat dairy and eggs in small quantities
— Green tea, water, coffee

That's it! It is truly as simple as that. And eating this way will not only finally get you to your goal weight (without obsessing over calories), but this is the only way to reverse diabetes and other chronic illnesses associated with a processed food diet of (1) high fructose corn syrup, (2) gluten, (3) oils, (4) sugar, and (5) trans fats.

We know what to do. But we're addicted.

So what do you have to do to get clean? You have to give processed foods up and realize there is a better way. As a former addict, I can honestly say there is nothing better than getting free from it. I hated being addicted to cigarettes. It controlled me, it stole from me, and it made me feel bad about myself. If that's your experience with food and your weight, maybe it's time to get clean. Stop messing around with high quantities of addictive substances. Watch your ingredients —I like the rule of thumb: if there are more than five ingredients or if you can't pronounce them, stay away!

Look, our old way didn't work. Eating over-processed diet foods that get the calories low so that we can still have cookies, cheesecake, muffins, and chips doesn't work. These are Frankenstein foods that don't deliver. They aren't satisfying and don't lead to weight loss. If diet foods worked, wouldn't we all be there already?

If you get defensive about your pleasure foods and can't imagine what life would be like without them, I want you to consider the possibility that you are an addict. Quit now while you are still healthy. Eat your salads and veggie stir frys and egg white omelets even if you don't love them. Not every nutrition experience needs to be a level 10 experience; sometimes you are just eating for fuel. But if you get off this stuff and start eating whole foods, something wonderful happens. You start feeling amazing. You have sustained energy all day long and don't need the kick anymore. No more rides on the sugar roller coaster. Hop off, my friends. Peace and freedom await you.

★★★

Last week I talked about how we can become addicted to what we eat. I hesitate to call this stuff food, because it's more like concentrated parts of food, not whole foods. Sugar, flour, oil, trans fats, gluten, corn syrup, processed meat.

What do you do if you are addicted and stuck? The only thing to do is get clean and sober. Why is this so tough to do?

I believe we live in our comfort zones most of the time. We eat foods we know that we like and are quick and easy. We skip exercise to watch TV or spend time on the computer. But after some time stuck in that old comfort zone, we feel ready to change. Maybe because we've received results back from a medical test that scared us. Maybe we hit a number on the scale that we never thought we'd see. Maybe we are just beyond sick of feeling bad about ourselves. Whatever the case, we build up the courage to step out of that comfort zone and make a change.

Anytime we do that, we are automatically hit with a bunch of false beliefs. I'll fail if I try to make this change. It's too hard. I can't live without whatever it is I'm trying to quit (crap food). I'll be deprived. I'll be too uncomfortable. I won't have any way of dealing with stress. My family won't support this. It won't be fun to go out anymore. It's too expensive. Why bother? I wasn't *that* miserable. I can live with the extra weight. I can live with the bad test result. Anything is better than being hit with all the lies and fear that's coming at me right now.

So, we bolt right back to the comfort zone. Stuck. But safe from the attack for now.

It may take a while, but the desire to be our best selves always comes back up to the surface at some point, and we work up the courage to try again. We step out, make a change, and get hit with the same wave of fears and lies! What the heck! So we run back to Stuck. It's a terrible cycle.

For me, the breakthroughs started to come when I understood that the waves of fears and lies were coming no matter what. But they were lies. I didn't have to listen. So I braced myself and prepared for them. I armed myself with the truth. The truth was that none of these things ever made me happy or got me what I wanted. I never felt good about myself even when I was eating cheesecake or smoking a cigarette. They were escapes from uncomfortable feelings I couldn't deal with. The truth was I was starting to have health problems. The truth was these substances had me in a prison. They were not my friends even though they appeared to offer comfort. They offered only moments of escape in exchange for my life. The truth was I was stronger than I realized.

My last attempt to quit smoking after 17 years was in 1999. I decided for the hundredth time that I was going to quit. I had tried before and failed so miserably that I swore off quitting. It was just too hard to fail like that over and over. But I had never tried quitting in a group, so I went. I got plugged in. And what I learned is there is power in sharing your story. There is power in sharing your fears and hearing others'. I saw myself reflected in other people's words. I saw the fear on their faces, and knew I was seeing my own fears. And they lost their power.

There is an old saying that you can't get sober in a bar. I have this vision of each of us sitting at a bar ordering a drink while begging the bartender to tell us how to get clean and sober.

If you want to get healthy, you have to eat healthy. Throw out the junk. Stop buying it. If you want to feel better, you have to stop eating so much processed food. You can't stock your kitchen with crap food then hop on Spark People or Weight Watchers and hope to control the amount. Addiction management is just as much of a prison as addiction. Get free.

The way to get clean is to change. And the way to change is to identify all your fears and false beliefs. Know beyond a shadow of a doubt that they are going to come at you when you try to change. But you will not be shoved back to Stuck because you will be armed with the truth. And you will not bolt back to comfort because you will get plugged into the people and the power that will give you the strength to change. And when you do, you get to move forward to freedom. Freedom from scary test results. Freedom from living at a weight you can't stand. Freedom from feeling bad about yourself and never truly letting your light shine.

It is your time. Freedom and confidence are the rewards of this work. It may be tough to experience the attack that comes at you when you decide to do it, but it is worth the fight. Arm yourself for battle and don't ever give up.

★★★

Have you been searching for THE diet?

There are a lot out there to choose from. Here's a quick search from Amazon:

Adkins Diet

South Beach Diet

Best Life Diet

Ultra Metabolism Diet

The Biggest Loser Diet

Eat Right 4 Your Type

Sonoma Diet

Body For Life Diet

Eat This Not That

The Paleo Solution

You On A Diet

The 4 Hour Body

The Kind Diet

The China Study

Ultimate Weight Loss Solution

Protein Power

Wheat Belly

The 17 Day Diet

Crazy Sexy Diet

The Zone

The Thin Commandments

The Glycemic Index Diet

The Raw Food Detox Diet

Volumetrics

The G.I. Diet

Fat Smash Diet

Flat Belly Diet

French Women Diet

I'm willing to bet that most of us have a few of these books in our collection. I know I do. I was one of those dieters that would get so excited each time a new diet best-seller swept the nation. I would think, "Finally. This is it!"

But it never, ever was it.

Back in the mid-90s before I quit smoking or lost any weight, I was having pretty bad lower back pain. I went to the doctor and was told I had a kidney stone that was stuck somewhere en route. My family doctor sent me to a urologist who scheduled me for a lithotripsy, the procedure where they use a sonic blast to break up the stone so it will pass. I was scheduled for Tuesday of the following week and was told if I happen to pass the stone, to save it for analysis.

I was married and lived in Virginia Beach at the time, and we went to Busch Gardens that weekend. Minutes after riding the Loch Ness Monster roller coaster, I felt a sharp pain and headed off to the public restroom at the park. After a few very uncomfortable minutes, I passed a pretty big kidney stone and then passed about 45 smaller ones after it. This process took about a half hour. Every so often my husband would holler in, "You OK?" Yep, be out soon.

Remembering what the urologist told me, I held my breath and plunged my hand into the water and retrieved all the stones, wrapped them in a piece of toilet paper and put them in my pocket. When I finally came out of the bathroom, all I said was, "We gotta go."

Bear with me, there is a point to my story! (Besides making you all say ewww when you imagined reaching your hand into the public toilet).

I followed up with the urologist and told him the story, then handed him my Ziploc bag full of stones. It's kind of fun when you can shock a doctor like that. I saved a lot of money by riding a roller coaster instead of getting a lithotripsy, he told me, and he sent me on my way.

About two years later, another stone got stuck. I passed this one more quickly, before there was time for a bunch of others to line up behind it. But this time the doctor said, "I wonder why you are getting all these stones?" I was referred to a nephrologist (kidney specialist), and thankfully, he diagnosed me with the kidney disorder that was turning my kidney tissue to stone. In the time between the Busch Gardens incident and this diagnosis, however, I had lost significant kidney function; well over 50%.

Fast forward to 2001. I finally quit smoking and I'm starting on my weight loss and fitness journey. What should I do? Adkins? South Beach? What is the answer? I know it's out there. Often weight loss diets stress protein and limit carbohydrates. I read over and over that you need lots of protein to build muscle. But I was now a kidney patient and supposed to limit protein. That's like blasphemy in the fitness world. Limit protein? Bite your tongue.

I really struggled. I believed carbs were bad. I didn't believe in plant protein. I thought the more chicken, the better. Then I learned a really important lesson that I wish everyone knew. There is no "one diet" out there because we're all different. What works is finding your personal formula that honors not only weight loss, but your overall health and well-being.

For me, that means a lot more plants and a lot less animal protein. It means being very aware of recommendations for kidney patients and how those foods sometimes conflict with the basic lower carb, higher protein fitness diets. A good example is avocado. I love avocado, especially on my salad. Protein and healthy fats, right? But avocado is one of the highest potassium foods out there, which means I have to restrict it. Same with bananas and tomatoes. But guess what kidney patients can have in unlimited amounts? Rice and pasta! It's hard to build a good fitness diet on rice and pasta but I'm doing it.

My kidney function has been stable now for 14 years, and even though I don't get the nutrition right every day, I get better and better. Progress over perfection.

Would my personal formula be right for anyone else? No, it wouldn't. It takes into account my fitness goals, my health issues, my customs and traditions, and my likes and dislikes. I can tell you things I've found that have helped me along the way, but it is still your responsibility to find your personal formula.

So, *Forks Over Knives* may seem extreme in its plant-strong recommendations, unless you have a diagnosis of heart disease. Then this information may be extremely important for you to design a nutrition approach that helps your body heal and recover from the damage done to your blood vessels.

A mostly raw food diet may seem impossible unless you were just diagnosed with cancer and want to fight with every weapon available. Then this type of food plan may be part of your holistic plan to get well.

The lean animal protein, low carb diet may be perfect for you to lose weight and conquer diabetes. But it's not right for us kidney patients. And it's not right for distance runners and endurance athletes.

You must find what is right for you. It's not out there. It's in you. It is in your creativity and your expression. It is in your ability to look at several variables and factors and come up with an approach. That approach may ebb and flow with trial and error. It will evolve over time. You will learn new things and discover new foods. But they will be yours, not someone else's. You will take those recipes you find and make them fit your formula. You will substitute ingredients so that each meal honors your health goals and helps heal your body.

When you do this—when you take radical responsibility for

your health and wellness—something wonderful happens. You stop hoping and searching for that *one thing* to come along. That old fear that you are missing it vanishes. You are filled with peace knowing that it is right here, present, in this moment. And the miracle is it was here all along, just waiting for you to discover it.

★★★

Sometimes getting moving can be the toughest part.

The alarm rang at 7:00 this morning—a Sunday morning.

"Oh, how I would love to sleep in right now! Then, get up and relax, drink coffee, and read and ease into the day. It feels like I just lay down but I am committed to walking today, so I have to get up."

"Maybe it's raining. No, it's not. Get up."

Finally the coffee kicks in, I have breakfast, find my workout clothes, and get ready to go. Make my recovery drink (coffee, vanilla almond milk, ice). Fill my water. Find my heart rate monitor. Out the door.

It's nice because there is no traffic on Sunday morning so it doesn't take long to get to Highbanks. It's quite muggy when I arrive, and some of the members of our walking group are there ready to go. It's on! I step out onto the trail, and we're on our way.

Something about the humidity makes this walk a tough one. The sweat and the breathing tell me we're working hard. We climb and climb until we reach the first stop on the observation deck where we rest, drink water, and check out a very large, majestic bald eagle.

After our short break, it's tough to get moving again. Even that small stop makes it difficult, and as we head back, it's uphill. But we carry on.

After an hour and eight minutes, we finish. Drenched in a kind of sweat I can only describe as cleansing, we check out our heart rate monitors to find that almost 600 calories were burned and time in zone was excellent.

I grab my recovery drink and head home to get ready for church. And as I drive home, I think about the fact that I have the freedom to choose to do almost anything with my Sunday morning. I could relax, drink my coffee, and read. I could sleep in. And I could come to Highbanks and sweat.

I take a deep breath in and smile because today, I made the extraordinary choice; the one that makes me feel the best about me. I get to say to myself, "I did it, way to go!" and I get to carry that with me all day. After a lifetime of failures and not feeling good about myself, this is the best thing ever. I've slept in before. And I've sat and relaxed and read before. They are both great but not at the expense of the walk. Never at the expense of the walk.

My transformation really started when I realized that walks = self-esteem for me. And although sleeping in and relaxing are great, they aren't as crucial to my self-esteem as exercise. So I made a promise, a commitment that I would walk as long as I am able. In those moments when I don't feel like it and would rather not, I reach for that promise and let it empower my extraordinary choice. It is a matter of taking care of myself, of showing love and respect for myself. If you are stuck, you can't wait until you feel like doing it. It is doing it that holds the magic. It is doing it that changes us and heals us. When you decide that you are not going to let anything come between you and your exercise, you will change.

★★★

I have had some pretty intense experiences out on the trails.

Picture me walking or running the loop at Sharon Woods. It's a gorgeous day, and I made the extraordinary choice to get outside and take care of myself. My music is going. The trees are reaching towards the heavens. The sky is alive with light. Then the music and my breath hit me a certain way, and next thing I know, I am stopped, bent forward hands on knees, crying from deep in my core.

This has happened a hundred times in the last ten years. People pass me by and look the other way. Or sometimes they ask if I am OK. "Yes", I say smiling through tears, "I am OK."

What healing! To connect with that authentic feeling and express it is such an amazing thing. For each of you who have cried during your workout at the studio, you know what I mean. It is common and it is wonderful.

I believe what is happening is we are, just for a moment, fully present. No escapes, no distractions. Something about holding a yoga pose or lifting a weight or walking the trail does this. Becoming aware of the breath does this.

We all need healing. We don't know how to grieve well in this culture, and so we walk through life wounded and sad, keeping it all to ourselves. We may need to grieve the loss of a relationship, the death of a loved one, or a child leaving home and headed to life on his or her own. We may need to grieve the loss of our youth or our health or a dream.

What we can't do is escape to TV and hope to get through it. We can't lose ourselves online and wait for it to go away. The only way out is through. Grief is a river that flows whether you want it to or not. Pretending it is not there doesn't make the water any less powerful.

I was very bad at grieving. I held it all in and pretended I was fine. Then I discovered fitness and began to inhabit my body more authentically. Turns out that my body is more than flesh and when I connected with physical movement, emotion came forth as well. I moved; my heart moved. I moved; my soul moved. I ran; I cried. And I began to heal.

Sometimes exercise can seem like just another thing on a very overwhelming to-do list. It can seem impossible to find the time and motivation to do it. But I believe if you truly knew its healing power, you would think differently. Instead of feeling the need to push yourself to do it, you would feel it pull you at the soul to move: to breathe, to cry, to celebrate, to grieve and to fully inhabit your body in the present moment.

I am passionate about fitness because it helped me change my life in a radical way. It helped me transform from a person who was scared all the time and stuck in her grief, to someone who is willing to inhabit the present moment without need to escape or withdraw. The role of exercise was to allow me to feel what was really in there. You can't heal it until you feel it. I found that in the busy daily life

I had created I was never connected enough to my breath and my body to even feel what was in there.

If you feel stuck in your weight loss or your fitness or your life, carve out some time and create a practice of becoming present. Walk, pray, stretch, meditate, write, sing. Become aware of your escapes. Food is a big one. It is easy to get lost in the pleasure of food and wine and never have to go beneath the surface. But if you do that every time something comes up, you will stay stuck. They key to moving forward is to allow the river to flow. Give yourself the gift of authentic connection with your soul. Put your hands on your knees and cry to the woods if you want to. Peace and joy await you.

★★★

Cravings are a glimpse into our hearts.

I believe that our bodies are perfectly programmed to eat the right amount of food for a healthy life. But something is overriding our programming.

Healthy programming looks something like this: Eat, burn, rest, eat, burn, rest while one's body weight remains very stable. But it has become this for many of us: Eat, gain weight, diet, lose weight, eat, gain weight, diet, lose weight. It is broken.

Changing our eating behavior (dieting) without changing the underlying thought processes will not work long-term. It can't. The underlying thoughts will eventually resurface and bring us back into the cycle of eat, gain weight, diet, lose weight, eat, gain weight, diet, lose weight. There is a way to stop the cycle and return to your body's healthy programming.

It takes practice.

Last week I talked about the importance of being present and the freedom I have experienced by becoming present with some authentic feelings during exercise. A daily practice of yoga can bring you to present. A daily practice of walking can bring you to present. Or prayer, meditation, singing, chanting, or humming.

Here is a letter I received this week from someone asking for help; it is a great illustration of how we can get stuck:

"This is a situation that arises for me frequently: I eat a healthful, light meal and I know that I'm '"done." Lean protein, vegetables. But, still, I have a strong urge to keep eating.

This is what I can think of to do:

~ Get myself exercising or otherwise out of there ASAP
~ Clean, sort papers, do dishes, laundry, etc., to distract myself for 20 minutes and maybe I will feel full and be engaged in another activity
~ Try to talk myself out of it by saying that I am not a person who has to eat more just because that is what I've always done
~ Drink a whole glass of tomato juice with a bit of sparkling water in it for fizz before eating anything else
~ Imagine how great it would be to get all the pressure off my joints while aging and how that will allow me to live more actively longer
~ Have a low-glycemic fruit and non-fat Greek yogurt if nothing above worked.

OK, that's it, I'm out. Do you have other things I could add to the list or comments on these strategies?"

Can't we all relate to that? An attempt to manage cravings is common. I had a list of my own similar to this for quitting smoking. But this kind of list ignores the possibility of healing the cravings completely instead of living with a constant need to manage them.

Here is my response:

I believe to busy or otherwise distract yourself is what will keep you stuck. Once you are "done" but still craving food, sit. Turn everything off. No phone, no TV, no computer. Get present. Now feel.

What do you feel? You might say to yourself or out loud I am craving. I feel empty. I feel anxious. I feel restless. I am bored. I am lonely. I am unfulfilled. Find it. Get real—remember radical responsibility. Whatever you feel is the truth. There is no wrong answer.

Once you find it (which might take practice), then choose.

If you feel empty, yes you can continue to eat and temporarily fill. Or you can sit with being empty and learn that you do have the strength to sit with it after all, and it passes. Radical responsibility—you get to choose what to do with that feeling that right now in this moment.

If you feel bored, yes, you can stay busy or you can sit with bored and realize that you have the patience to sit with it after all, and it passes. Radical responsibility—you choose.

The lie is that you have to do anything. Just sit with it. Pray, meditate, sing, chant, hum. Ask for healing. "God, I ask for divine help and strength to be with this feeling. Send your miraculous grace and peace. Please make me whole. Amen."

And her beautiful response:

"This brings tears to my eyes as hearing the truth often does. What you have explained here just feels so much more real, and like the truth than my list (which I was not hopeful about). I think I knew that my list wouldn't work (hasn't ever worked yet), but I just didn't know what to do. Thanks for knowing this. Thanks for sharing this. I'm going to try this even though in the recesses of my mind I can feel the beginning of the scheming about all the reasons I can't do it; I know that scheming and denial is false belief, as you would say. I am kind of excited, and really scared about it. Who would think that deep feelings could be that scary and powerful?"

Is another diet really what any of us need to move beyond the broken cycle of weight gain and loss? Isn't it possible there is something very powerful waiting to be discovered if we are willing to sit with it? I often have women ask me how I lost weight. I'm sure it's not the answer they expect, but I finally developed a practice of looking within (often while walking), even when it felt uncomfortable, and allowed the stuff that had been in there all along to come to the light, where it loses its power. It is there you get to make extraordinary choices and you are empowered to create the life you've always dreamed of.

★★★

You can't cross the sea merely by standing and staring at the water.
—Rabindranath Tagore

Who are you in your journey to fitness?

I used to think that when I finally got focused and disciplined on my diet and workouts, I would get thinner and happier. I thought with each pound down, I would automatically jump one notch up on the happiness scale at a 1:1 ratio. But that's not how things work. Fitness and health is an outcome, not the actual path. The changes that must take place happen on the inside.

For example, when I learned how to deal with my feelings in a real way, I no longer used food to escape and numb myself.

When I stopped making excuses and took radical responsibility, exercise and activity became consistent things in my life without having to force myself to do them.

When my need for approval was healed, and I felt worthy without so much striving for perfection, I suddenly had much more time to devote to health and fitness and the life I wanted. I started cooking, and I got organized once I slowed down.

When I started to believe that I could make changes in my life, change came much more easily.

One common scenario looks like this. A woman decides to get really focused and lose weight. She joins weight watchers and gets a food journal out. She throws away every carbohydrate in her pantry. She joins a gym or signs up for personal training and starts working out. Then she forces herself to restrict her food. She forces herself to eat food she doesn't like. She forces herself to be hungry. She forces herself to work out. After she loses several pounds, the part of her that is still heartbroken and afraid starts screaming something like, "Hey! You are taking away my only comfort and safety in this world. Why are you doing this to me?" And soon she's on an all-out binge, thinking, I'll eat what I want, when I want, and no one is going to deprive me ever again."

Forcing ourselves to change on the outside while these waters still rage on the inside is impossible. If you have been trying to make a change in your life and something in you won't let you, I suggest you stop and listen to what this voice within is trying to tell you. It's not that you are failing at focus and self-discipline. It's that something in your heart needs tended to.

I struggled with this especially when it came to smoking. Smoking was a big thing for me. It wasn't just a nicotine addiction, so all the nicotine replacement therapy in the world wouldn't help me quit. In my heart, I was a smoker. To me, that meant I was a rebel, a strongly independent freedom fighter with every right to smoke if I wanted to. My identity was attached to it. How could I quit smoking? Who would I be then? How would I know who I was?

I have had this conversation about weight loss with dozens of women. What would I be without my struggle with weight? It has identified me my whole life. It has been my purpose my whole life.

We need to remember who we really are. We are not our addictions. We are not our struggles with weight. Remember, we may have a broken story but we are not our broken story. When our hearts need tended to, let's tend to them. A miracle awaits you if you are brave and do the internal work. The miracle is this: much of the struggle and the battle falls away once the heart truly believes in its comfort and safety. The need to search outside of ourselves (in food, substances, other people) for these things is healed and without finally finding laser focus and radical self-discipline, we begin to get fit and healthy from that wonderful place of peace.

★★★

Outcomes are so different depending upon intention.

When I was going to Youngstown State doing my undergraduate work, I took a lot of classes. Some I liked; some I didn't. I went to class (sometimes), I studied and I took exams. But I didn't really apply anything I learned to my life. Organic chemistry has limited application to a 19-year-old living at home and working at Fast Check. I liked learning it, but there was really nothing to do with the information. My whole goal was to graduate. My intention was focused on passing class and getting my degree.

Years later, I got the opportunity to go back to school

for a graduate degree. I was working as a quality manager at a manufacturing facility at the time, and it seemed that every class I took had an immediate application at my job. I went to class, I studied and I took exams, but I also got excited about the material and put my new knowledge to use as soon as I could. Being able to use what I was learning made me hungry for more. I really enjoyed school the second time around when my intention was to learn as much as I could and apply it to my job immediately.

Fitness can be like this.

Without intention, we can be undergrads who just want to get through each class so we can get back to our friends and start partying. We might not miss a single class and we might get good grades, but we don't really connect what we are learning to our life. There is no intention to apply any of the knowledge until after graduation.

With intention, we can be grad students of fitness. We can approach each class, workout, walk, or personal training session as an opportunity to learn something new about ourselves, about exercise, or even about humanity. We can approach the material with excitement, knowing it has the power to change lives. Then we can take what we got from that workout and apply it to our lives right away.

This is the difference between getting some exercise in and changing your life.

There is nothing wrong with getting some exercise in. But if you are miserable, frustrated, scared, desperate, stuck, hopeless, and feel like you're never going to conquer this thing, then exercise isn't enough. That workout also has to function as the catalyst that shakes things up in your life. That workout has to stay with you, and the spirit of it must be brought home to the kitchen, the pantry, and your walking shoes. The knowledge must be applied.

Maybe on a particular day, your workout is just a workout. That's cool.

But maybe it is just what you need to light the fire of motivation in your gut and take radical responsibility, do the work, and finally feel good about yourself.

Maybe it is your trail marker on a long and winding path, and although at times you may feel lost, you know that you have that trail marker each week, and it inspires you to make extraordinary choices all week long to honor your best life.

Maybe it is time with a community of women who know and understand the struggle and are with you every step of the way, and you bring their love with you when you head to the grocery store this week.

Maybe it's not just a workout. Maybe it's there to teach, inspire, and motivate you. Maybe the real intention is to get you to believe that you are worth taking care of, and you can do anything you set your mind to. Anything!

★★★

What is your favorite comfort food? I'd have to say mine is ice cream. When I eat it, I feel good! For some people it's all about sugar; for others, it's a carb-fest like macaroni and cheese, a home-style dish like meatloaf, or bread.

There's nothing wrong with having a few favorite comfort foods. But what happens when you can't get through a day without them? What happens when the stress or discontent is so bad at work that the only way to cope is with comfort food? What happens when the stress, loneliness, or the lack of peace is so bad at home that the only way to cope is with comfort food?

It is usually not the desire for something that causes imbalance, it is the over desire. When food has too much meaning and value, it can cause a real problem. The outcome is being overweight, which, in turn, can cause many health problems, which we all know.

The other thing that being overweight can cause is discomfort. I remember being so uncomfortable in certain clothes, in most clothes, actually. I remember being uncomfortable having my picture taken. I remember being uncomfortable if I wasn't covered up. Swimsuits were very uncomfortable. I remember feeling like I was being squeezed when I sat and found it difficult to take a deep breath. Going up stairs was hard, and running felt like I was jiggling from head to toe.

So if comfort food leads to all this discomfort, why do we hold onto it so tightly?

If it's all we know, there's no way we can let go. There is no way to get through a stressful day at work with an awful boss without some form of stress relief. That is true. But what's the lie?

The lie is that the only stress relief available is food. Or that any other stress relief is too difficult, takes too long, or is ineffective.

I believe the key to taking the power away from your comfort foods is to have a variety of strategies that work to sooth what you expect sugar, bread, or macaroni and cheese to sooth, whether it is exhaustion, anger, loneliness, boredom, or any other experience you are having. Here's how.

First, own your experience and become intentional. If you are having a bad day, name it. I am stressed out. I am angry. I am sick of doing everything for everyone and want my reward for it now. Whatever you are experiencing, name it and own it. Radical responsibility.

Second, state your belief. I want food right now because I believe it will sooth this discomfort. I don't believe anything else will work.

Third, recognize this as a false belief. State the truth. The truth is there are a hundred ways to sooth stress or to comfort myself at this moment, many of them being much more loving than feeding myself some junk. The truth is food is a quick fix with some pretty major consequences. The truth is I am sick of feeling so uncomfortable in my own body.

Fourth, recognize you have choices. Think about what the healthy people that you know and love do to relieve stress, loneliness, and anger. They work out, drink tea, walk, knit, do yoga, make ceramics, create art, write, sing, dance, hug, talk, play music, read something inspiring, pray, hang out with a pet, hang out with a friend, tell their story, ask for help, vent on Facebook, take four deep breaths, stretch, play Words with Friends...there are hundreds of choices. It is a big lie that food is the only option. It is not. It is just a common drug of choice.

Fifth, access your higher self, invite the spirit, and make a loving choice. Your wounded, pissed off self is not a good choice-maker. She has a very difficult time seeing the big picture and the consequences of her choices. She just wants comfort now. But your choices do not have to be made by your wounded, pissed off self. There is a part of you that is able to rise above and make a better choice; a choice based in love, not fear. A choice that not only soothes now, but contributes to your self-esteem and feeling comfortable in your body down the road. A choice that's good for you.

The more you practice, the easier it gets. The way I look at it, food is always an option if I need comforted, but I have lots and lots of other options as well. And when I keep up my daily spiritual practices that keep me from spiraling into that wounded, pissed off woman that only wants to eat and smoke, I tend to choose other things most of the time. Trust me, it feels so much better to choose an exercise class over a pint of ice cream. It really does.

If you feel stuck in this cycle, I want you to know there is hope. You are not destined to be stuck in it forever. There is a way out and it starts by taking radical responsibility. Name it! Then state your belief and really look at it. Is it true? What is the truth? Look at your choices. What do you need to do to make a better choice? How can you access the part of you that chooses for your long-term good? Do you invite the spirit to help? When you are faithful to this process, self-confidence starts to grow. As your belief in the process grows, good choices become much easier. And soon, comfort food doesn't have any power at all.

★★★

Getting in shape and losing weight are all about food and exercise, right?

It is true you have to make extraordinary choices when it comes to food and exercise to get in shape and lose weight. But food and exercise aren't the whole picture. Food and exercise are an indication of what your deepest beliefs are. Your behavior reveals your beliefs.

Why do beliefs matter? Beliefs matter because when we are

making choices based on a set of false beliefs, we are going to get lost or stuck. It just isn't possible to navigate and progress when you're being guided by a set of lies.

What are the big lies that keep women stuck?

I don't have time to prepare healthy food.

The truth is whatever you are in the habit of doing is what takes the shortest amount of time. My healthy foods are just as easy to prepare as my old, unhealthy foods were. It was making the switch that was difficult. I had to get in the habit of buying all new foods at the grocery store. I had to get in the habit of chopping veggies and preparing things ahead of time, so they are ready for the week. I had to get in the habit of reaching for these things instead of reaching for old standbys that I relied on before as my quick-and-easy don't-need-to-think-about meals.

I don't have time to exercise.

That is never true. The truth is I have not prioritized exercise in my weekly schedule. Often, that is due to a lack of belief that it will do any good, so why bother? The people I know who exercise consistently do so because they believe in it as a way to weight loss or maintenance, better health, and greater self-esteem. It is very difficult to devote the time and energy to exercise when you really don't believe in its benefits.

I can't make good choices when I'm stressed.

I disagree. I believe that we can all continue to make healthy, life-affirming choices even when we are challenged by our circumstances. The lie is that everything must be calm to make progress in this area. The truth is that anyone at any time can decide to make this a priority and begin making different choices. The truth is that choosing healthy food and consistent exercise can help get your through difficult circumstances or stressful times in your life.

There is a quick-and-easy way, and I'm going to find it.

This is the biggest lie of all. There is no quick, easy way. I do believe anyone can lose weight. Anyone can switch into deprivation mode and drop several sizes. But only about 5% of people who lose weight keep it off. 5%! What do you need to do to be part of the 5% who keep it off instead of the 95% who gain it all back plus some?

You need to change. The thinking, the beliefs that got you to the overweight, unhealthy place have to be tackled from the inside out. Fear of disapproval has to be calmed, so you can take time away from your family or job and go exercise. People pleasing has to be conquered, so you begin treating yourself like you matter (because you do.) Compulsive eating has to be healed, or you will continue to turn to food for comfort as soon as life gets stressful.

It took me many years, but when I started doing the hard, internal work I realized that my beliefs were keeping me stuck. I believed that I got a raw deal in life. My parents were dead by the time I was 23, and I made a series of bad choices in response to that. These choices left me feeling even more worthless, and I got to the point at which I just didn't care anymore. My heart was hard and I just didn't care. I was going to seek out pleasure in every way I could, including eating anything I wanted, and ride out my remaining crappy years until the whole miserable thing was over.

Then a miracle happened. I learned the truth. What had happened in my past did not have to dictate the rest of my life. My past choices did not have to dictate my future choices. I was free to start over, no matter how lost I had gotten. I was free to adopt a new set of beliefs, so I did.

Now I believe that anyone can start again at any time. I believe that you can start over as many times as you need to. I believe that radical grace is there for when you struggle or get lost. I believe it is available in infinite supply. And I believe we each are unique and beautiful and are here on this earth for a purpose. I believe we all matter. Because we matter (a lot!), we need to learn to take care of ourselves and make extraordinary choices so that we are free to live out our unique purpose. I am quite certain that purpose was not to spend a lifetime wishing we were thinner.

Knowing Who You Are

When I was a kid, I liked almost everything made by Hostess; Ho Hos, Twinkies and cupcakes. When I was old enough to eat whatever and whenever I wanted, I ate a lot of this stuff. To me, having a car and a driver's license was more about being able to drive to Fast Check and get snacks and pop than almost anything else. I liked it, I wanted it, so I was going to get it. Ahh, freedom!

Uh, freedom?

Why didn't I feel free? I felt really deprived and restricted, actually. Not of the food I could eat; no one was stopping me from eating whatever and whenever I wanted. I was feeling deprived and restricted from life as it was intended. I felt overweight and awful.

You would think being able to satisfy every craving, every physical appetite would bring peace. If I want chocolate, I can have it. If I want pop, I can have it. If I want pizza, no problem. I can literally eat whatever and whenever I want. Most of us can. So why doesn't this satisfy? Why aren't we ever done?

Smoking is a good example, too. Have any of you been smokers? You wake up and want a cigarette. You pour a cup of coffee and smoke with it. You light one up to drive to work. It is endless and never satisfies. There is always another craving around the corner.

There are two sides of me. There is the girl who can't wait to get a car, so she can have all the junk food she can imagine. She binges while driving. She hides food, so no one will eat her treats. She constantly feeds herself, but it is never enough.

Then there is the girl who knows truth and has found peace with food. She makes choices based on what will feed her soul more than what will feed her physical cravings. She has a goal of taking care of herself and honoring and respecting her body.

I have learned that one of these two parts of me will be making my choices. If I am triggered back into eating junk food, it usually means I am feeling those old emotions and need to stop and do some soul work. If my cravings feel out of control, I know that I am feeling far away from the source of my peace.

When I know who I am and I am walking with the truth, I know that freedom will never come from satisfying every craving. Freedom comes from healing those cravings and taking their power away. Ask any heroin addict, "Does satisfying your every craving bring you peace?" No.

There is an easy way to tell where you are with this. Look at what you eat and ask yourself, "Did I choose this mainly because I like it, or did I choose this because it shows honor and respect to myself and my body?" It is a very big lie that you have to eat something just because you like it and that if you don't eat it, you are being deprived.

Freedom came when I stopped choosing food based on "But I *like* it" and started choosing based on honor and respect. On what is good for my body and soul. I still like Ho Hos, but I've probably only had two in the last ten years and I do not feel deprived. I could stop at any store and eat whatever I want, whenever I want. But I don't feel the need anymore. I can choose anything on the menu when I go out to eat. No one will stop me. But instead, I choose something healthy because I want to live life as it was intended. Free of the burden of compulsive dieting, broken body image, or over-desire for food.

If you are struggling, look at your food choices. Look at the quantity. Look at your snacks. Looking at your food choices is a way to see who is making your choices—a brokenhearted, insecure little girl or an adult woman who understands her worth and knows how to honor and respect it? And if you feel like your cravings are controlling you, don't work on your food. That's not the issue. Focusing on the food will only make cravings stronger. Focus on the truth. Be reminded of who you are. Embrace your beauty and your value. Feed your soul. When you do that, you can make choices from a place of peace, and the freedom in that is delicious.

★★★

As many of you know, I am in recovery. I am recovering from nicotine addiction. I am recovering from a painful addiction to people pleasing. And I am recovering from a lifetime of food and body image issues.

I remember my first diet. I was about ten years old. I had gotten hold of a book and was following it by sitting in yoga poses while trying to eat an apple instead of a stack of Thin Mints. It wasn't working. I would stare into the mirror, standing sideways, and picture how great my life would be if only I didn't have fat around my belly. I somehow believed that if I didn't have this belly, I would feel loved, important, and happy.

Fast forward to my return from hiking out West last month. I felt more fit and in shape than I think I have ever felt in my life. I couldn't wait to get on the scale to see confirmation of all those calories burned. (How many of you just screamed, "Don't do it!"?) Exactly.

Being the woman with food and body image issues that I am, I ignored my own screaming to stay off the scale and got on it anyway. It was a number that made me smile. Then, guess what happened next? I know those of you in recovery with me know what happens when you get a good number on the scale. Yes, I started eating out of control. The binge was on.

It went on for about three weeks. I kept eating my basic healthy foods. I kept working out. But I was also adding crazy things to my normal daily choices. One night I ate six slices of pizza, then saved the last two slices for breakfast the next day. I had a huge pancake breakfast one Sunday. I had lots of ice cream and chai tea lattes.

After a few weeks of this, I started feeling gross. Sluggish. Bloated. My jeans were no longer comfortable. My body felt uncomfortable. I had sugar cravings, calf cramps, headaches, and all kind of stuff. Good Lord, how did I ever eat this way all the time? I must have felt horrible back then if I was feeling this bad after only a few weeks of it.

As soon as I became consciously aware that I was feeling bad about myself, I said "Stop!" I made a commitment to myself a long time ago to change my life and make healthy choices, not to look better or to weigh a certain number, but to feel better about myself. That has always been at the core of my reasons for changing, and it was my trigger to get back to what I know.

I know that I had to get off the sugar. Drink more water. And eat my vegetables. I know that when I am eating recklessly, it only takes three days of really clean eating for the cravings to go away. So three days it was. Grilled chicken, lettuce, almonds, pecans, carrots, peppers, egg whites, and not much else to get back on track. I felt so much better by the end of the first day! I guess I have to be reminded over and over that junk food is poison to my body and my soul. I don't feel good physically when I eat too much of it, and I struggle to feel good about myself.

Yesterday I decided to get on the scale to see how much farther I had to go. I was right where I normally am. Not post-hike super-fit, but just at my normal weight that I've been hanging out at for the last five or six years. Huh! That's not what I expected, but great. My three days of eating clean and getting back to normal did the trick. I have no idea how many pounds, if any, I had actually gone up during my sluggish, bloated weeks. Who cares, really?

My message today is this. For many of us, recovery is a lifelong battle. It's not easy. But it can be done. If you are struggling, that's OK. There are a lot of us that understand completely.

But listen. You don't have to live that way. You can change. Change is possible! For me, it took finding a very personal reason for making the change. I hated feeling bad about myself all the time. I reached the bottom, if you will, and couldn't take another day of self-hatred. Knowing that I feel better about myself when I'm making good choices helps me to get back on track when I slip and helps keep me on track when I'm moving forward. I've learned that I don't get fat in a day, and so if I fall off the wagon, all I need to do is climb back on.

If you feel like you've been off the wagon lately, that's OK. But don't keep going in that direction. There is nothing but pain and struggle down that road. Turn around! Go in a different direction. Make the choices that build your confidence. Make the choices that feed your soul. Make the choices that reflect what a valuable, unique person you are. When you treat yourself with honor and respect despite your past, you have learned what it means to overcome. And isn't that what we all must learn to do whether we are in recovery or not?

You know what to do. Get off the sugar. Eat more veggies. Drink your water.

★★★

I find it fascinating that any of you think I have it together and figured out or that I don't have to make a conscious effort to stay on track. I struggled with the way I felt about myself for many years, and I have received a lot of healing in that area. But some days I still struggle. The difference now is that I know the fight is worth it. And I believe that if I keep going, it will be worth it.

Here are some of the strategies I have found that work for me. I encourage you to find your own personal strategies that work for you.

The main thing I try to remember is that my overeating is a symptom. If I keep focused on that, then I know where to work when I become aware that it's happening. There are many excuses I use to eat more food than my body needs. It tastes good. I like it. It's cold outside. It's dark in the evenings. I'm bored. I'm out to eat with friends. It's a party. I'm busy. I'm tired. This list goes on and on. But if I'm willing to get real with myself, these excuses aren't the root. The root is I believe that food will make me feel better right now at this moment, whether my body needs the fuel or not. And I believe that I need to feel better right now much more than I need to feel better long term.

But there are major consequences to that kind of thinking. If I eat more than my body needs, it gets stored as fat. Period.

How is the switch made from constant short-term gratification to long-term health and wholeness? I believe the answer lies in taking radical responsibility.

So a few weeks ago, when I became aware of my overeating, I first had to stop and remember that this symptom (overeating) points me to what's out of balance in my life. What's wrong? Why am I using food? What am I using it for?

I had a few things going on. I felt sadness after coming back from the hike. I didn't want it to be over. I got myself twisted up over feeling good and getting on the scale. When the scale is good, it is always some weird permission to binge. And I wasn't organized. I was behind from being gone for a week, and didn't have my groceries stocked or my food made.

To restore sanity to my life, I didn't go on a diet or start logging my food. I took responsibility and then put my strategies back in place.

Step 1: Name it. I named my current problem. I'm eating crazy, and I'm feeling bad about myself.

Step 2: Stabilize. I told myself "Everything is fine." You do not get fat in a few days. You can recover.

Step 3: Feel. I gave myself a little time to feel sad about the hike being over. It's OK to feel that way. Then I sat with the feeling of self-esteem downslide. I let it in instead of escaping from it. Blah!

Step 4: State my belief. When I eat like this, I feel very bad about myself.

Step 5: Act on it. I ate very clean for three days. Lots of water. Stocked up on good stuff. Took the time to make food for the week. Got organized.

Step 6: Get moving. Working out is a natural antidepressant for me. One of the first times I went to counseling, my therapist gave me a choice of medication or exercise. I chose exercise. That one thing lifted me up enough to deal with my pain and it is still vital to my well-being.

I am not exaggerating. After two or three weeks of making bad choices, it only took three days of making extraordinary choices to feel much better. Oh yeah! I remember now. This is why I choose to eat the way I do. This is why I exercise consistently. This is why I deal with my feelings rather than running from them. The difference is incredible.

I know I will never go back to my old way of living. But I also know I will slip and struggle. I believe this is crucial to all of our long-term health and happiness. We must know how to get back up when we fall. If all we know to do is beat ourselves up when we're down, it will be impossible. But if we have strategies in place to lift ourselves up and to have others help us up, we will be free to move forward. And we may never reach perfection, but who cares? That has never been the goal.

★★★

We all have some struggles. Sometimes you just can't see it.

I have found while talking to clients one on one, there is a common misconception that we are alone in our struggle. It can feel frustrating. Maybe the other women you work out with can do a lunge, and you can't because of your foot or knee. Maybe someone working out next to you has better balance than you. It may look like your workout buddies don't struggle with their weight or body images.

I challenge you to see it differently. I believe comparison can cause us to feel stuck and alone. The kind of comparison that says I am; you're not. The truth is we all are.

We are all on the same path, just at different places on that path.

You may feel frustrated, overweight, and out of shape.

The woman next to you is struggling with her balance and coordination.

The woman next to you is grieving the loss of her mother.

The woman next to you has chronic kidney disease.

The woman next to you is at a healthy body weight but can only see the overweight girl she used to be.

The woman next to you is diabetic.

The woman next to you has joint problems that make simple tasks scary and challenging.

The woman next to you is a breast cancer survivor.

The woman next to you has artificial knees or hips.

The woman next to you doesn't believe she will ever conquer her food addiction.

The woman next to you hates her body.

The woman next to you is addicted to people pleasing.

The woman next to you has a chronic illness.

The woman next to you struggles with depression and anxiety.

The woman next to you has been dieting since she was ten years old.

The woman next to you is worried about her husband's recent diagnosis.

The woman next to you is overwhelmed.

The woman next to you struggles with her self-confidence.

You know all these women.

It is amazing to watch when the walls of separation come down to let each other into our lives and our struggles; when we stop comparing ourselves to others and start seeing how we all share the journey; when we stop judging ourselves so harshly and receive grace for our struggles.

You are not alone.

You are part of a community that celebrates fitness at any age. That may mean having to deal with all sorts of challenges. That's what exercise modifications are for! So what if you can't do a lunge. There's an alternative. The important thing is that you keep moving, stay strong, work on your balance, and make better choices. The important thing is to know you are not alone in your struggle. The important thing is to have the courage to share your journey with others and receive the encouragement and support you need to keep going. And by doing so, you provide that same encouragement and support to someone else.

★★★

Halloween reminded me of that old commercial. This is your brain. This is your brain on drugs. And the egg hits the hot skillet and sizzles.

This is my brain. This is my brain on Halloween.

Me: I am going to have two pieces of candy tonight and really enjoy them.

(ha ha.)

Me: I just had a mini KitKat and a Nestle Crunch. They were good, and now I'm done. Good job. (ha ha.)

Me: Oh, just one more. That KitKat was yummy. And it was really only half of one normal KitKat. (Have two.)

Me: Be quiet. One more is plenty. It wasn't that good.

(Yes it was.)

Me: I should stop eating sugar. [Eats KitKat] I should go vegan. I should try CrossFit. [Eats Nestle Crunch]

(Told ya.)

Me: Told me what? That I have no self-control around this stuff? I already know that. But I really like it.

(Me too.)

Me: Fine, I'm done. I could eat the rest of that bowl of candy. I'm thirsty. How long ago did I quit smoking? I should try Paleo. I should run a marathon.

(Have a KitKat.)

Along with all that internal drama, I had 400 calories worth of candy. That night. But some leftover Reese's Peanut Butter Cups came home with me.

Me: I'll put them in the back corner of the freezer and have one a day until they are gone.

(HA HA!)

Me: Be quiet. I can do that. I like Reese's. Everything in moderation.

(They're good cold.)

Me: Yes but I already had my one for today.

(Have two.)

Me: Be quiet. You're not helpful.

(It's only one more.)

Me: You're right. What difference does one more make? Yum.

(There's a pumpkin, too.)

Me: What? Oh I see it. A Reese's Peanut Butter Pumpkin. I just had a regular peanut butter cup.

(You deserve both.)

Me: Be quiet. I had plenty. They were *so* good. I really just want one more. If I have one more, I think I'll be done. I can set the alarm for 5:30 a.m. and go work out and burn them off.

(ha ha.)

Me: I think they need to be gone from here.

(Eat them.)

Me: SHUT IT! I don't want to eat them. I should just toss them out. I had plenty.

(That's a waste.)

Me: What are they, four cents each? I should toss them out right now.

(Eat one more first.)

Me: I could just finish them then I would not have to deal with you anymore.

(Good plan.)

[Eats the rest.]

You know what can happen. "Just one more" can turn into five, eight, ten pounds gained. The foods we encounter are high in calories, salt, sugar, and fat. Expect to experience the battle in your mind. Maybe not quite as crazy as me, but there are two parts of us that battle.

One part just wants the candy and will use any tactic to get it. Then the consequences come, and you all know what these consequences feel like and what they do to our self-confidence.

The other part takes radical responsibility for every choice. This is the part of you that needs nurtured and loved. This is the part of you that is capable of change. This is the part of you that knows the truth.

The truth is every choice matters. The truth is it's hard work to make extraordinary choices consistently. It is hard work to take radical responsibility for your choices every day. But we can do it. We know what to do! (Exercise, eat clean, drink water, sleep.) We are all capable. All we need is the belief that it is possible, the knowledge that it matters, and the passion to make it happen. Once we have that, there are no more limits. We are free.

★★★

I ran three miles this morning. It was a great run, my second one this year. I took a year off to see if running was causing my back to hurt, and I found that it wasn't.

Very often, there seems to be a common phrase or theme in the studio. This week, the theme was "I should." I should be able to do this on my own. I should be able to hold myself accountable. I should be self-disciplined enough to get consistent. Or, as I was running today, I should be able to run faster. I should be able to breathe easier. I should be able to run longer.

I want to challenge this thinking. I don't think it is healthy.

One of the problems is that it implies such criticism. If the way I interpret my workout this morning is that I should be a better runner, that is pretty critical. Judgmental. Shame on me. How hard do you think it will be next time I go to lace up my shoes to run? Will that root of shame motivate me? Will I be pulled to go outside by the harsh judgment? No. I am never motivated to change or improve by criticism and judgment.

Another problem with *should* is that it implies it's only you who struggles and that is not true. How many of us do exactly what we tell ourselves we won't do? And how many of us don't do what we promise ourselves we will? I take such comfort that the Apostle Paul was writing about this exact thing in his letter to the Romans in chapter 7. If he was writing about it, then I am sure it wasn't a "broken me" issue, it was a humanity issue. We just don't have it in us to always do what's good for us on our own. We need help and that is OK.

Should also implies falling short and that is a lie. Just because I'm breathing heavy during my run, does not make it a failure. Just because I'm slow, doesn't mean I suck. It is a victory every single time I get out there. You may believe that you should be doing it faster, better, easier, more consistently. I understand completely. However, it can't stop you from doing it anyway. It can't keep you from making a commitment to take care of yourself.

So I run anyway; breathing hard, heart rate too high, for 3 miles. I'm just getting started and I know it will get easier. But in the meantime I am going to override those thoughts of criticism and judgment and find the victory in each run. I got up today and did it! I felt good about myself after. I felt proud of myself all day long.

Do it anyway. Take a new class. Start personal training. Try boxing. Go for a fitness walk. Ask for help. Override all the shoulds, the judgment, and the criticism, and see the victory in doing it. Claim it. Own it. You become more empowered to make extraordinary choices every time you make your choice from the place of acceptance and not judgment. From the place of love and not fear. From the place of grace and not shame.

This kind of thinking takes practice. It is tempting to jump on the merry go round of all the shoulds and just spin around but never get anywhere. Or you can see them but let them go. Just let them fly right past without ever connecting with them. They are critical and judgmental. They aren't empowering. And they aren't true. Let the thoughts that guide you be centered on the truth. You are on a journey to be the best that you can be, and there are challenges and obstacles. But you're doing it. And it doesn't matter where anyone else is on that journey. We are all in it together, just perhaps at different places on the path.

★★★

I love the conversations that we have at the studio. The more we talk about struggles we share, obstacles we face, and how we're overcoming them, the better. Working out is only part of the reason any of us are at Clear Rock. For most of us seeking to make changes, lose weight, and get healthier, we are also there for motivation, consistency, and accountability.

This week one of my fitness warriors came to me after her workout, and said she would like for me to issue her a challenge to help her get back on track. My challenge back to her was for her to create her own challenge and share it with me, so I can hold her accountable. The challenge wouldn't mean anything coming from me. I can issue challenges all day long. The challenge must be personal and it must come from you. And it must, must, must be met. No matter what.

If you put a challenge out there and then don't feel like it, you must do it anyway.

If you put a challenge out there and don't have time, you must find time.

If you put a challenge out there and feel scared, frustrated, or unmotivated you must overcome.

If you put a challenge out there and your leg falls off, you must find a way to do it with one less leg.

The discipline of fitness is not about fitness alone. It is about learning to do what you ask of yourself. It is about learning to trust that you know what to do, and you'll do it. It is about learning to value yourself and then backing that up with action. To build self-esteem and confidence in this area of our lives, to change our beliefs about what is possible, we must do something. Change something. Reach for something. And then make it of utmost importance to get it done, not because of the pounds lost or any of that. Because of the new beliefs that will be formed. I can do this. I will succeed.

This is not a time to sit around passively, wishing life were different. It can be! But, you have to take steps towards your goals. Make them small, doable steps. Don't sit on the sidelines wishing and hoping to feel better. There's only one way to get there. Get moving.

★★★

I personally find it inspiring and am grateful to be around women in their seventies who are doing cardio four days a week. I want that to be me! I want every one of us, no matter what age, to be fit and healthy. To be strong and balanced. To be doing the things we love. And to be doing cardio four days a week.

I spent years wishing and hoping I would change, but never being able to follow through. I just couldn't understand what was happening. What I didn't realize was I wasn't failing others, I was failing me. I was the one treating me like I didn't matter or that I wasn't good enough.

Then I learned the biggest lesson in life. I matter. That means I must do what I say I will do. That means my choices all matter. That means my health is important. That means how I feel about myself is important.

I truly believe that if any of us actually knew how important we were, we would never make a self-destructive choice again. We would become unstuck and care passionately for ourselves. We would naturally be as consistent and motivated as we were meant to be. Once the struggle was gone, all that would be left is purposeful and authentic living. No more fights with food, exercise, or our bodies. Can you imagine for a moment how bright your light would shine if you didn't have any of this to fight with, obsess about, or wish for?

It is possible. And it is never too late. Remember who you are, and it will be yours.

★★★

We are over half way through December. I know it's tough. I know there is food everywhere. But you can do this. Listen. I want you ready for what's coming in January. Every quick-fix product and service you've ever heard of will be advertised. Every magazine cover will scream about 100 ways to lose ten pounds this week! Every other commercial will be Jenny Craig or WW. Fitness equipment will go on sale everywhere. None of these things are the answer. I am not the answer. Diets are not the answer. Equipment is not the answer. There is only one answer to getting fit. Get right with food and exercise.

Everything that pulls your attention away from that simple truth is just adding to the amount of time it will take you to get right with food and exercise.

No diet can do it for you. You have to learn to make healthy choices in all circumstances.

No piece of equipment can do it for you. You have to learn to choose daily exercise, and fitness equipment does not come with radical responsibility built in. That part is up to you.

No gym can do it for you. You are the one that decides to go or not.

No trainer can do it for you. You have to want to change so badly that you decide to let nothing stand in your way.

I want you ready for the lies. They are coming. I want you armed with the truth. You can do this!

The way to be set and armed is to stay on track. If you get off track and start feeling crappy about yourself, you're vulnerable. Vulnerable to the lies. Vulnerable to the old quick-fix way of being.

But you aren't like that anymore. You know better. You've learned this one.

Even if the first half of December has been off the rails for you, stop and turn around. Don't buy into the lie by telling yourself you'll focus on your fitness when January comes. Do it now. Today is much more important than a day in January. Today matters.

If you need to mark a turning point, do it today. Repeat after me. I receive forgiveness for not taking care of myself lately. I let go of the past and make a new commitment. Starting today, I will honor myself by making good choices when it comes to food and exercise. I will take radical responsibility for my choices and keep moving forward. I will do this with the intention of being strong and ready to start a new year without feeling like I somehow have to improve myself or become good enough. I am already good enough.

How cool to start 2013 like that.

★★★

"Here is my big issue: the scale. I have been working hard on my training goals and have been succeeding. I have also been watching the food and said "no" to a lot of the bad stuff, but I cannot get away from the scale. It seems I live and die by the scale, and I hate that! The weight has not moved much, and I get down on myself. Intellectually I know my goal should be feeling good and knowing

I am healthy, but I still think the scale is the ultimate indicator of my success or failure. Should I just hide it away or what should I do with it? Why is it that we get so caught up on something so stupid and let it stand in the way of feeling good about ourselves?"

—from client email

Don't we all struggle with the damn scale? I used to, until I realized that the scale is full of lies, and I want to live my life in truth.

Here are the lies.

Lie #1—My issue is the scale.

Lie #2—I cannot get away from the scale.

Lie #3—I live and die by the scale.

Lie #4—The scale is the ultimate indicator of my success or failure.

Here is the truth.

#1—The issue is not the scale. The scale is a mechanical instrument made of metal and plastic with absolutely no power. The issue is we give it power, ultimate power.

First, own it. I'm sorry that I gave the scale ultimate power over my well-being and self-worth. The truth is I don't trust myself and the scale gives me a (false) sense of control. I want to feel in control of this scary process of changing.

Next, come out of agreement with the lie. I come out of agreement with the lie that a scale has any power over my well-being or self-worth. I come out of agreement with the lie that I cannot be trusted with my own health and wellness.

The truth is, with a little faith, I can trust myself and trust the process.

#2—You can get away from the scale. We all can. It is not a stalker, and it cannot follow you. You choose every time you step onto it.

First, own it. I chose to put myself through this abuse daily, even though I knew the chaos it created in my mind and my heart.

Next, come out of agreement with the lie. I come out of agreement with the lie that I cannot get away from the scale.

The truth is I can choose to stay off the scale today, then tomorrow, then tomorrow.

#3—You actually don't live and die by the scale; you just believe that you do.

First, own it. I have a compulsive need for external validation. I don't believe my own heart. I can wake up feeling fantastic about myself, get on the scale, and all that joy can vanish in an instant. I'm sorry that I haven't honored that joy.

Next, come out of agreement with the lie that I need to know how much I weigh to see if I am succeeding or failing. I come out of agreement with that lie that I must get external validation for my success to matter.

The truth is you matter. The measurement is just a measurement. It's irrelevant and has zero ability to impact your choices in a healthy way. Your choices come from your heart.

#4—The scale is not the ultimate indicator of anything. Look at it like this. Imagine if you asked me if I love you, and I pull out a tape measure and measure the circumference of your head. Absurd.

First, own it. I gave away my worth to an object or measurement.

Next, come out of agreement with the lie that the scale is an indicator of anything relevant. I come out of agreement with the lie that the scale means anything to me.

The truth is, what we all want is to feel good about ourselves. We want to belong, to matter, to be loved and to be at peace. We want to be strong, healthy, fit, and beautiful.

You are all those things already. Throw the scale away and put the lenses on that allow you to see yourself as you really are. You belong, you matter, and you are loved. You are strong, healthy, fit, and beautiful. If you don't believe me, I'd be happy to measure your head.

I love you. Throw your scale away. It is a LIAR.

★★★

I know what to do, I just don't do it.

I know that an apple is a better choice than a Reese's Cup. I know that broccoli is healthier than French fries. I know that grilled chicken has fewer calories than pizza. Yet I eat Reese's Cups, French fries and pizza. I have gone to the grocery store and filled my cart with fresh, whole foods. Then on the way home, I've gone through the Taco Bell drive through.

I've gone out to eat and taken half of my meal home in a to-go box, only to eat the rest of it while standing at the kitchen counter thinking how I should put it in the fridge or throw it away.

I have gone out to eat and ordered a grilled chicken salad with the dressing on the side, only to eat two or three rolls or pieces of bread while waiting for my salad to come.

I ate eight Reese's Cups the day after Halloween all the while telling myself that I would only have one more and that it was better to get rid of them this way than to have them in the back of my freezer.

I order the same thing every time I go to a Mexican restaurant, so I don't get tempted by the high-calorie platters on the menu, and then mindlessly devour half a basket of chips.

I know what to do. Sometimes, I just don't do it. To me, as a trainer and as a seeker of truth, this has always been the interesting place to work. Why don't I do it?

I can work on what to do forever and not get anywhere. I can buy fitness equipment and join gyms. I can hire a personal trainer and read a book on nutrition. I can learn form and progression in strength training. I can get a heart rate monitor and calculate or measure my zones. I can buy whole foods at the grocery store.

I do all those things. But what good is all that if I stop at Taco Bell on the way home? I'll let that be my personal metaphor for I know what to do; I just don't do it. (Since this one annoys me most when I do it.)

I believe there is a small group of people who are overweight or out of shape because they really just aren't aware of how many calories are in certain foods. After these people learn to track calories, a light goes on in their heads regarding how much they have been eating and how much a high-calorie meal costs them; they change and lose their excess weight. I believe that is a very small group.

The rest of us learned to track calories, but it didn't stop us from making high-calorie choices. We came to look at calorie or point counting as a means to gain some control over the compulsion we have to eat more than we need. We didn't become aware and then suddenly change into healthy eaters. We may have started exercising, but mostly what we do is use exercise to hang onto where we are. We never get anywhere. We don't move forward, and we don't break free of the compulsive eating. I am in that group.

What took me a long time to own was there were emotional reasons underneath my desire for too much food that no amount of awareness about exercise and nutrition was going to fix. I am a user. I use food for comfort. I use food for love. I use food for loneliness. I use food to calm my fear.

That is not easy to own.

But when I owned it, I brought it into the light. When I owned it, it lost its power over me. When I owned it, I no longer felt out of control. I felt empowered. I had a choice!

I never would have guessed that my fitness journey would lead me to that. Turns out, it wasn't about fitness at all. It was about healing. It was about bringing what was in darkness into the light.

If you have been struggling for any amount of time with your weight or how you feel about yourself, I understand completely. Please don't buy the madness that is out there. You will not feel better about yourself once you reach your goal weight. That is backwards. You will reach your goal weight once you feel better about yourself, and the irony is you will be so happy in your new freedom that your weight won't mean much to you at all.

Truth: If counting points or calories didn't teach you about whole foods, eating clean, and proper portions the first time...then there are deeper issues that no diet can ever fix. What are you using food for? Be brave and seek the real issue. I know what to do; I just don't do it. That is the issue. That is the interesting, life-changing work.

★★★

I cleaned out my closet the other day. What a job! You would think it would be as simple as going through item by item and deciding whether to keep it or not. But it took all day. And it was emotionally draining.

I couldn't donate my pink sweatshirt that doesn't fit right (and I never wear) because I got it in Hawaii. I couldn't get rid of several pairs of jeans because they might fit someday. I had to keep the dress I wore on my honeymoon in 1996 even though one, it doesn't fit and two, I'm divorced. I saved clothes I wore when I was in love. I saved clothes I wore when I felt fat that I believed helped me hide. I saved clothes I wore when I was starting to feel good about myself.

Many items had an emotion or memory attached. I could have written these things on strips of paper and pinned them to the pieces of clothing. It might have a feeling written on it, a place, a person's name, a number on the scale, a life event.

I'm not sure I was ready to be confronted with all of that when I decided to clean out my closet. I'm definitely not aware on a daily basis of all that energy tied up in a bunch of clothes. But I knew it had been several years since I had done it, so I made a decision to get through all the memories and the drama to fill up six big bags for Goodwill.

When we try to make a change in health and fitness, there is a similar process. We may not realize the attachment is there on a daily basis, but once we step out and decide to make a change, there it is. It just comes up.

For example, say I want to change the way I order when I go out to eat. I eat consistently healthy at home, but can go off the rails at a restaurant. I'm sitting at the table looking at a menu. Pasta and bread is just pasta and bread. Grilled fish and broccoli is just that, right? Or, is there something more attached? If my pattern is to order rich, high-calorie meals at a restaurant, and I decide to try to order something say 550 calories or less, what happens?

"You hardly ever come to this restaurant. This is a special treat. You should order whatever you want. You may not be back here in a long time"

"I'll work it off tomorrow. Five miles, I promise."

"This is a special occasion. I should get to eat something special."

"I want to be able to eat like everyone else and not worry or care about how much or what I'm eating. I want something I like."

"OK, ten miles. I swear."

"Life is short. I don't want to be deprived of all the good stuff. We were meant to enjoy life."

"I never make progress anyway, why bother making a healthy choice?"

"Healthy food doesn't taste as good."

"But I like bread."

"Everyone will comment and I won't be accepted if I order something healthy."

"I can't make a public proclamation that I am trying this again, I've done this too many times and failed."

"OK; fine; I'll run a marathon. Just give me dessert."

No wonder we give in. If you don't know this is coming at you, it is very difficult to confront all the stuff that comes up. And it only comes up when you try to change. My closet wasn't yelling all this emotional stuff at me every morning; I have those attachments buried deeply and well-contained. Until I try to change, that is.

So, the question becomes: Are you ready to confront whatever is attached and make a change?

What happens when we confront the lies with the truth:

The Lie: "You hardly ever come to this restaurant. This is a special treat. You should order whatever you want."

The Truth: You can come here or a place just like it whenever you want. Food is abundant. Love is abundant. You are not deprived anymore.

The Lie: "I'll work it off tomorrow. Five miles, I promise."

The Truth: You cannot exercise your way out of consistently unhealthy choices.

The Lie: "This is a special occasion. I should get to eat something special."

The Truth: Life is the special occasion. Time to live it free from this broken relationship with food.

The Lie: "I want to be able to eat like everyone else and not worry or care about how much or what I'm eating. I want something I like."

The Truth: The people you are wanting to eat like are struggling with the same compulsion as you. Emotional freedom is way better than any food I've ever had.

The Lie: "OK, ten miles. I swear."

The Truth: Over-training in an attempt to compensate for compulsive eating is a very dangerous cycle. Break free.

The Lie: "Life is short. I don't want to be deprived of all the good stuff. We were meant to enjoy life."

The Truth: Life is so much better once the broken relationship with food (compulsion) is healed from the inside. It changes everything. The fear of deprivation goes away completely.

The Lie: "I never make progress anyway, why bother making a healthy choice?"

The Truth: Every choice matters because you matter.

The Lie: "Healthy food doesn't taste as good."

The Truth: BULL. Make my chili recipe. Get creative. Find healthy food you love. It exists, I promise.

The Lie: "BUT I LIKE BREAD."

The Truth: Bread has no power. I can choose based on whether it is good for me, not whether I like it. I like Salem Slim Lights. Doesn't mean I smoke them anymore.

The Lie: "Everyone will comment and I won't be accepted if I order something healthy."

The Truth: Your peeps will love you no matter what, and if they have any reaction, it is just a projection of their own issues onto you. It's not about you. You have my permission to ignore their comments. They love you!

The Lie: "I can't make a public proclamation that I am trying this again. I've done this too many times and failed."

The Truth: You absolutely can do this. We all can. Just be willing to confront the junk.

I know it can seem like a lot. Why do I have to go through all this just to order better at a restaurant? This is the process of change.

If you can change without confrontation, awesome! You didn't have a lot of emotional stuff attached to what you were trying to let go of. But for most of us, those attachments are there. It is time to confront them.

The first few times are the toughest. Get plugged in. Get support and encouragement. Access your strongest self when you try to make a change. Then, the next time you are looking at a menu, although you may be confronted again, this time you have more truth to plug in to. You know how you felt after making a good choice last time. You felt better about yourself! That is the truth. Remember that as you begin to string several good choices together.

Once you have a few successes, you begin to heal. The attachments begin to break and eventually, if you stay committed (left foot, right foot), you are just sitting in a restaurant looking at a menu while enjoying the time with family and friends. It's about the people, not the food. It's about love, not fear. It is no longer a confrontation with your wounded self. You are healed and free.

★★★

I started my college class this week. What an experience! I am taking an online class called Creative Writing Non-Fiction. This is my first time in a college class since 1998. This is my first ever online class. And this is my first writing class since 1984. As much as I love the class so far, I'm more excited that it is giving me a chance to get into the process of change and confront my fears.

When I teach my Break Free seminar, I start in the small box which I call "stuck" or "my comfort zone." In the case of writing, I could certainly stay in my comfort zone. This class is not required to write my newsletter or to train at Clear Rock. I feel comfortable writing about the topics that I choose, and I feel like I know my audience. I'm very happy doing what I do, and I could stay right here.

But so many people have said to me, "I love your writing. You are a good writer. You could do more." So I've decided to step out of the small box into the bigger box of "change." I would love to write for magazines, and I dream about writing a book.

The first step I decided to take is this class. It's so fascinating. From the moment I stepped out of my little bitty comfort zone, the fear and lies started chattering to me. This is what I hear:

You're not a good writer.

Who are you to write anything?

You'll never figure out this online learning.

Do you really want to share your story?

No one cares about what you have to say.

This will be humiliating.

You will be vulnerable.

A book: are you serious?

You will never succeed.

You're not safe.

You don't matter.

So I think to myself, "Hello, voice of fear. I know you! And I know you are a liar."

Just a few years ago, that voice of fear would have driven me right back to the comfort zone, the small box, stuck. I couldn't take it. The churned up feeling in my gut. The anxiety running through my arms and legs. The sense of insecurity.

But not anymore. I know it's coming at me. I know what it is. And I'm ready for it. No jumping back to stuck.

So how do you deal with the voice of fear if you want to make a change and get unstuck?

I start with the truth. I know I matter and that I am safe. I know the first few steps are scary, but they will be worth it. I've learned the lesson that feeling insecure or scared is no reason to quit. In fact, if I want to grow, I must do precisely that which I am afraid of.

So I access my courage. I know it is there, I've accessed it before. My family and friends have helped me know my own courage and strength. Then, I plug into my community of support. I am connected to others who encourage me. I tap into that unlimited source of empowerment, by sharing what I'm doing and asking for help. And finally, I connect deeply to the Spirit of Love. It is my main source of strength and with it, I take the next steps: left foot, right foot.

I am afraid. I am also safe and I matter.

Making the choice from the Spirit of Love and from my authentic self (not from the wounded part of me that believes the list of lies above), I step into freedom. Freedom to choose something new. Freedom to live a more purposeful life. Freedom to change.

I am afraid. Do it anyway.

If you are stuck, I understand completely. I know how stuck feels: frustrated, sad, desperate, tired, giving up, and defeated. I know how it felt to be stuck at a weight I hated. I know how it felt to be stuck in a cigarette addiction I hated. I know how it felt to be stuck in self destructive patterns that brought me pain. I believe that we can all overcome these patterns, compulsions, and addictions. We can be free.

The only thing that can stop you is fear. Don't listen to it. It is a liar.

So try that new boxing or spinning or hip-hop or yoga (or writing!) class.

Try a new healthy recipe or two.

Try getting consistent with your cardiovascular exercise: walk, use the elliptical, bike.

Try to add a strength training day.

Try eliminating processed foods for three days.

Step out. It is the only way to confront the fear.

The likeliness that your attempt to change ends wildly successfully is much more likely than you ending in a heap, humiliated. Confront the voice of fear and go with confidence towards the best case scenario. That is where you make changes that last. That is where you finally let go of unhealthy patterns and strongholds. That is where freedom is.

And if I can do it while afraid, believe me, you can too.

★★★

It is all or nothing with me sometimes. Either I am confident and at peace, or I am scared to death. Either I am doing my cardio consistently, or not at all. Either I am making clean food choices, or

I am eating ¾ of a pizza and a pint of ice cream. I've had to learn to understand this all or nothing tendency because I found it was one of the things really keeping me stuck.

Picture pulling a pendulum way up as high as it will go. Now let it go and watch it swing wildly way up the other side. It takes a long time to settle down at the center.

This is what we do to ourselves when we attempt to restrict, diet, or do anything in the extreme. We start pulling that pendulum upward, upward, and upward. "Alright", we say to ourselves, "It is time to get serious." So, we get out the notebook or the phone app, and we start tracking every piece of food that goes in. We look up the 17 Day Diet or the South Beach Diet or the Paleo Diet and we stock up on nothing but nuts, leaves, and meat. Then, we decide upon a six-day-a-week workout plan, one hour of cardio a day, and we set up the column in the notebook or the app to track calories burned.

Here's the problem. Day one. Told myself I wouldn't eat any carbs. I was absolutely starving by lunch and the thought of salad with tuna on it made me want to slap someone. So I got macaroni and cheese and bread. And a cookie. Fine, forget Day One. I'm not working out after a crap day like that. I'll start again tomorrow. Commence a night of eating every carb in sight. I might not get to eat them again. Ever.

Day two. Oh my God, I might not ever get to eat carbs again! I better stop and get a bagel at Panera and start this tomorrow.

Day three. I let the pendulum go. It flings itself up the other side. I don't want to live a life of restriction!!! What kind of life is that, anyway? We were meant to enjoy food! I'll just live with being this size. I don't even care anymore. Stop taking my only treats. I like this stuff. I don't know why I try. I hate this. Why do I struggle with this? What is wrong? What's happening?

Believe it or not, this is very common. We all go through this. It is a natural reaction to pulling the pendulum up way too high; of attempting to change everything at once. I understand the reasoning. If I can do all this at once, I can return to the life I know and not have to think about it ever again. But with that thinking, we always end up where we started.

The only way to move forward is to lift the pendulum gently.

When you lift the pendulum gently, and think about making a small change or a small step forward, you minimize the chance of the all-out rebellion or the wild swing to the other side. It's more peaceful. It's calmer. It's slower. But it is how to move forward.

Pick one small step. If your mind rebels and wants this all done right now, tell it to hush. You're trying to get something done. Do your one small step. Actually succeed at it. Sit with how that feels. Pretty good, huh? Yes, indeed.

Now, while maintaining that sweet little change you just made, pick another one. If your mind rebels and wants this all done right now, tell it to hush again. Then do your small step. Succeed. Then commit to it. Can you stick with it? Can you make it part of your life forever? If not, it was too big. Go smaller.

Imagine doing one small, doable step a week for a year then committing to the change. Can you imagine how different your life would be a year from now? Close your eyes for a moment and just imagine it. Imagine you with fifty two successes under your belt. A huge lesson learned about how to make incremental changes that last.

Now just for a second, imagine one year from now, having gone through the torment of the pendulum over and over without getting anywhere. Still stuck, still trying to figure it out. You do not have to live that way. Give up the pendulum. Let go of all or nothing thinking.

Here's how. First, own it. Say to yourself or write in your journal, "I see that I've believed the lie of all or nothing thinking." Then turn around! "I come out of agreement with the lie of all or nothing thinking. I am willing to go through the work required to make these changes."

Then take your first small step. You're on your way to freedom.

★★★

In fitness, there are always two things going on at once.

The first one is knowing what to do.

There is a lot of information available on what to do. For nutrition, there is ample guidance on how to eat clean and why. Calorie counts are available online for almost any food or restaurant. There are research papers written on what combination of carbs, protein, and fat is healthiest and supports your specific goals the best. There are entire articles written just about kale, blueberries, and almonds. There are hundreds of healthy recipe sites online and at least that many recipe books.

For exercise, you can find everything you ever wanted to know in textbooks, research papers, magazine articles, blogs, books, and websites. If I decide to run a half marathon, I can download a training plan. If I want to do a workout today that focuses on back and biceps, I can download one or even view one on YouTube. I can have an entire shelf dedicated in my house for workout DVDs. I can have the simplest or the fanciest home gym, treadmill, gym membership, workout shoes, clothes, heart rate monitor, etc.

None of this makes it happen.

The second thing that must be going on is doing it. Just because I know what to do, doesn't mean I do it.

I have had gym memberships that I rarely used. I've had a treadmill that sat in my basement for months at a time while I complained about how it was too cold to walk outside. I have lots of workout DVDs, workout clothing for every season, the best shoes. None of it matters unless I can light the fire of motivation, carve out time, and do it consistently.

I think the most interesting question in fitness is not what to do, although those discussions are fun. What heart rate zone is best for your goal? What is the optimal way to set up a strength training program? CrossFit or BodyPump? Zumba or HipHop? Boxing or running? Insanity or Biggest Loser DVDs? Vegetarian or Plant-Strong? There are an infinite number of choices and combinations to personalize a lifestyle that works for you.

The most interesting question (to me) is: if I know what to do, why am I not doing it?

When we ask this question, we have to make a shift from external to internal; away from all that information straight to the heart. What is in my heart, in my mind, in my set of beliefs that is keeping me from doing what I ask of myself? Even though not doing it has caused me pain in ways it is hard to even explain.

Do we really not know what to do? If not, that's easy. Here it is. Walk or do some other form of cardiovascular, aerobic exercise almost every day for an hour. Do strength training at least twice a week. Stretch. Sleep. Drink a lot of water. Eat whole food, plant-strong. No processed sugar or fat. Stay within your appropriate caloric intake for the day, every day. That's it. How you do it is up to you.

If you are still struggling to do just a small part of it after 10, 20, or 30 years, then you are in the category of I know what to do; I just don't do it. Just like I was. This one thing held me back for so long. I was not in control of my choices. No matter how much I wanted to make good choices, this force inside me would take over and convince me otherwise. I made excuses, I thought I had no self-discipline, and it really wore away at my self-esteem. It doesn't feel good to be unable to choose well.

Then I stopped looking outward. I stopped thinking that the answer was in the next gym, diet, piece of equipment, super food, or workout outfit. The answer was in me.

There is only one reason I am going to carve out an hour to exercise. And that is if I believe it (and myself) to be worth it.

There is only one reason I can choose to eat an entirely different way than I used to. That is if I believe it will get me to where I want to go.

If I believe that giving up that extra hour or my comfort food isn't going to get me to my goal, there is no way I can make that change. But think of a time when you knew, when you absolutely knew, that something you were working towards was going to pay off; that it mattered. Maybe it was marriage, college, career, or parenting. Because you believed in it, you showed up 100%. You made a commitment.

If you are stuck, look inside. Have you lost your faith in the process? Have you failed too many times to really believe it can happen for you? I've been there! I understand completely. Don't give up. A dramatic shift can occur when you shine a light on all the false beliefs of your past. When I started really looking at mine, turns out, none of them were true. The truth is I am capable of doing anything I ask of myself, as long as I believe it will matter.

★★★

Do you own "beautiful"? Because you are. Absolutely beautiful. Go ahead, practice saying it out loud over and over. I dare you. Say, "I am beautiful." No matter what size. No matter what weight. No matter what anyone else thinks. No matter what. If I believe that I am beautiful only at a certain size or shape, I am destined to stay stuck. We will do anything to prove ourselves right. Let's prove to ourselves, instead, that we're drop dead gorgeous.

Do you own your progress? When someone tells you you're looking stronger, leaner, toner, tighter, do you say "thank you"? Or do you argue and say, "Yeah, but I have a long way to go—you should see my thighs; I hate my chin; my stomach is still fat; look at these arms, these wrinkles, this skin. Try "thank you." Own your progress. Even if it is a small success, you did that! No one is holding your progress up to measure against perfection. No one expects that of you, except possibly you.

Do you own your meltdowns? I had a horrible week of eating. I had McDonald's fries and an entire bag of candy. It was my choice. I can do the work to figure out why I ate compulsively, because I did that. I ate things I really didn't want to. But the bottom line is I made the choice. No one forced me except my little ego telling me I needed some comfort, reward, sugar kick, treat, or whatever.

Do you own your fears? I am afraid. I am afraid of trying something and failing. I am afraid of stepping out of my comfort zone. I am just as afraid of being stuck there. I am afraid of looking like an idiot. Don't we all share this? Don't we all battle fear? Let's empower ourselves with the mighty truth and step out anyway. Do it afraid. It's the only way to move forward.

Now that you've owned it, you can do it. Do your cardio! Get on the treadmill and get creative. Knock out some awesome intervals.

Get outside and walk at one of the parks. Try hip-hop or Zumba. Whatever your preference, doesn't matter. Just get your heart rate into your Zone 2. Work up to an hour of cardio 4–5 days a week.

Now that you've owned it, you can do it. Lift! A minimum of two strength training sessions a week. Find a way to make it happen. If you don't do it on your own, get help. Hire a trainer or take a class. Make it heavy, push yourself. Feel those muscles work and get stronger. Don't skip this. It is your metabolism as well as your strength, endurance, and balance. Not to mention the self-esteem kick.

Now that you've owned it, you can do it. Eat cleaner! That means eat more chicken, fish, and vegetables. It means less fried food, processed food, sugar, flour, alcohol, and salt. That means changing. It means finding ways for your authentic self to show up and make the choices. It means healing compulsive eating, emotional eating, and stress eating. It means confronting whatever keeps getting in the way of you making extraordinary choices.

So own it. Empowerment is what leads to change. Empowerment comes when we get really honest with ourselves and then make choices based on the truth. No more thinking about it, it's time for action.

★★★

Lent began this week, the season leading up to Easter in the Christian faith. I used to think Lent was all about giving something up. I would pick chocolate or chai lattes and restrict myself from having any from Ash Wednesday to Easter. Sometimes I would make it through that time, sometimes not. Sometimes I would tie it into my compulsive dieting. (Ooh, the Lent diet! I'll eat no sugar for 40 days and lose 20 pounds...spring is coming!) It eventually lost its meaning and became a religious ritual and then nothing at all to me.

I realized recently that Lent is not supposed to be about restriction. It is supposed to be about making room for something better.

Health and fitness can be like that. We can go through restrictive ritual after restrictive ritual. They may last days or week or even months. But they never really produce any lasting change. How many times have you done Weight Watchers? Did it change you? How many diets have you tried? Did they change your relationship with food or your body?

Dieting is like Lent without any meaning. Just restrictive ritual. I thought it was about giving up food I really liked for bland, tasteless food I didn't like. I thought it was being hungry all the time. I hated the diet cycle. It was awful, and it wore away at my belief that a healthy body and healthy body image were possible for me.

But then I realized what I really wanted was to feel good about myself. I hated feeling so awful about myself all the time and hiding it from everyone. I realized that if I was going to change, I had to connect with what I was changing FOR.

I can be in a pit of low self-esteem, or I can be full of courage and confidence, depending on the day. I hate it when I'm in the pit. I feel bad about my body, I'm critical, and anxious, and lonely. But when I am standing in empowerment, I feel amazing. I feel good about myself, I'm accepting and supportive, and I feel loved. Life is so much better standing in that power.

There is only one way I know how to get there, to get out of the pit, to stand in my power. It is through daily practices that keep me empowered and rooted in the truth that I am good enough exactly the way I am. Some of those practices will be different for me than for you. But I believe we share some of the same needs to keep us rooted in the truth.

Think about how you feel on your best day. For me, it usually means I've had a great walk outside or workout with friends. It means I made extraordinary food choices. I took responsibility for my choices and feel great about myself. I am ready and willing to be my absolute best, authentic self.

Now think about your last self-esteem meltdown. When you try on five outfits and still feel awful. When you are melting down about a number on the scale, how tight your pants feel, or a depressing shopping trip. For me, it usually involves food binges and self-hatred.

I am useless to be of any kind of service to anyone when I'm in that state. I'm all needy and drama.

Fitness plays a key role in this.

The role of fitness is to contribute to being our best self, so we each can express our authentic gifts and live our life's purpose full on! It is not meant to deprive us of pleasure or force us to work out against our will. Imagine if your best day was every day. What would your life be like if you had that level of confidence, joy, and peace? Maybe that's what taking this journey is all about: finding the path that leads to the full expression of your very best life and remembering what is worth changing for.

★★★

What is it that happens to me when I am doing well, making good choices, feeling good about myself, and then BAM! I'm off the rails. Often there has been a trigger. For me, there are two kinds of triggers; food and emotional.

Food triggers are things that, once I eat them, I crave them. These are things I just don't keep around the house because when they are here, I can't seem to control how much or how many I eat. Something physiological kicks in that feels like that old nicotine craving. It's clearly physical. It takes only one cigarette to create enough of a craving to become an addict. But it is impossible to get addicted to smoking if I never have one.

For me, some junk food is the same way. I was in CVS last week to buy some Tylenol, and I passed the Reese's Easter Eggs. I wanted to get one but started having a mental battle about it. By the time I went to the back of the store for the Tylenol, I was in my crazy mode. There was no way I was going to allow myself a peanut butter egg. I don't know why not. So, little miss rebellious saboteur got flared up and said, "Fine, if I can't have the Reese's, I'll get a bag of Dove chocolates with peanut butter." Which I did.

Clearly the egg would have been a better choice. Now I had a bag of candy at home. All of you who understand and experience compulsive eating know what happened next. Yes. I ate the bag in a day and then felt like...you know, pardon my French.

Emotional triggers happen when our old wounds get poked at. Mine is usually my "I don't matter." It may be entirely in my head, but if I start feeling like someone is treating me like I don't matter, I get flared up. I have come a long way, so I rarely rage at people anymore. I know that it's my issue and I own it. But sometimes it still takes a pint of ice cream and the subsequent meltdown to remember that what I was feeling could have been dealt with honestly instead of escaped from with the ice cream. I use ice cream to escape feeling that way, and it usually takes me a day to figure out what I am really feeling and deal with that instead.

Another trigger for me is a restaurant menu. I am usually fine if I go to a restaurant knowing what I'll order. Ask my friends and family. I have a tendency (more like a strategy) to order the exact same thing every time because as soon as I open a big menu filled with pictures, I go back to the days (decades) when I could not afford to go out ever. My old fears that this may be my only chance to eat out get triggered, and I start looking at options like double cheese fettuccini Alfredo with cheesecake on the side. But if I can calm down and get honest with myself, I remember that I can go out to eat every day of my life now. The days of scarcity are over, and everything is great. Then I can take radical responsibility and make a better choice.

Triggers are part of this process. They will come at you in the form of foods, people, and circumstances. What I've learned is I can blame the triggers all I want. I can try to control them. But that won't change anything. What really helped me heal was to understand what they were triggering in me. These old wounds and false beliefs were causing me to make bad decisions. The irony is they aren't true, they are lies! The truth is I could have had a Reese's Peanut Butter Egg, I do matter, and I live an abundant life. Making choices based on the truth instead of false beliefs and old wounds is the only way to healing and the freedom we all desire.

★★★

What are your food rules?
Eggs are good.
Eggs are bad.
Dark chocolate is good.
Chocolate is bad.
Red wine is healthy.
Alcohol is bad.
Protein is good.
Meat is bad.
Whole grains are good.
Carbs are bad.
Dairy is healthy.
Butter and milk are bad.

I could make list after list of judgments that we carry around in our internal belief system about how to lose weight. Yet despite all these rules, are we happy? Do they work? Do rules have the power to take you to the life you want? I believe the more rules we have, the farther we are away from our healthy body weight and peace with our body.

I think of food rules like I think of religious rules. People love to go on about rules. This is good, this is bad. Judge, judge, judge. But a long list of restrictive rules misses the whole point. The point is to make choices and live your life lit up from the inside out with joy, health, and light. I don't follow a rule to avoid being bad, I am obedient to the truth because I know that it will lead me to the life of my dreams.

Same with health and fitness. A long list of food rules is just "graceless religion." But that misses the point. There is a way to relate to food, exercise and your body that leads you to your healthiest, authentic self. Not the self shrouded in too much body weight or the shame you carry with that. Not the self that you label lazy or lacking self-discipline. No! The you that shines. The you that is full of life, hope, energy, and gratitude. *That* you.

Look, I've read all the magazines and books that you have. I could cite a new research article every day and add a new rule to the list. The issue for me is this; the rules never worked. In fact, all they

I KNOW WHAT TO DO, I JUST DON'T DO IT

did was cause shame. Yet, I was convinced I had to hold onto them. Maybe because it was the only belief system I had. Maybe I feared eating three gallons of ice cream and a pizza every day and nothing else if I had no rules. None of those fears are true.

There is a better way. You must find something to move towards. Add things to your day that affirm your health and your life. Fill up with goodness. The truth is if you eat enough plant-strong whole food, you get feeling awfully good. The truth is if you make healthy choices to fill up on, the rules start to fall away. Try it. Take a week and let all the controls go. No counting, no weighing, (yes, I said no scale), no measuring, no rules, no restriction. What you will find is much less shame, judgment, and self-condemnation. A person who is not under that kind of wrath of judgment is much more likely to take positive steps than a person who feels constantly judged. No one was ever criticized into changing.

If you find it impossible to let go of restrictive, controlling processes, try to understand why. Do you know what you are afraid of? It is OK to trust yourself, even if you went off the rails in the past. The energy you are spending thinking about how to keep holding this beach ball under water is going to exhaust you. Let it go.

The way to freedom is to find your vision. What is the life you want? What does it look like? Then, without rules, by grace, step towards it. Find your courage and make a positive change. Create daily practices that honor your life. Deal with what comes up! (Because stuff will come up when you try to change.) Then take another step. Left foot, right foot. Rules keep you stuck where you are. You have to get moving forward towards the life you want. It's there just waiting for you to let go.

★★★

We had another transformational experience at the Break Free from Dieting seminar on Saturday. Thank you to everyone who attended. I feel like we're building an army of empowered women who know the truth and can stand strong when the moment arrives.

Actually, the moments arrive constantly.

We are making choices all the time. When we have weight issues, we can get fooled into thinking we're choosing whether to eat or not, or what to eat. But really, it's not about food at all. It's about staying or escaping in the moment.

Let's take stress eating, for example. The morning is going OK, and then your boss-spouse-client-child-principal-crazy driver-girlfriend-plumber-Starbucks drive through line-flat tire-bad hair day- ___ (insert stressor here) throws your stress hormones into a frenzy. Suddenly, you are angry, and your mind is racing. All you want is your peace of mind back.

There's your moment. You can (A) work through the stress to get to a place of authentic peace or (B) escape to a place of counterfeit peace.

(A) takes longer and involves more effort. All (B) takes is a spoon and some ice cream.

This is not a choice about food. There are many other ways to escape. If I am suddenly stressed, angry, or terrified, there are many means I can use to escape. Food is a big one because it is quick, easy, and cheap. And it works. You absolutely leave your frenzied mind and go to your happy place. But only as long as there is ice cream on the spoon.

When you choose to run away, it is no different than if you shoot up heroin. Your brain takes you just as far away from the issue that you were only a moment ago standing in the middle of. But just like the junkie, the issues are still there once the high is gone and the emotions still need to be dealt with. If we keep putting them off, it's like going into emotional debt. We keep spending and shifting amounts around on different credit cards, but eventually we have to pay. We have to face what we were escaping.

And if we were escaping for a long time, now we have to face our original issue plus the feelings that come with being overweight and using food.

The moment of choice when you are hungry is what to eat and how much. This is where your strategies, your awareness, and your knowledge come into play.

The moment of choice when you are not hungry but are feeling something uncomfortable presents you with three options: eat comfort food, shoot up heroin, or deal with the issue. It takes a lot of strength to deal with the issue. It may mean telling someone no and feeling afraid they will disapprove. It may mean finding your voice and telling someone what you need. It may mean taking some time to just sit with your fear and letting God do some healing work in you.

Even if you choose to eat carrot sticks, if you do it to escape, you are still escaping. That is why it is not about food and why a diet will never fix this.

So, what can you do? You can get strong; physically, emotionally, and spiritually. Because when you are in that moment and those feelings get uncomfortable, you must be empowered to stand against that discomfort and fear! You must stay put. You must know who you are and that you are enough. You must know that there is a power at work in your life that is stronger than anything that might be coming at you. You must know that you are connected to other women who encourage and support you being fully real in those moments.

Then, as that automatic tendency to escape yourself heals, you will find that the issues that resulted from that—the weight, the food, the scale, the clothes, the health scares—all begin to heal as well. And soon you find that food is just food, peace is actual peace, and real comfort is way better than the counterfeit version ever was.

★★★

I want you to do an exercise with me. It's about labels.

Imagine you have a plain white coat. Think London Fog, knee length. Now take a thick, black sharpie and begin to write all the labels you've put on yourself. Don't forget anything that has been spoken to you. Never good enough? Write it down the sleeve. Where would the words "too fat" go? Mine would be across my belly. Abandoned? Write it. Ever been called lazy? Write it. Ever thought to yourself, "I don't have enough self-discipline"? Write it. Ever thought you weren't important? Write it. Too old? Write it.

Failed too many times? Write it. Others always have to come first or I'm selfish? Write it. You get the idea.

Now... feel what it is like to put this coat on. All I ask is you wear it for a minute. Feel how heavy it is. Feel how constricting it feels.

Now take it off. Feel the freedom?

Those labels are lies. I started thinking about all the stuff written about progress. Progress over perfection. We have to progress. We have to change. I get that. We might really want to. But what would happen if we wanted to change because we felt so amazing instead of so unworthy?

What if we knew the life that was intended for us? Without the heavy coat.

Take it off!! I mean it. Get rid of it. Throw it away. Burn it. Bleach it.

Is it off?

Now, we need to make a new one. Actually, feel free to write directly on your body with that sharpie now because you're going to keep these new labels. Or if you prefer, a new coat; brand new and all white. But before you write, take a few deep breaths and connect to the truth. I want you to feel what it is like to wear radical acceptance. Because the truth is you don't have to progress at all to be OK. You are OK right now. In fact, you aren't just OK, you're amazing. So write it. Amazing.

What else are you? Empowered. Strong. Beautiful. Compassionate. Loving. Write it!! Creative. Inquisitive. Powerful. Nurturing. Generous. Kind. Write it!! Daughter. Mother. Wife. Friend. Sister. Heart. Soul. Write it!! Fierce. Determined. Gentle. Peaceful. Hard Working. Caring. Worthy. Enough. Significant. Safe. Free. Accepted. Enough. Write it!!

Now put it on. Wear it. No eye rolling or resisting or "yeah, but..." or back talk. Put it on and wear it.

How does it feel? Feel empowered? Feel strong?

Are you wearing your new coat?

What you wear matters. Put on failure and never good enough, and you will walk out failure and never good enough. Put on radical acceptance and absolutely good enough, and you will walk out radical acceptance and absolutely good enough.

Just because it was spoken to you in the past, does not make it true. Just because you may have experienced something painful in the past, does not mean that is who you are.

You know who you are! Live it. Don't hold back. Wear the label proudly of your awesomeness, and you will see what happens next. Choices line up with your belief about who you are and next thing you know, those old struggles to eat food as you were intended and to move your body as you were intended fall away. They fall away. When you wear the labels that match who you really are, you become who you were intended to be.

And trust me, that is *not* a woman who is consumed with whether she is fat or thin. Let's live life!

Truth: The compulsive behaviors I had in place were there to keep me from having to deal authentically with what was going on inside. That is why, when I would try to quit them, it felt like all hell was breaking loose. It kinda was. It was when I was finally willing to sit with the uncomfortable feelings that came up that I started to heal.

★★★

There is a big obstacle out there, and it comes in the form of a lie that weight should be lost quickly. I'll use my experience at Clear Rock as an example. A woman will come to me ready to work out. I explain that what we will be focusing on is strength training. We all know what the benefits are. She buys a package and starts working out the following Monday. She comes in apprehensive and nervous but gets through the first session and feels great. She comes back the following Monday and does it again. She feels great!

After about five weeks and 35 times on the scale, she starts getting frustrated. No weight loss. It's not happening! Then, here it comes: "See, it's not going to happen for me. There's something wrong. This is too much time and effort and money to be spending if I'm not getting anywhere. This was a mistake. It's my metabolism, it's menopause, it's my genetics. I'll never lose weight. It doesn't work. I'm failing again."

I understand completely. I really do. It took me two years working with my training before I lost significant weight. I got frustrated. I didn't believe it would happen for me. I wanted to quit.

I am so very grateful I didn't. What I didn't know was during those two years, amazing things were happening that I just couldn't see yet:

I was maintaining my health.

I was boosting my metabolism.

I was building muscle.

I was getting strong.

I was developing core strength.

I was developing consistency and accountability.

I felt so much better about myself.

My brain chemistry was healing.

I was becoming more confident.

I was feeling empowered.

I started giving up my excuses.

I was dealing with my past.

My heart was healing.

As all this was happening, something else started to happen. I started wanting to walk. I started to want different food. And my compulsion to eat when I was stressed or upset began to heal.

I started to believe this was possible after all.

Then I lost weight. Slow and steady. Maybe two pounds a month for about two years. A little slower than that towards the end of the two years. I am not sure really, I stopped caring how long it would take somewhere in there. I realized that the gifts that came with each pound lost far outweighed the pounds themselves.

Every pound lost represents something that must be dealt with first. These are personal to each of us. If you are someone who is stuck in all-or-nothing thinking, you cannot lose weight without dealing with that. Deal with it first, then watch that pound fall away. If you are someone who makes excuses and doesn't take responsibility, you cannot lose weight without dealing with that. Deal with it first, then watch that pound fall away.

This is the truth. This is how weight loss works and why diets and weight loss surgery don't. You can't will it to happen from the outside in. You can't control it with counting and tracking. It is an inside job.

For most of us, this is great news. (I know it doesn't sound like it yet, but trust me.) For me, food and inactivity and all my other self-destructive and compulsive behaviors were in place to keep me from having to deal authentically with what was going on inside. That is why, when I would try to quit them, it felt like all hell was breaking loose. They were like Band-Aids keeping the wounds and pain at bay. Had they been ripped away from me all at once, I'm pretty certain I would have died. There was just too much stuff underneath.

Authentic weight loss is a slow process, but it is an amazing process. It has so very little to do with food. It is about learning how worthy we are of respect and care. It is about knowing we are strong enough to sit with very painful or uncomfortable feelings without needing to escape into food. It is about learning we are empowered to make any change we want in our lives and believing that it is possible.

Don't miss out on the gifts by wanting to be thinner right now. Being thinner won't change your life. The gifts absolutely will.

★★★

My weight loss story involved starting and stopping; trying again and quitting. It was frustrating and slow as I learned to deal with my feelings and not eat them (drink them, smoke them...) numb.

I remember one of my first meltdowns. I was working out with my trainer alongside another woman about my age. She had been training for several years and was chatting away while I was huffing and puffing. I had on a hoodie, and I remember feeling like I was just bursting the seams of that sweatshirt. And I was hot. But I was not going to take that layer off and reveal what I felt like was disgusting me. Especially after seeing her toned arms and thin waist. I started getting really upset during the workout as my self-esteem meltdown began to envelop my thinking, and I couldn't imagine a day when I wouldn't feel so bad about myself.

Looking back, I realize that the spirit of comparison that I was bringing to the party was wrecking me. And that woman's arms triggered my worst feelings about my body to come right up to the surface. That wasn't her fault, although I wanted so badly to find things about her to dislike. (This wasn't easy, she's a great person.) Having these feelings triggered and brought to the light was extremely uncomfortable. But it was one of the biggest gifts on my journey to health and fitness.

I wasn't able to do it the day I had the meltdown, but eventually, I began to own and understand my comparisons. They revealed many of the false beliefs I was carrying around with me. I will never be good enough as long as I'm fat. I'll never be truly loved as long as I'm fat. My weight determines my worth as a person. I will be accepted once I get thin. Toned arms must equal happy life. Look at her, she is fit so she must be accepted, loved, worthy.

If I could go back in time and tell myself one thing only, it would be this. "Beautiful girl, you are accepted, loved, and worthy right now. Just as you are. No matter what weight, body fat percent, size of clothing or amount of arm jiggle. You do not have to do anything to earn love. It is a gift. And you can't become unworthy of it by being overweight, out of shape, or anything else we believe damages us."

My healing came not as I lost weight, but as I learned the truth. The better I felt about myself, the more likely I was to honor that by making a healthy choice. The more I understood my worth as something I was born with that couldn't be ruined by bad choices, the more I affirmed that by showing up for walks and workouts.

I am on a mission to convince every single woman I have contact with that her worth is not in any way determined by her weight. This is the truth and without belief in it, we will always (subconsciously) find a way to prove ourselves right. Yes, we are sent this false message from many sources, often very trusted sources. But if someone spoke this lie to you and you're struggling to believe you are accepted, it is time to come out of agreement with that lie. You do not have to live your life in its grip.

Freedom comes when you claim the truth at the core of your being, and then walk it out. Prove it right. So every time I take a walk, I'm honoring the belief that I'm worth it. Every time I lift a weight, I'm affirming the truth that I am worthy of love, respect, and care. You have to take the walks and lift the weights to be healthy and fit. But it must be done as an expression of the truth to create lasting change.

Next time you are standing at the bathroom mirror and the voice starts berating you with words like fat, disgusting, jiggle, rolls, cottage cheese, flab, or anything else—I want you to claim the truth right then and there. Say "no!" out loud if you need, but do not allow the voice to keep attacking. What is the truth? Are you really not as good of a human being because you store 5, 10, 50, 100 extra pounds of fat on your body? That's ridiculous. This is the moment of change. Take radical responsibility and state your worth. Claim who you are: a fabulous, beautiful, kind, loving child of God with unique talents, passions and gifts to share with the world. Keep telling THAT to the woman in the mirror and watch your life change.

★★★

This has been a week of struggle for many of us. I don't know why. I wrestled with fear (I *am* afraid) this week. Many of the women I talked to struggled with feelings of failure and frustration.

I'm sorry it is a struggle at times. I know that it is. I don't believe there is any way to avoid the obstacles on this journey, but I do know that so much of what keeps us stuck is that we think about things backwards.

We do not have to figure out how to change our bodies to be a certain shape or size before we can feel good enough. That is radically backwards. We must feel good enough at the shape and size we are right now, then our bodies will become healthy, fit, strong expressions of that.

The body follows the mind. If you see a flawed body when you look in the mirror, look for something in the mind that needs healing.

I know how hard this is to believe. I know many of us will keep looking outside of ourselves for the answer, the program, or the means of control. I am so thankful that being victorious has nothing to do with control or willpower. If that was the answer, I never would have gotten anywhere. Ever. I am just not good at forcing myself to do things that I don't want to do, like control and restrict my food, count my food, write down my food, etc.

I want freedom.

Look, a food journal can be a great tool to become aware of what the heck you are eating. If you do not know how many calories are in what you're eating, get out your food log. Write it down. Learn. This tool is so you know how to make a good choice. But be clear. This tool is incapable of giving you the ability to make a good choice.

What does give us the ability to make good choices?

An identity rooted in the truth. We must know that we are OK, enough, accepted right now, no cleanup work required. Otherwise, we may rise up for a moment and make a good choice, but those false beliefs are always there to sabotage every long-term effort. If you feel like two parts of you are fighting for victory in this, they probably are. One part of you knows you are an amazing, unique woman and makes choices as an expression of that acceptance and worth. Another part of you never feels good enough, rebels against anything that shows love and respect to your body (like positive words, healthy food, or exercise), and eats for comfort.

It is a painful, conflicted way to live.

The only way out is to replace the lies with truth. If you could diet your way out of this, you'd be done already. Some of the lies that need a big, bright light shone on them are:

Lie: I will be accepted once I lose weight.

Truth: You are absolutely accepted right now, any weight, any size.

Lie: I won't be good enough until I lose weight.

Truth: You are already good enough.

Lie: I can't dress up, spend money on clothes, etc. until I look better or can buy a different size.

Truth: You are totally worth having outfits that fit your body right now and make you feel awesome. Express your beauty at any shape or size.

Lie: I can't have the love/job/body/life of my dreams until I fix some things.

Truth: Nothing in you needs fixed to live the life of your dreams. Imagine if Oprah had decided she was too fat to be a talk show host, if Susan Boyle thought she'd better never sing in public because she didn't feel beautiful, or if Meryl Streep decided she would have to have a perfect body before she could try acting.

It is our minds and our hearts that need healing. We have been through a lot and have taken on a lot of beliefs about ourselves that just aren't true. The shift can happen in an instant. All it takes is seeing the lies for what they really are. Release those lies and come into agreement with the truth.

Start by being kind to your body! Learn how to graciously accept a compliment. It is not your body's fault you feel the way you do. It was a long process of creating a set of beliefs that no longer serve. It is time to say goodbye to them and live as you were intended, unshackled and free to be beautiful you.

Lie: We will be good enough as soon as we change our appearance, our weight, our body fat percentage, our face, our hair.

Truth: As soon as we understand that we are already good enough, then we will express our healthiest weight and our beauty will shine.

The truth will set you free.

★★★

I used to think weight loss was a mysterious formula that only a few people understood. I was struggling with 50 extra pounds and a lot of women I knew were struggling, too. I tried "everything." I was stuck and frustrated.

I see women all the time who are like I was, looking for the answer out there in a program or product that will fix the problem quickly and without too much effort. It doesn't work like that.

I had a conversation at the studio this week that sounded like this:

Client: "How do I lose this weight?"

Me: "Are you walking regularly?"

Client: <sigh> "I know..."

We know the answer. We just want the other answer, the one that is quick, doesn't require our time and energy, and doesn't ask us to dig into our issues.

But there is only one true answer. Fitness and health comes from eating healthy and exercising almost every day. It seems impossible to some of us. How? I've tried and failed. There are two things that you must do to get moving towards success in this area.

1. Walk almost every day in your aerobic zone (or bike, swim, run, dance, do your cardio!).

2. Either stop eating more food than your body needs or deal with why you eat more food than your body needs.

If you do that, you will lose weight.

I believe these things fall into the category of "I know what to do; I just don't do it." That's where I was stuck. I knew daily exercise would help. I knew I wasn't consistent. I knew I ate too much crap. I knew I ate compulsively to numb my feelings. I knew this because I would be eating as I was telling myself not to.

Weight loss and fitness are about daily practices. It is about looking honestly at your excuses for what they are: obstacles to your health and happiness. It is about figuring out what deeply rooted lies are keeping you stuck in this awful, unhealthy cycle of overeat, diet, overeat, diet. It sounds like bad news, but it is really great news. The answers are within you. No magic needed, no mystery to solve. You add a walk this week, and you're one step closer. You figure out why you were making unhealthy choices every evening, and you're one step closer. You understand why you eat for stress and break the power compulsive eating has had, you're one step closer. Then left foot, right foot you are on the path to what you've always dreamed of, but never believed you would achieve. Complete healing of your issue with weight.

And with that comes freedom and it is sweet.

Truth: When I felt my absolute worst, I didn't feel worth taking care of, and so I didn't. Understanding my worth helped me break that cycle, but so did taking care of myself even when I didn't feel like it.

★★★

It's just one hour around the loop at Sharon Woods. Is it really a workout? My leg muscles have worked continuously for an hour, propelling me up and down hills. My heart rate has held steady in my zone 2 except when I push myself up the hills, which is when I got some awesome high intensity training. I drip sweat, I breathe heavy, and I push myself. I burn an amazing 500 calories in the zone that is perfect for weight loss as well as heart health, mental health, joint health. I share the path with deer and wild turkeys. I leave exhausted and feeling amazing. But it's just a walk.

It's just a path in the woods at Highbanks. Is it really a workout? There are hills I come to where I have to dig deep within to push myself to the top. So I lean forward, make two fists and pump my way forward. There are stretches of trail I come to where I have to dig deep mentally to keep my pace. All the while, sweat is dripping off of me, and my heart rate monitor is racking up calories burned past 600...650...I stop for a moment at the overlook to see bald eagles flying over the river, a large nest perched in a treetop above. When I get to the car, I feel like a changed person, inside and out. Legs exhausted. Heart full. Mind at peace. Spirit soaring. But it's just a walk.

It's just a walk. Is it really a workout? I think about walking, but I struggle to get it done. Some walkers are ahead of me, others are behind. It doesn't matter. We're all walking. Before I know it, we are done. I did it! I hear someone say to me, "good job!" I feel proud of myself. I feel good about myself. Because instead of thinking about it but never actually doing it, I did it. I take that confidence with me for the rest of the week. I start to become a person who knows what to do and does it.

But it's just a walk.

★★★

One evening a few weeks ago, I left the studio around 7:00 p.m. to head home. I stopped at City Barbeque to get take-out on my way. Love their pulled chicken and southern-style green beans! I got home and unpacked my bag of food. I scooped about half the shredded chicken onto a large dinner plate along with a heap of the green beans and coleslaw. The plate was packed.

As I sat down to eat, I thought about how grateful I was that I had enough food left over for lunch the next day. I needed to get to the grocery store, but that would give me until the next evening to do it, which worked out great with my schedule.

I enjoyed every bit of my dinner. I ate slowly and really savored it. When I was done, I sat back feeling very happy and satisfied. Even felt a little proud of myself that I ate half and saved half. I got up, took the plate and silverware to the kitchen, and cleaned up.

About 15 minutes later, I walked back into the kitchen, opened the refrigerator, and scooped the rest of the shredded chicken onto a clean dinner plate along with a heap of the green beans and coleslaw. All of it. The rest of the food. On the plate.

Then I ate it.

As I finished, I sat back feeling stuffed full and sick. Why did I just eat all that? I felt awful and had to go lay down and hold my achy belly for a while.

A few days later, I was telling a friend this story. I told her how good I felt about myself after the first plate, and how awful I felt after the second. I was telling her how I felt a total loss of control, like a zombie, shuffling to the kitchen to mindlessly shovel a second plate of food into my mouth. Wanting to stop it, but unable, it was like I was watching it happen to someone else.

As I was telling her the story, in the back of my mind I started to see myself as a young girl. I saw myself standing at the refrigerator, looking in, only to find all the food my mom had bought gone already. There's not enough. There's not enough! That's the thought that goes through me. If I wait too long, I don't get any more.

I stopped talking for a second to acknowledge what was

coming up from my past. I told my friend about it. She nodded in understanding. What did I believe about food? What did I believe about there being enough?

As we talked through it, I remembered a fight (an ongoing one) I had with my ex-husband when we were married. I didn't drink beer often, but once in awhile I really liked one so I would buy a six pack of Heineken to keep in the back of the refrigerator for times like that. It never failed. When I would go to get one, they were gone. What did I believe about there being enough? There's not enough!

Bringing this shadow belief to the light, I began to understand it. No amount of control was going to stop me from going back for that second plate. No shaming weigh-ins. No counting of points. No smart phone tracking apps. No chain lock on the refrigerator door. Control was not the answer.

I needed to heal. I needed to make the shift from lie/fear (I am afraid there's not enough!) to truth (I live in incredible abundance). I needed that miracle. I needed to replace the false belief with truth.

So what is the truth? The truth is I can eat whatever I want, whenever I want, as much as I want. Period.

Thursday night, after the group walk, I went back to City Barbeque for dinner. I got my favorite pulled chicken, coleslaw, and green beans. I ate about half and took the rest home in a to-go box. I told my friend I was sure I was going to eat the rest before it ever got to the fridge. She said "remember to pray." So I did. I prayed that my old fear (I am afraid there's not enough!) would be replaced with the truth (I live in incredible abundance) and that I would be grateful.

I got to eat my leftover chicken and green beans for lunch the next day. Healing is possible for all of us, but we must learn to work at the root. We must replace the old beliefs (lies/fear) with a new understanding of our world. We are safe, we have enough, we ARE enough, we matter greatly, and we are loved.

★★★

How did subcutaneous fat get so much power?

Subcutaneous fat is the fatty or adipose tissue lying directly under the skin layers. Subcutaneous translates to "under the skin." Subcutaneous fat is a shock absorber, helping to cushion our skin against trauma, and also stores energy, which the body uses during periods of high activity.

But somewhere along the way, we decided to come into agreement with the following:

The amount of fat I have determines my worth as a woman.

The amount of fat I have determines my beauty.

The amount of fat I have says something about my character.

If I have a certain amount of fat, I'm not fit.

Think about it. How much power does fat have over your life?

Some of us have lived most of our lives obsessed with the food we eat in an attempt to control how much fat we store on our bones. I believe we're doing this because we desperately want to feel good about ourselves. I know I do.

But removing subcutaneous fat doesn't make anyone feel better about themselves.

That's not where self-esteem comes from. If you think about it, that's just so ridiculous, we should all be laughing hysterically right about now. But we're not because there is a painful truth underneath all this. We've given up a lot in life in an attempt to lose fat.

I have many clients who struggle to celebrate how fit they are, because they still feel like they have too much stored fat. How about shifting perspective and owning that you lift weights like a madwoman twice a week and have been consistently for years! How about owning how long you can hold a plank! How about owning that you can get out and walk a 5K any day of the week!

I also know women who struggle to own their worth and beauty because they still feel like they have too much stored fat. How about owning your beauty and knowing your worth! That is life-changing stuff. Slogging off a few pounds of subcutaneous fat is not. We've interwoven the two things to such a degree, we've got it backwards.

We've come to believe that the fat we carry is the cause, and when we finally conjure up enough self-control to get rid of it, we will be happy, beautiful, worthy and fit.

That is backwards.

The truth is, and you have to reflect on this deeply for it to sink in, this: The fat we carry is irrelevant and meaningless, except to point us to where we have come out of balance with the way we were created and how we were intended to live. As happy, beautiful, worthy, fit women.

Become that, know that, and watch the power fat has over you disappear.

★★★

I just came back from vacation. I traveled with a large group of friends, and during dinner one night towards the end of the cruise, one of my fellow travelers, having overheard something I said about the fitness center onboard, said to me, "You worked OUT on vacation??" I smiled and said, "Yes I did, four times."

Listen, I have learned this lesson. My body does not know I am on vacation. It burns and stores fuel and fat the same way it does any other day of the year. I have been on vacations where I took my free-pass with me (eat everything and anything) and felt terrible for weeks after the trip. I don't do that anymore. There is a way to be completely on vacation, yet bring choices that honor and respect your health and your journey.

Here are some of my strategies. I would love to hear yours and share them with our fellow travelers.

Water, water, water. I took a water bottle with me and kept it full and in my bag. It helped a lot.

Every meal does not have to be a level ten food experience. Breakfast can just be breakfast. Save the level ten experiences for special meals while traveling.

Make lunch mostly plants. Every day I had a big salad or a plate of veggies with a little protein added. I skipped the carbs at lunch. It really helps to tell myself that there is nothing special about rice, potatoes, pasta, or bread. I can have them anytime. This kept me from getting into the carb cycle of eat too many, then crash and crave.

Dinner is meant to be savored with the people you love. I went to dinner every night with the intention that this gathering was about the people I was with, not the food. As a healing compulsive eater, this is hard but it helped a lot. The purpose of dinner is not to stuff myself full of as much food as possible, but to fill myself with as much love as possible.

Remember that food is abundant. I had to keep from getting into a feeding frenzy. I ate whatever I wanted for dinner, but kept portions small. If you have been on a cruise, you know you can get an appetizer, bread, soup, salad, entree and dessert every night. Think protein and veggies when you order. Then you can relax and eat all the courses.

Enjoy dessert! Keep it small, that's all.

Just like in daily life, find time to exercise. It was easy on the cruise. There is a beautiful fitness center with a treadmill that overlooks the ocean. I did an hour of cardio in my target zone and felt fantastic. I knew I was splurging on dinner, but it felt good knowing I was burning it off.

Lift weights. Yes, I lifted on the cruise. It was harder to do than cardio, but once I got started, it felt great. Keep that metabolism up, up, up and burning. And keep those muscles strong, so when you get back, it's not like starting over.

I used to believe that vacations, holidays, and gatherings were a free pass to eat anything and everything. That was one of the beliefs that kept me stuck. That is a lie. It doesn't take away anything from vacation to treat yourself well. A food frenzy is not treating yourself well, it only feels like that if you are stuck feeling deprived in some area of your life. Fill up on the adventure, the people, the love that is in front of you, and you won't need to fill up on food.

The best part is when you return from your vacation, you don't feel the compulsion to hop on the scale or go on a diet. You just keep on going on your journey. You stay on the path since you never got off the path. That is the key. Stay on the path of self-respect whether you are at home or traveling. The reward is a feeling of self-confidence and peace that is well worth the mindfulness needed to get there. Leave the free pass and take care of yourself wherever you go. You are worth it.

★★★

On being a wuss.

I love how hard all of you work at the studio. You amaze me, and I am very proud of you. Thank you for bringing your best to every workout. But I want to talk to some of you who tend to push too hard. There are several ways to do this.

The first is to work a joint beyond what it is capable of on a given day. So, if the knees are hurting, you have to modify. If the hip is bothering you, you have to modify. If the back is cranky that day, modify. And it varies from day to day, so you have to be very aware of your body.

There are always lots of levels, including level one versions of your exercises. You are not being a wuss if you choose level one, you are being wise. It is your responsibility to know what is appropriate for you that day.

I have heard many of you say, "But I don't want to be a wuss." I get that, I really do. But I also know that an injury can take you out for quite a while. Stay safe, protect your joints! We can work around anything.

The second way of working too hard is to let your heart rate get too high. The best way to keep an eye on this is with a heart rate monitor, but it can also be done with what's called perceived exertion. If on a scale of one to ten, you start feeling like you are hanging out at seven or eight, it might be time for a break. You might feel like you are huffing and puffing, struggling to catch your breath, and your mind is usually flashing a warning light saying, "Slow down."

The way to take a break is to stop lifting weights and to get on a cardio machine at a nice, easy pace until your heart rate comes down to your zone one, or your rating of perceived exertion comes down. You should be able to breathe easy. All warning lights should stop flashing. You should feel ready to go again.

When I say during a workout, "If you need a cardio break, take it," I mean it. Again, you are not being a wuss by doing three minutes of cardio, you are working out wisely. I've talked about this in detail, but working out at too high a heart rate is counter-productive to most of our goals. Stay in your zone. This is your responsibility.

The third way of working out too hard is overheating. This is not hard to do when the humidity is high, which it certainly has been lately. There are several strategies used to prevent this, such as staying hydrated before your workout and dressing appropriately for the heat. A good sweat is one thing, heat exhaustion is another. The signs to watch for are: lightheadedness, nausea, tunnel vision, cold sweat. These are not symptoms to work through. If you feel any of these, stop what you are doing and let your trainer know. Walk or sit, but do not lie down. It should pass as your body temperature cools, but it can often leave you with quite the headache.

Once again, there is nothing wussy about stopping before you get to that point. Dizziness and nausea are not normal parts of working out. They are warning signs that something is off. It might be you didn't sleep well the night before or are dehydrated. It might be that you don't exercise consistently between training sessions and therefore aren't acclimated to the weather. Whatever the reason, stop before you get to that point.

It is a challenge for all of us to work out with others without feeling judged. When I went to Body Pump class yesterday, I used very light weights for class, and I just knew that's what I needed. I am over worrying if people think that the trainer has enough weight on her bar. No one thinks that way! No one cares!

I believe all this is extremely important, not only because it keep the paramedics from visiting the studio too often. I believe it is extremely important because the key to fitness is consistency. And the risk with overworking is it often leads to quitting.

The beauty of fitness is that your highest level of intensity is never required to see results. There is a zone, whether you are doing cardio or lifting, that is appropriate to work within. It takes practice to find, but you will know it by this: you will leave your workout feeling better than when you started. And you will not dread the next workout. If you have a sense of dread, you are working at too high an intensity. Back it off. Get over the fear of being a wuss.

There is no such thing! Find that level that works for you and stick with it. That is how to honor the dedication to hard work that is already within you.

★★★

We all have false beliefs (lies, fears, excuses) to deal with, don't we?

I know I do. My false beliefs are like lottery balls. You know; the white ping pong balls in the clear box that they use to pick lotto numbers. When I am in my comfort zone, doing what I've always done, it is like the machine is off. The balls just sit at the bottom of the machine. Nothing moves, nothing comes up.

But then I try to make a change. It's like someone fires up the lottery machine. Suddenly all the numbers are bouncing around, fighting to pop out of the tube at the top.

So for example, I might decide to start walking regularly. Sounds like a good thing to do for myself. Shouldn't be too hard, right? And if I don't have any false beliefs to deal with, then it won't be too hard. But if I do, it is like someone flips the switch on, and all of a sudden all those ping pong balls are bouncing around like crazy.

This is where it becomes much more than just a walk. It becomes an opportunity for healing. My decision to walk has triggered a false belief to pop up to the surface. "I don't have time. It is too hot, too cold, too wet, or too humid. My mother, daughter, sister needs me. I'm too tired."

Now at any point, we can take these thoughts as truth, and skip the walk. That is how to stay stuck. Change is impossible if you keep making the same choice.

But at some point, we can challenge the thought. Is it true that I don't have time? Is it true that it is too hot or too cold or too wet or too humid? Is it true I can't work out how to balance the needs of others with the needs of myself? Am I really too tired?

Change comes from hearing the lies, and replacing them with truth.

I don't have time becomes I'll make time.

It's too hot, cold, wet, humid becomes it's fine, I am strong and I can deal with it.

Someone else needs me is replaced with I can take care of myself and others.

I'm too tired becomes I can do it.

One of the beautiful things about this process is as the lies are replaced by truth, they stop coming up. It is like in the lotto drawing. Once the number is picked, it can't be picked again.

I spent many years of my life miserable and stuck. It was so hard to understand why. But then I saw it. I believed every thought I had was some basic truth, when in fact, most of my thoughts were not true. Thoughts like, "I'll never matter" or "It's too late for me." "I can't quit smoking or lose weight, I always fail." "I don't have time, I can't do it." When I took that sidestep to see these thoughts from the perspective of an observer instead of identifying with them, I realized they were rooted in lies and fear. My journey has been so much less about fitness, exercise and nutrition and more about learning how to *not* identify with the lies I was carrying around. I needed to learn who I really was.

And the only way to do this is to try. What comes up, the false beliefs, lies, fears and excuses are gifts. They will lead you to so much more than fitness. They are a wonderful path back to your authentic self.

★★★

We walked in the rain Saturday. It was a steady rain. No lightening, no thunder, no downpour. Just rain. It was quite beautiful.

Inside my backpack, I was carrying a 10 pound dumbbell. I'm training for the long hike in September, so I want to mimic what it will be like to carry food and water on my back. Ten pounds makes a huge difference! The hills were definitely harder. Everything was harder.

Sometimes we load up our backpacks without even realizing it. With an appropriate amount of weight, we build strength and endurance. Too much weight and we lose the benefits and risk injury. Too much weight and we can't even move.

Throughout my life, my backpack has been filled with some heavy weight: grief, people pleasing, unworthiness, brokenness, self-hatred, addiction, unforgiveness and shame. What I am learning is carrying all this doesn't make me strong. It keeps me stuck.

Taking radical responsibility for what I am carrying is hard. It asks me to unpack these things and own them, then look at them through the lens of truth. It takes work. But it is the kind of work that strengthens me, whereas carrying this load will not.

Taking radical responsibility for unpacking requires that I find my voice, my authentic voice. And use it, even when I am afraid that I will be judged, criticized, or rejected.

I'm not there yet. But I am beginning to know what it will be like. It will be like when I took my backpack, with that 10 pound weight, off my back and set it down next to me on the ground. I felt so light. I felt so unburdened. I felt free.

★★★

I don't want to be last. I don't want to look stupid. Today I was thinking about how many awesome things we miss out on when these fears are our guide.

Today I was signed up for a half marathon at Three Creeks MetroPark. I signed up months ago, planning to walk it as part of my training for the Grand Canyon hike, figuring it would help me get long walks in. Then I got a message yesterday about something that was going on today at 11:30 a.m. with my niece that I really wanted to attend. I switched to running so I would get done on time.

Well, I haven't been training to run long distances at all in the past few years. I've been walking. So my run was slow, and I was near the back. Way back. And you know what? Everyone was so awesome and supportive. No one would have cared if I was absolutely last. No one cares! I got thumbs up and high fives regardless of my finish time.

And what I got to experience was so far beyond any finish time.

I had made up a playlist for the event and loaded it up on my iPod the day before. So as I was slowly making my way to the turnaround and back, sometimes by myself where I couldn't even see other runners in front of me, I got to experience a flood of memories and joy as the sunlight filtered through the trees on this beautiful morning.

When the song "Able" by NEEDTOBREATHE played, I remembered the first time I heard it while getting ready for work one morning and just stopping to listen to the words.

> Find your patience, find your truth
> Love is all we have to lose
> I'm not able on my own

Then a song called "Healing Rain" by Michael W. Smith came on, and I remembered my dear friend Sharon sending me this song while she was going through chemo. I remembered what she told me about being afraid.

> Healing rain, it comes with fire
> So let it fall and take us higher
> Healing rain, I'm not afraid
> To be washed in Heaven's rain

"Paradise City" by Guns N Roses took me back to the days of spin class. He sings that last "take me home" and you think it's over. Then Slash keeps going for about two minutes on guitar, my legs would burn, and I would push, push, push finally making it to the end of that song feeling like I was unstoppable.

"Thunderstruck" always reminds me of my mom. She would watch that AC/DC video and shake her head, commenting on Angus and his nonstop head banging for the entire video. Her nickname for him was appropriately, "Headache." How can I not smile and feel so incredibly lucky when that memory comes up?

And then "When We Were Beautiful" by Bon Jovi. I love this song, but at the end of it when you see them in concert, the band stops and the crowd just keeps going with sha la la, sha la la hey sha la la. I have a vivid memory of singing it with my sister at one of the concerts we've gone to, and every time I hear this song I think of her (and usually text her "sha la la hey"). I hope she knows what it means to me, and as I thought about that today, I got so choked up I had to stop and walk for a while.

You can't tell me this is just about the exercise or the calories burned. If you believe that, then you need a better playlist. This is about showing up and being you. Whether you're first or last; whether you're slow or fast. Open your heart, become radically present with your amazing authentic self, and experience the gifts of this life.

Crossing the Canyon

I was in the Grand Canyon and it was cold and dark. I was struggling and ready to quit. Thoughts about wilderness survival crossed my mind. Why had I risked so much to do this? I had spent so much of my life dying a slow death inside, chained to my comfort zone by fear. I knew the time had come to fully live. And for me that meant doing this.

Two of my fellow hikers went on to the top of the north rim trail while one came back for me and began talking me through each step. He said, "I know how you feel, I've been there." He walked very slowly with me as I took my ten small steps. Then he waited as I bent over, hands on my knees, trying to catch my breath. He tried to carry my backpack for me, I wouldn't let him. He tried to get me to eat something. And he said, "You are going to finish."

We made our way slowly to the north rim of the Grand Canyon. I was exhausted. Upon reaching the top, I learned from my fellow hikers that the lodge where we were staying was two miles from the trail. All we could see was the trailhead sign, a water pump, and a wilderness highway surrounded by spruces and pines.

It was now cold and dark. The stars were bright, but we weren't in the mood to enjoy them. Eventually, we got a ride from a family who was looking for a campsite and gratefully we climbed into the warm vehicle that deposited us at the lodge entrance.

I walked into the building, sat down in a leather chair and immediately fell asleep.

My fellow hikers took care of getting checked in and finding out if we were too late for dinner. Thankfully, we weren't and I perked up at the thought of bread, pasta and a big diet Coke. I ate as much as I could and took the rest with me. After I got to the room and got cleaned up, I had to decide whether I was OK to hike the next day or not. It was about 10:00 p.m. and the alarm was set for 4:30 a.m.

The question in my mind was, "what happened?" If I knew the answer to that, I would know what to do the following day. We planned to hike back on the same trail to the Colorado River, and then take a different trail up to the south rim. The second day would be three miles longer than the first. Now that I was no longer climbing and had eaten, I felt pretty good, just tired and cold. I fell asleep.

When the alarm rang, I was surprised that my energy was back and I wasn't too sore. This was a good sign. My kidneys also seemed to be functioning normally. That was one of my biggest concerns. Were my kidneys OK? Was it the altitude? Or was it a problem with fuel?

I talked it over with my friends as I ate my leftover pasta and bread. Bill was pretty sure I had bonked (ran out of fuel). Since I felt so good after eating, I agreed and loaded up my backpack. This time my strategy would be different. I needed food more often, more of it, and I needed liquid calories once the climb got tough, because I learned that I don't want food once I'm working that hard. Bill set his timer to chirp at me every 20 minutes as a reminder to eat, and I loaded food into my front pockets where I could easily access it without taking the pack off my back.

We took the shuttle to the north rim trailhead and hopped out. It was gorgeous! I had missed all the views the night before, so to arrive and begin hiking as the sun came up through the pine trees was fantastic. And this time instead of looking up wondering when the top would ever get here, I was looking down and out over the entire canyon.

As I started down the trail, I decided to let yesterday go. I had stumbled, but it was time to turn around.

As I did that, as I let it all go, I felt alive again. I felt the cool air of the canyon hit my lungs and fill me up. I gained my footing and found my stride. Now this I did not expect. My fear all summer while I was training for this hike was day two, yet here I was feeling great. I decided not to get ahead of myself, because we were hiking down not up, and up is where I ran into trouble. Then I heard "chirp chirp" - take a bite of food. Eat.

After many magical moments, we arrived at Phantom Ranch campground, where they have the world's best lemonade. I drank a big glass with my Oreos and then filled up an empty water bottle with it, to take with me for the end. We had 11 miles to go, all uphill, gradual at first but then steep switchbacks for the last few hours.

As we walked along the Colorado River, I was flooded with thoughts about Clear Rock, this conversation we've had, and our journey together. I suddenly believed that it was possible to climb boldly out of this canyon. I knew the truth because I had written about it for years.

Take small steps.
Drink lots of water.
Eat plenty of healthy food to fuel the climb.
Go your own pace.
Keep going.
Stop and turn around often enough to see how far you've come.
Get encouragement.
Don't hide from the pain. Walk with it.
Receive healing, forgiveness, and grace when you stumble.
Believe in what's possible.
Know the truth.
Remember who you are.

Turns out that's all we need to know to accomplish *anything*. And to remember that no matter how far we have gotten away from where we would like to be, we can turn around. We can start again. We can learn and grow and let yesterday go. And we can stand in confidence with our arms held high knowing that we didn't give up.

We have stood on the edge looking across for long enough. It is time. Cross whatever canyon you must to honor your beautiful, messed up, authentic life and don't ever give up. You are loved, you matter, and you are already good enough.

CPSIA information can be obtained at www.ICGtesting.com
Printed in the USA
LVOW13s0542311013

359319LV00002B/5/P